The Pennysaver Cookbook

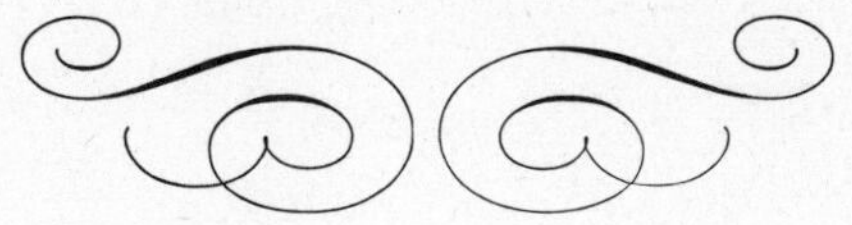

Also by Inez and Dan Morris:

A FAMILY GUIDE TO SALTWATER FISHING

THE SAVOR OF THE SEA
(by Dan Morris and Matilda Moore)

THE STERLING COOKBOOK
(by Jack Sterling with Dan Morris)

THE MIKE DOUGLAS COOKBOOK
(by Mike Douglas with Dan Morris)

THE PENNYSAVER COOKBOOK

Inez & Dan Morris

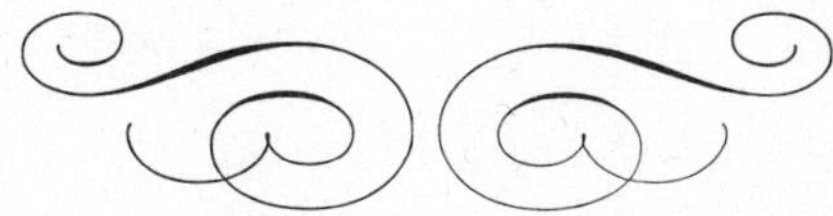

FUNK & WAGNALLS / *New York*

Library of Congress Catalog Card Number: 68–22165

Published by Funk & Wagnalls, *A Division of* Readers Digest Books, Inc.

Printed in the United States of America

Acknowledgments

Our thanks to the following for sharing their expertise with us and thus helping to make this a much better book:

Mrs. Velma Seat, Home Economist and Food Marketing Specialist for the Oregon State University Cooperative Extension Service; Mrs. Alice Scott, Director of the Homemaking Department of the Long Beach, N. Y., Anti-Poverty Program; Rhea Zinman, Public Information Specialist, New York City Consumer and Marketing Service of the United States Department of Agriculture; Mrs. Gloria I. Barry, Extension Home Economist, Phyllis Goodman, and others on the staff of the Nassau County, N. Y., Cooperative Extension Association; Herbert Saal, member of the American Dairy Science Association, lecturer, and editor of the American Dairy Review; Marie Gifford, Manager, Consumer Service Department of Armour and Company; Reba Staggs, Director, Home Economics Department, National Live Stock and Meat Board; Clarence E. Mueller, Department of Public Relations, American Meat Institute; Patricia Myles, Director of Home Economics, Poultry and Egg National Board; John Von Glahn, director of the Fishery Council at New York's Fulton Fish Market; all those whose names we do not know at the United States Department of Agriculture, Consumer and Marketing Service, and the United States Department of Interior, Bureau of Commercial Fisheries, Washington, D.C. And last, but by no means least, Arthur Petry, our friendly neighborhood butcher in Long Beach, L.I., N.Y.

Contents

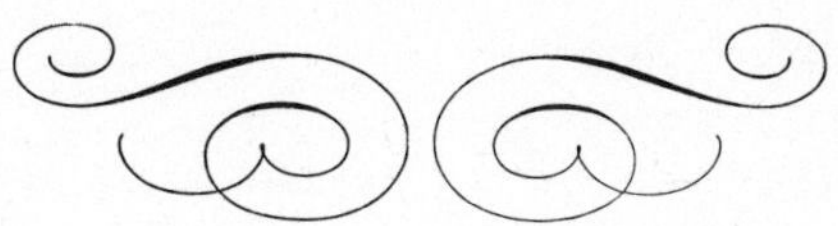

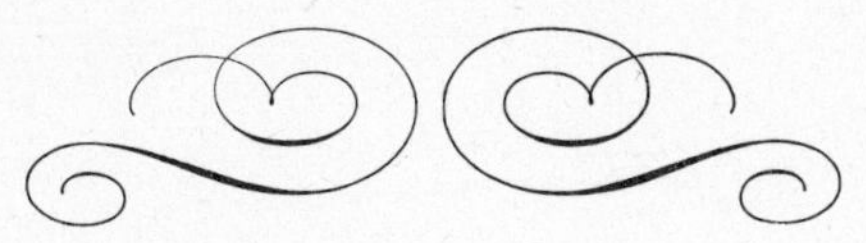

SECTION I
Things You Should Know if You Want to Save Money on Food

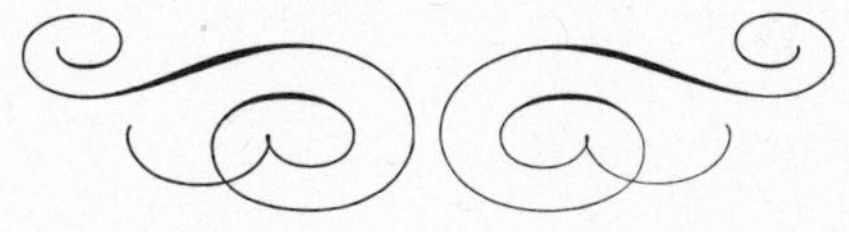

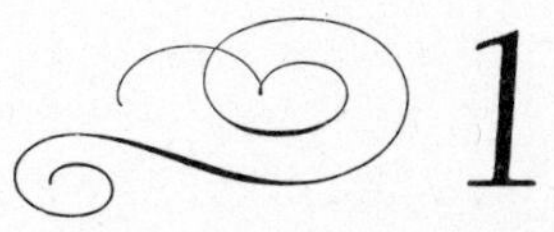

1 SOME OF THE FACTORS AFFECTING FOOD PRICES

Whether your income is $25,000 a year or much farther down the scale, you undoubtedly think your food budget is too high.

What can you do about it?

There are many ways of saving money on food without cutting corners on quantity or quality, and without lowering the appearance and taste-appeal standards of your meals. This book tells you what they are.

The way you use it depends on how much money you want to save and how healthy you want your family to be.

We are in the midst of a scientific revolution that is continually changing methods of growing, processing, packaging, shipping, and marketing foods, thus constantly changing our ideas about what is and what is not economical.

Aside from the enormous changes being wrought by science, other factors affect the cost of food. Some are stable and easily understood; others baffling and confusing to most family purchasing agents.

Demand for particular foods, caused by advertising or eating habits, makes them more expensive than other foods.

Sometimes eating habits that affect food prices are regional; sometimes they are based on religion; sometimes they started out as a preference taste and got in a rut.

Sometimes food production and marketing are affected by transportation problems, strikes, bad weather, disease, large-scale purchases by branches of the government, government control of production, and large-scale government shipments to foreign countries.

Making the most of your food dollar under these conditions cannot be accomplished simply by buying the cheapest food you can find. You must keep abreast of what is happening that affects food prices. One of the most important things you must do is become flexible in your eating habits, change them if necessary, in order to take advantage of shifting patterns in food prices. This is by no means bad; it can shake you and your family out of a dull eating rut into exciting culinary experiences.

We hope to introduce you to some of these culinary experiences in this book.

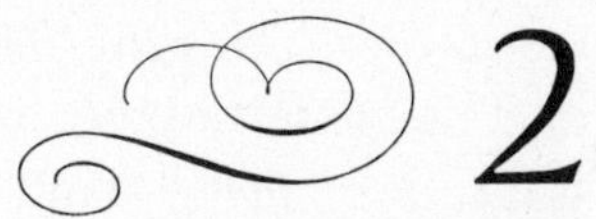

2

HOW TO PLAN MEALS AND MAKE SHOPPING LISTS USING BASIC FOUR FOOD GROUPS

Know your needs and plan for them. The family that doesn't spend more money than necessary under today's changing conditions is the one that goes about its shopping in some kind of an organized way.

Let the food experts do your research. Start your shopping trip in a comfortable chair. You could go to the store and try to figure out what's the best buy. Don't. That's too expensive. Instead, pour yourself a cup of tea or coffee, turn to a good newspaper food column, relax, and read it. If your local radio station has a food program, listen to that, too. Other good sources of information are your neighborhood butcher and your vegetable, fish, and poultry market managers.

If your food guides said you might expect some unusually good specials of about 40¢ a pound off on loins of pork or half hams, get out your food circulars to see if any of the markets are carrying that type of special. You'll probably find that they all are, including your regular market and the neighborhood butcher. So start from there and build your week's menus or your week's supply of food around those in-season (so they'll taste best as well as being cheapest), best-buy foods.

Then look at the recipes in Section II. See if you can perform a little culinary magic, giving your family what it likes, while using needed ingredients. You can double-check yourself on the needed ingredients by using the Pennysaver Food Check Lists described on pages 8, 10, 16, and 20 as shopping lists. (Use Food Check Lists in Pennysaver as a pattern and make up a supply of each of the four to write out your weekly shopping list.) They are arranged according to the four basic groupings in the United States Department of Agriculture's *A Daily Food Guide* in a way that serves as a reminder of recommended serving sizes as well as nutritional requirements. Most supermarkets divide their products into roughly the same grouping, which gives the Lists another advantage over helter-skelter shopping.

Food Check (and Shopping) Lists with Built-in Good Nutrition

The Really Big Savings of Good Nutrition: Good foods don't come labeled "4¢ off doctor bills" but maybe they should, since food is absolutely necessary for the growth, reproduction, maintenance, and repair of the body. How we feel, how we look, whether we walk with a cane after a fall in middle age, how long we live, in short, our general well-being and that of our offspring are greatly influenced by our ability to provide our bodies with the right food in the right amounts at the right time.

Federal Studies Show All Economic Groups Neglect Nutrition

Teachers and school nurses tell us that children do not do as well as they should in school if their breakfasts and lunches are inadequate.

Although such evidence is more noticeable in the lowest socioeconomic groups, studies show that many Americans in all walks of life do not get the recommended amounts of some nutrients. For the "average" American the effects of improper or inadequate nutrition are not dramatic enough for us to pay much attention.

Nutritionists who study foods and their relationship to physical and mental functions have, to date, identified well over fifty substances in food that the body is known to require. Those substances are known as nutrients. Fifty nutrients are not easy for busy homemakers to memorize . . . and on top of that learn and remember their major sources; how much of each is required; how many times a week they should be eaten; or that some nutrients are so temperamental they refuse to work unless accompanied by another, different one.

Nature used a nutritive cross-indexing system to sneak just about everything necessary into our daily diet, providing we eat a wide variety of food; and providing we don't cross up nature, and ourselves, by destroying the nutrients somewhere between the harvesting and the eating. *We list short descriptions of the functions of the four basic food groups in their individual sections* (see pages 6, 9, 12, 18). *It should be noted, however, that new discoveries are constantly being made and that the functions of our food nutrients overlap in complicated ways that would be too lengthy and confusing for us to describe in detail in this book.*

If we are careful to include a wide variety of types of foods—milk, meat (including poultry and fish) and eggs, grains, fruits and vegetables are their four groupings—colors, tastes, and textures in our daily diet, we will probably get a fairly adequate supply of nutrients.

The trouble is, there is a big one-word problem in this happy-go-lucky system of selecting food for a family . . . MONEY.

It can be, and it is, very expensive to go wandering through a supermarket which displays several thousand food items if we haven't worked out, as they say in the military, some Standard Order of Procedure in advance.

The United States Department of Agriculture, through its Institute of Home Economics, has reduced the SOP to its basics for us. You'll see here a Four-Group Plan Chart. The foods in our Pennysaver Food Check Lists are divided according to the same Four-Group Plan. The recipes in Section Two are also so arranged, as nearly as possible.

Make the Four-Group Plan Chart your Standard Order of Shopping Procedure. Simplify food buying still more by using the Pennysaver Food Check Lists. *Be sure to mark down advertised prices on your lists and refer to them when paying for your purchases.*

FOUR-GROUP PLAN CHART
(An adaptation of the USDA "A Daily Food Guide")

MEAT GROUP

2 or more servings daily of:
beef, veal, pork, lamb, poultry, fish, or eggs
*As alternates: lentils, dry beans, dry peas, nuts, or peanuts

VEGETABLES-FRUIT GROUP

*4 or more servings daily** to include:*
A citrus fruit or other fruit or vegetable important for Vitamin C
A dark green or deep yellow vegetable or fruit that is important for Vitamin A
Other vegetables and fruits, including potatoes

MILK GROUP

Some milk daily for everyone:
Children . . . 3 to 4 cups
Teen-agers . . . 4 or more cups
Adults . . . 2 or more cups

BREAD-CEREAL GROUP

4 or more servings daily of those products made from:
Whole, enriched, or restored grain

Plus other foods as needed to complete meals and to provide additional food energy and other food values.

* Alternates are more effective when used with even a small amount of meat, eggs, poultry, fish, milk, or cheese.
** The fruits and vegetables important for Vitamin A may be eaten every other day, rather than daily, if taken in sufficient amount.

The Meat Group

The Four-Group Plan: This pattern recommends that we have two or more servings of meat every day; that, instead of eating it all at once, we spread it over the day by having some at each meal.

The Meat Group includes not only meat, the top-quality protein; it also includes the not-quite-so-perfect "legumes," the vegetable-source meat alternates. The human body, nutritionists tell us, makes better use of vegetable-source proteins if even just a little animal protein is eaten at the same meal.

Considering that eggs and fish are grouped with beef, veal, lamb, pork, and poultry as meat, it's not too difficult to follow these recommendations.

Function of Meat in the Body: The proteins in meats and in the meat alternates are needed, in the words of governmental home economists, "for the growth and repair of body tissues—muscle, organs, blood, skin, and hair" and, they add, "these foods also contribute iron and the B-vitamins—thiamine, riboflavin, and niacin." (See comment, page 5.)

Pork is an exceptionally rich source of thiamine, B1. And liver . . . well, what more can we say than that besides being an outstanding source of all of the foregoing, two ounces of fried beef liver also supplies an adult male with approximately six times the Recommended Daily Dietary Allowance of Vitamin A. But first, of course, he has to eat those two ounces.

About Meat Recipes: Section Two of the Pennysaver includes recipes for (1) dishes that contain some meat in combination with meat alternates, vegetables and/or bread crumbs, sauces, and eggs; (2) ways to cook economy cuts of meat; (3) vegetable, salad, and soup dishes that contain meats.

MEAT GROUP FOOD CHECK (AND SHOPPING) LIST

WE SHOULD EAT TWO OR MORE SERVINGS FROM MEAT GROUP EVERY DAY

What Constitutes One Serving of *Cooked* Food:

TOP-QUALITY PROTEIN (Animal Source) — 2 to 3 ounces of *lean, boneless,* cooked meat, fish, or poultry; two eggs*

NOT-QUITE-SO-PERFECT MEAT ALTERNATES (Vegetable Source) — 1 cup *cooked* dry beans, peas, or lentils; 4 tablespoonsful of peanut butter

Recipe Page	*Kind of Meat*	*Amount*	*Adv. Price*	*Store*

* Serving sizes on all Pennysaver Food Check and Shopping Lists are those suggested by the Human Nutrition Research Division of the USDA which points out: "The size of servings can be suited to the needs of family members." The American Meat Institute recommends buying anywhere from one-quarter pound of raw, lean, boneless meat up to one pound of meat that has a large amount of bone per serving. See Section II for more specifics.

The Vegetable-Fruit Group

There are three parts to the Vegetable-Fruit Group lists: "Important Sources of Vitamin C," "Important Sources of Vitamin A," and "The Other Fruits and Vegetables, Including Potatoes." The last list is for you to write down any of those in-season fresh or on-special canned or frozen fruits and vegetables not included in the first two lists because they contain lesser amounts of vitamins A and C. This list will help you round out the variety of your meals—and variety, as we've been pointing out, is very important to our systems. Just one example why:

Greens are listed as suppliers of both Vitamin C and Vitamin A. We shouldn't ignore them and instead eat only oranges for C and carrots for A, because greens also make a valuable contribution to our supply of calcium (among other things), much more so than either carrots or oranges. Here's an interesting breakdown:

1 cup milk contains 288 milligrams of calcium (less than half the recommended daily allowance for an adult male)

½ cup cooked collard greens—145 milligrams of calcium

½ cup cooked turnip greens—134 milligrams of calcium

1 California navel orange—49 milligrams of calcium

½ cup cooked, diced carrots—24 milligrams of calcium

Function of Fruits and Vegetables in the Body: "Vitamin C," say our governmental home economists, "is needed for healthy gums and body tissues. Vitamin A is important for growth, normal vision, and a healthy condition of the skin and other body surfaces."

Some fruits and vegetables contain a lot of one nutrient and a little of another, some contain a medium amount of several things, thus contributing in too many different combinations of ways for us to list here. (See comment, page 5.)

The following Food Check Lists can help you check off the supplies you have on hand and serve as a reminder of what fruits and vegetables you should be eating that you may be overlooking. Used this way, they can be effective shopping lists with built-in good nutrition.

THE FRUIT AND VEGETABLE GROUP FOOD CHECK (AND SHOPPING) LISTS

PART 1: IMPORTANT SOURCES OF VITAMIN C

Include at least one serving of a Vitamin C fruit or vegetable daily. One serving equals ½ cup fruit or vegetable, or one med.-size fruit, or ½ grapefruit.

Sources	*Recipe Page*	*Quantity*	*Price*	*Store*
Asparagus tips				
*Broccoli				
*Brussels Sprouts				
Cabbage (raw)				
*Cantaloupe				
*Grapefruit				
*Grapefruit Juice				
Greens (Collards, garden cress, kale, kohlrabi, mustard, spinach, turnip)				
*Guava				
Honeydew				
Lemon				
*Mangoes				
*Oranges				
*Orange Juice				
*Papayas				
*Peppers, Green				
*Peppers, Sweet red raw				
Potatoes and Sweet Potatoes cooked in jacket				
*Strawberries				
Tangerines				
Tangerine Juice				
Tomatoes				
Tomato Juice				
Watermelon				

* Starred items are good sources; others are fair sources of Vitamin C. (Lists of important sources of Vitamins C and A are from the USDA's *Family Fare,* Revised in 1968.)

PART 2: IMPORTANT SOURCES OF VITAMIN A*

Serve a dark green leafy or deep yellow fruit or vegetable at least every other day.

Sources	*Recipe Page*	*Quantity*	*Price*	*Store*
Apricots				
Broccoli				
Cantaloupe				
Carrots				
Greens: (Chard, collard, cress, kale, spinach, turnip greens, and other dark green leaves)				
Mangoes				
Papayas				
Persimmons				
Pumpkin				
Sweet Potato				
Winter Squash				

PART 3: THE OTHER FRUITS AND VEGETABLES

Include enough of these fruits and vegetables to give you a good variety and to make sure you have four or more servings of fruits and vegetables every day. Try to fill up this list with in-season fresh or on-special canned or frozen foods.

Fruit or Vegetables	*Recipe Page*	*Quantity*	*Price*	*Store*

* To avoid confusion, we have followed the example of other publications and refer to the above fruits and vegetables throughout the book as being "sources" of Vitamin A. The National Academy of Sciences National Research Council, however, states in its Publication 1146 that, "The average American diet is considered to provide about two-thirds of its Vitamin A activity as carotene and one-third as preformed Vitamin A. Carotene is converted to Vitamin A in the intestinal wall."

The Milk Group: (Milk, Cheese, Ice Cream, etc.)

The constantly upward fluctuations in the retail price of milk are much too complex to be dealt with in any book, cookbook or otherwise, that does not lend itself to continual revisions. But milk is one of our greatest blessings and, no matter what the price, *it is cheaper for you to buy it than not to buy it.*

Everyone, not just children and teens, needs some milk every day. Again, we quote our government home economists who say, "Milk is the leading source of the mineral, calcium, which is needed for bones and teeth. Milk also provides protein, riboflavin, Vitamin A" (in the cream), "and many other nutrients." (See italicized comment, page 5.) "Cheese and ice cream also supply these nutrients, but in different proportions."

The Forms in Which Milk Is Sold

There are Federal standards for some forms of milk. Other forms are covered by provisions of a model milk ordinance, a law adopted, sometimes with modifications, by many jurisdictions.

Whole milk is the form to which the average consumer is most accustomed. It contains from 3 to 3.5 percent butterfat, the exact amount varying from state to state and in some places it may go as high as 4 percent.

A quart of fortified whole milk has had about 2,000 U.S.P. units of Vitamin A and 400 U.S.P. units of Vitamin D added to it: Vitamin D, by the way, is the so-called "sunshine vitamin" that helps your system to pass the calcium and phosphorous from the milk to your teeth and bones.

About 50 percent of the whole milk bottled in the United States has Vitamin D added to it. The same is true but to a somewhat lesser degree with nonfat or skim milk in liquid form.

The most popular substitute for whole milk, both for those who must watch their pennies and those who must watch their pounds, is nonfat, or skim, milk. It contains about 0.5 percent butterfat and a proportionately low amount of Vitamin A, but otherwise it retains all the nutrients of whole milk. And, the big factor for calorie counters, it contains only 90 calories per cup as against whole milk's 160. Fortified nonfat milk also has had added about 2,000 U.S.P. units of Vitamin A and 400 U.S.P. units of Vitamin D per quart.

As of the time this book is being written, fortification of powdered skim milk varies with the different brands. However, Standards of Identity have been established for a product to be called "Nonfat Dry Milk Fortified with Vitamins A and D." Powdered skim milk has the advantage of keeping very well without refrigeration, before being reconstituted, so that you can always have a supply on hand. (Dry whole milk must be refrigerated.)

"U.S. Extra Grade" (see label above) is an instant nonfat dry milk that must meet the USDA standards for that grade. This means, according to the USDA bulletin, *How to Buy Instant Nonfat Dry Milk,* that it must have a sweet and pleasing flavor and a natural color. It must also live up to its name—that is, dissolve instantly when mixed with water.

A comparative newcomer to the marketplace is two percent milk (in some areas called "low fat" or "partly skimmed" milk), which has 10 percent solids and only 2 percent butterfat. It costs more than nonfat milk but less than whole milk.

Then there are these other milk-rich products:

Half and Half: a mixture of milk and cream with a minimum fat content of about 11.5 percent. (Model milk ordinance specifies minimum fat content of 10.5 percent.)

Whipping Cream: it contains upwards of 30 percent fat.

Cultured Buttermilk: made of cultured skim milk, sometimes with small amounts of butterfat added.

Sour Cream: sweet table cream with about 18 percent butterfat to which has been added a special culture which lends itself not only to scores of recipes but also to as-is eating along with such cut-up vegetables as green onions (scallions), radishes, lettuce, and cucumbers.

Yogurt: another cultured milk product, is made from whole, partially skimmed, or skimmed milk and has somewhat the same consistency as sour cream. Far less fattening than sour cream, it can sometimes be substituted for it.

Cottage Cheese: a skim milk product, small or large curd, creamed or uncreamed, with or without salt.

Chocolate Milk: pasteurized *whole* milk with chocolate and sugar added. If cocoa is used, it is called "Chocolate Flavored Milk."

Chocolate Drink: pasteurized *non*fat or two percent milk with chocolate and sugar added. If cocoa is used, it is called "Chocolate Flavored Drink."

Canned Evaporated Milk: whole milk, usually homogenized, with about 60 percent of the water removed by heating but with about 400 International Units of Vitamin D almost always added to every pint. A can with the same amount of water added has about the same food value as whole milk.

Canned Sweetened Condensed Milk: evaporated milk with sugar, which is added as part of the evaporation process and which constitutes about 40 to 45 percent of the product. This milk is sometimes used instead of cream (which costs more) in dessert making.

When you buy milk in any form, check the cap or label.

This advice applies just as much to ice cream as to other milk products, since it, too, should contribute to our nutritional needs. There are far too many kinds and flavors to list here; the label is your window into the contents of the package.

A Little About Cheese

Most cheeses in America are made from whole milk, but there are some made from skim, or a mixture of skim and whole milk. The individual characteristics of the various cheeses are the result of: (1) the kind of milk used, (2) the types of bacteria or mild cultures used in ripening, (3) the method used for coagulating the milk and forming the curd, (4) the conditions of ripening, (5) salting, (6) the length of time aged.

Mild cheese is cured two or three months; medium or mellow cheese is aged up to six months; sharp or aged cheese has been aged for six months or more.

"Aged" or "sharp" cheese is better for cooking than those not cured so long because it melts more easily and blends well with other ingredients.

Buying Butter (and sometimes cheese and sour cream) Bearing USDA Stamp

Of the dairy products, butter is most apt to carry the United States Department of Agriculture grade shield. This shield is your assurance that the butter was packed under sanitary conditions and has been tested by a Government butter grader. Following are the three grades and what they stand for, besides showing "when graded" and the statement each stamp bears that it was "packed under inspection of the U.S. Dept. of Agriculture."

USDA Grade AA butter is made from high quality fresh sweet cream, it has a pleasing aroma, with a delicate, sweet flavor and good spreadability.

USDA Grade A, the next grade, is almost as good and usually sells for a lower price. It, too, is made from fresh cream.

USDA Grade B butter is generally manufactured from selected sour cream and is readily acceptable to many consumers.

Cheddar cheese may bear these same three grade stamps, but at the writing of this book cheese grade stamps were not frequently seen.

Another USDA stamp at this time not too often seen is a "Quality Approved" one which may be used on cottage cheese, process cheese, and sour cream. It means the product is of good quality, manufactured in a clean plant.

THE MILK GROUP FOOD CHECK (AND SHOPPING) LIST

CHILDREN	3–4 cups daily
TEENS	4 or more cups
ADULTS	2 cups or more
PREGNANT WOMEN	4 or more cups
NURSING MOTHERS	6 or more cups

	Recipe Page	*Quantity*	*Price*	*Store*
Milk				
Whole Milk				
Buttermilk				
Yogurt				
Nonfat, Liquid or Powdered (Are Vitamin A and D added?)				
Canned Milk				
Cream				
Other				
MILK SUPPLEMENTS				
Ice Cream				
Ice Cream				
Ice Milk				
Other				
Cheese				
American (or mild)				
Cheddar (It takes approximately 10 lbs. of milk to make 1 lb. of cheddar-type cheese)				
Cottage				
Cream				
Swiss				
Grated				
Other				
Cheese Foods (check label to find actual amount of cheese)				
Butter				

The Bread and Cereals Group

The Four-Group Food Plan recommends that we eat four or more servings of whole, enriched, or restored cereal grain products every day because our bodies need them. The United States Department of Agriculture booklet *Conserving the Nutritive Values in Foods,* prepared by Consumer and Food Economics Research Division, Agricultural Research Service, explains some things about cereals we feel are so important to know that we are repeating them here:

"The cereals—wheat, corn, rye, rice, and oats—come to your table in a myriad of food items, including breakfast foods, hominy, breads of all kinds, macaroni and other pastes, puddings, pastries, cakes, and cookies.

"Cereals are nutritional bargains. They are economical sources of food energy, protein, minerals, and the B vitamins.

"*How much vitamin and mineral value your family gets from a cereal or a cereal product depends on how much of its original value remains after milling, what nutrients are added, and on how you prepare it for eating.*

"*Whole-grain* forms of cereals retain the germ and outer layers of the grain where the B vitamins and minerals are concentrated.

"Whole-grain products generally available on the market include: Whole-wheat flour, sometimes called graham flour; brown rice, dark rye flour, whole-ground cornmeal, and rolled oats or oatmeal, and bread and other products made from them. Milling whole cereal grains into refined products removes all or part of the germ and a considerable amount of the outer layers.

"Most consumers prefer white bread and other products made of refined cereal grains. Some of the milling losses are offset through enrichment of certain staple cereal products.

"*Enriched* cereals are milled cereals to which the B vitamins—thiamine, riboflavin, and niacin—and iron have been added within the limits specified by the Federal standard of enrichment. Provision is made for the optional addition of two other nutrients, calcium and vitamin D.

"Federal standards for enrichment have been established for wheat flours, white bread and rolls, farina, cornmeal, corn grits, macaroni and noodle products, and rice.

"Enriched flour has about seven times as much thiamine, nearly six times as much riboflavin and about four times as much niacin and iron as unenriched all-purpose flour.

"Many manufacturers of breakfast cereals add nutrients to their products. The amount and kinds of nutrients added vary widely since, except for farina, there are no Federal standards for the addition of nutrients to these products.

"A comparison of the nutritive values of different forms of rice shows that *parboiled rice* is intermediate in food value between *highly-milled, polished rich* and brown rice. *Brown rice* is the unprocessed kernel with the hull removed; from a nutritional standpoint, it is considered a whole grain."

Cooking Losses

"Some persons persist in washing rice before cooking. This is an unnecessary step because today's packaged rice has already been cleaned. Washing rice once before cooking can cause a thiamine loss of 25 percent in regular white rice, and a loss of 10 percent in brown or parboiled rice.

"The nutrients in rice are well retained if rice is cooked in just enough water to be absorbed during the cooking period.

"Baking, one of the commonest ways of cooking cereal products, permits good retention of thiamine. You can conserve thiamine by:

" • Baking the product only until the crust is light brown.

" • Limiting the surface area exposed to heat. For example, less thiamine is lost when cornbread is baked as a loaf than when the same batter is baked in sticks.

"Toasting causes additional loss of thiamine. However, the thicker the slice of bread and the lighter the finished product, the smaller is the loss of thiamine.

"Riboflavin, another B vitamin in cereals, is not greatly affected by heat but is sensitive to light. Experimental studies of riboflavin loss in commercially baked bread indicate that heavy wax paper or other translucent covering protects the riboflavin in bread very well."

THE BREAD AND CEREALS FOOD CHECK (AND SHOPPING) LIST

4 servings daily (whole grain or enriched). Count as one serving: 1 slice of bread, or ¾ to 1 cup ready-to-eat cereals, or ½ to ¾ cup cooked cereals.

	Recipe Page	*Quantity*	*Price*	*Store*
Bread				
White (enriched)				
Whole grain				
Other				
Flour				
White (enriched)				
Other				
Whole-wheat (or graham)				
Dark rye				
Whole-ground cornmeal				
Noodles (enriched)				
Macaroni (enriched)				
Spaghetti (enriched)				
Cereals (enriched or whole-grain such as rolled oats)				
Grits				
Rice, brown				
Rice, white (enriched)				
Cakes, cookies, etc. (enriched or whole grain ingredients)				
Other				

SHOPPING CHECK LIST FOR MISCELLANEOUS ITEMS

	Recipe Page	*Quantity*	*Price*	*Store*
Beverages				
Oils				
Seasonings				
Shortenings				
Other				

Remember to use all of the Food Check (and Shopping) Lists when reading your daily or weekly food column and other food advertisements. Mark down the advertised prices.

MDR and RDA

If you should have occasion to check to see whether or not a product has been enriched by a meaningful amount of nutrients, you should know the difference between MDR and RDA.

When foods are designed for use because of vitamin or mineral content, the Special Dietary Regulations of the Food and Drug Administration require that the label state quantities of these substances in terms of the "minimum daily requirement" (MDR), as established by the Food and Drug Administration.

The RDA, "Recommended Daily Allowance," is something else again. It is the recommended daily allowance established by the National Research Council, the standard commonly used by nutritionists. It is important to remember that this standard is more liberal than the minimum set by the Food and Drug Administration, especially in vitamins. In brief; the "minimum" amount is usually less than the "recommended" amount.

No one wants to spend much time adding and subtracting nutrients but there are times when it's helpful to know what the RDA of certain ones might be for the members of your family. If you're checking the label on a box of skim milk or a box of rice, for instance, you may find the following chart an easy reference source:

RECOMMENDED DAILY DIETARY ALLOWANCES

(Allowances are intended for persons normally active in a temperate climate.)

Age in years From Up to	*Weight in lbs.*	*Vit. A (I.U.)*	*Vit. D (I.U.)*	*Vit. C (milligrams)*	*Niacin* (milligrams)*	*Riboflavin (milligrams)*	*Thiamin (milligrams)*	*Calcium (grams)*
Infants								
0–1/6	9	1,500	400	35	5	0.4	0.2	0.4
1/6–1/2	15	1,500	400	35	7	0.5	0.4	0.5
1/2–1	20	1,500	400	35	8	0.6	0.5	0.6
Children								
1–2	26	2,000	400	40	8	0.6	0.6	0.7
2–3	31	2,000	400	40	8	0.7	0.6	0.8
3–4	35	2,500	400	40	9	0.8	0.7	0.8
4–6	42	2,500	400	40	11	0.9	0.8	0.8
6–8	51	3,500	400	40	13	1.1	1.0	0.9
8–10	62	3,500	400	40	15	1.2	1.1	1.0
Males								
10–12	77	4,500	400	40	17	1.3	1.3	1.2
12–14	95	5,000	400	45	18	1.4	1.4	1.4
14–18	130	5,000	400	55	20	1.5	1.5	1.4
18–22	147	5,000	400	60	18	1.6	1.4	0.8
22–35	154	5,000	—	60	18	1.7	1.4	0.8
35–55	154	5,000	—	60	17	1.7	1.3	0.8
55–75+	154	5,000	—	60	14	1.7	1.2	0.8
Females								
10–12	77	4,500	400	40	15	1.3	1.1	1.2
12–14	97	5,000	400	45	15	1.4	1.2	1.3
14–16	114	5,000	400	50	16	1.4	1.2	1.3
16–18	119	5,000	400	50	15	1.5	1.2	1.3
18–22	128	5,000	400	55	13	1.5	1.0	0.8
22–35	128	5,000	—	55	13	1.5	1.0	0.8
35–55	128	5,000	—	55	13	1.5	1.0	0.8
55–75+	128	5,000	—	55	13	1.5	1.0	0.8
Pregnancy		6,000	400	60	15	1.8	+0.1	+0.4
Lactation		8,000	400	60	20	2.0	+0.5	+0.5

* Niacin Equivalent (preformed vitamin and the precursor, tryptophan) Figures from the Food and Nutrition Board, National Academy of Sciences-National Research Council, *Recommended Dietary Allowances*. Revised 1968.

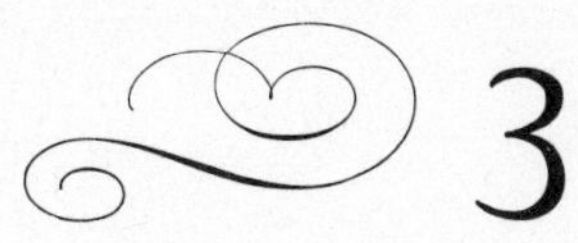

3

WHERE—AND HOW— TO SHOP

Choose the Right Store: If you kept a check list on such things, you probably would find that the store that advertised the lowest price on one item sold another item at the highest price. And chances are you would find that you bought the highest-priced item as well as the lowest-priced one, because who can keep comparative prices of hundreds of items in his head?

Stores are in business to make money and it stands to reason that if a store lowers the price on one item in order to attract customers, it may have to raise it on something else to offset any possible loss.

If you place any value on your time, you're better off narrowing your shopping down to one store (at least for staples and miscellaneous items) and pretty much sticking to it, rather than running from market to market trying to take advantage of every "special." Here are some of the things you should consider in choosing a store where you will shop regularly:

List of Qualifications for a Good Store

1. Does the store regularly stock a large variety of all the foods you need and at what have proved to be good competitive prices?

2. Are the meats, poultry, fish, eggs, fresh fruits, and vegetables dependably good quality?

3. Are sale-priced items hidden away at the far ends of shelves in a basket? If the answer is "yes," that's not your store.

4. Are the manager and various department heads courteous and willing to answer questions . . . even at the end of the day?

5. Does the store give "rain checks" on advertised sale-priced items it runs out of?

6. Does the checker call out prices as he rings them up, or is the cash register facing in a direction that permits you to watch the amounts being added?

7. What is the appearance of the store and its merchandise? Are they clean or do you sometimes unpack cockroaches along with your groceries? Do you often see a great many dented and rusted cans on the shelves? Even if the prices in a store that's dirty and has inferior merchandise seem low, it may cost you considerably more in one way or another to trade there than you save.

8. Is the store conveniently located? Near to a bus stop or a large parking lot, or your train station? Or, best of all, within easy walking distance of your home? Sometimes the location of the store means the difference between shopping at a convenient and an inconvenient time; between shopping only once a week or being able to buy such things as fresh fish, fresh eggs, fruit, vegetables, baked goods, and milk two or three times a week without any inconvenience.

Generally speaking, the rule "Do your shopping once a week" is a good one, if what we really mean is "Do your menu planning and shopping for staples, nonperishables, things that stay perfectly fresh in the refrigerator, and freezer foods once a week." This is the kind of organization that saves us from spending an untold number of additional pennies, nickels, and dimes buying staples at the delicatessen. But if any of the fresh produce is going to spoil after two or three days because of bruises or too long a stay in improper storage, why let it happen at your house?

Read the Labels on Cans and Packages

The first step in learning to read labels is to study those on the old standard products right in your own kitchen. Become familiar with the general label terminology and layout. Learn the various types of labels and how different the quantities of principal ingredients may be in similar-appearing cans. You will see that lists of ingredients are given in descending order of amount; the largest amount is listed first, second largest amount, third, and so on. You will note that some producers go far beyond the requirements of the law and even include recipes on their can and package labels. A discussion of *Standards of Identity* on page 26 will explain why some canned foods do not list the ingredients at all.

Compare what's in a can of Fruit "Juice," "Drink," and "Punch." You may discover, on reading the labels, that a can of "fruit punch" or "fruit drink" that cost you less than a similar-size can that's *all* fruit juice is half sugar and water. Really to be a better buy, the "punch" or "drink" that was half water might have to cost less than half as much as the can that is all juice, with no water added.

Compare the amounts of meat (usually the most expensive ingredient) in different brands of such things as canned stew, soup, or pork and beans. If two cans sell for the same amount, but meat is at the top of the list of ingredients in one can and near the bottom of the list on the second can, it's possible you haven't been getting your money's worth if you've been buying the second can. The presence of some expensive food such as mushrooms, of course, could account for a price difference.

Compare the contents of "Cheese" and "Cheese Foods" packages. The package with the most cheese is usually the best buy.

Check bread wrappers. Be sure the nutrients removed in the milling process have been replaced in the enriching process. (Enrichment will be declared in terms of percentages of Minimum Daily Requirements.) Besides checking the amount of enrichment on the bread wrapper, also check the "net weight" as appearances can be very deceiving.

Check labels on powdered skim milk. See which ones add vitamins A and D. Vitamin A is removed from milk with the cream. Therefore, there won't be much left in skim milk unless it's put there. Some of us rely on what is often added to whole milk, but not nearly so often added to powdered skim milk, for a sufficient supply of Vitamin D. So check. (See "The Forms in Which Milk is Sold," page 12.)

Federal Regulations of Canned and Packaged Goods

Federal law requires that all canned and packaged goods shipped across state lines must be labeled with the following:

Name or description of the product; the net contents in double labeling, if the package contains between one and four pounds or between 1 pint and 1 gallon (that is, 31 oz. and also, 1 lb. 15 oz.); name and address of packer or distributor, and all the ingredients in the container (except for some standardized foods). Further, when a canned fruit or vegetable product is marketed in various forms (whole, halves, slices, etc.), the form is considered part of the name and is to be included.

New regulations on the labeling and formulation of foods for special dietary uses were issued by the Food and Drug Administration in June of 1966, but, as of the writing of this book, the regulations have been stayed pending the outcome of public hearings.

Standards of *Identity, Quality,* and *Fill* are administered by the Food and Drug Administration. The *Standard of Identity* states kinds and amounts of the ingredients that either must, or may, go into a specific product and how the product is made. *Foods that exactly meet this standard of identity need not list all the ingredients on the package.* FDA standards of identity specify which ingredients *must* be declared on the label. Among these are artificial coloring, flavoring and chemical preservatives.

The *Standards of Quality* limit and describe the number and kinds of defects permitted. They do not provide a basis for comparing foods as to grades. They define drained weight, color, and such things as amount of peel per pound.

The *Standard of Fill* regulates the quantity of food in the container.

Federal Inspection and Grade Mark (or Stamps) on Canned and Packaged Goods

The United States Department of Agriculture (USDA) inspection mark is assurance of a good, clean, wholesome product, produced under the supervision of a Government inspector. This inspection mark must appear on all meat and poultry sold across state lines, whether it's fresh or canned. (Fish comes under the jurisdiction of the United States Department of Interior [USDI], but, at the writing of this book, it is not subject to such strict government regulations as are meat and poultry.) *See: Meat, Poultry, Fish, and Eggs in the introductions to each of these recipe sections for more complete discussion of both inspection and grading of these products and illustrations of the marks and stamps used. See page 12, in this section, for further information on milk and cheese and butter.*

The inspection mark above is used on *processed* meat products: canned, dried, frozen, or otherwise packaged. Processed poultry products bear the same mark as do the fresh ones that cross state lines. It appears under the discussion of buying fresh poultry, Section II, page 121.

Inspection stamps should not be confused with *grade stamps*. The best way to avoid confusion is to read them. Generally, the Federal inspection stamp is round, while the grade stamp is shaped like a shield.

However, one exception is the inspection stamp shown above which is obviously shaped like a shield and is not round. This stamp is not required by law but it does assure you that the product has been produced under the supervision of a Government inspector.

It may be used on fruit and vegetable products (fresh as well as processed), including jams and jellies—and also some nuts. Its use is voluntary by food processors to assure you that the label bearing this mark has been approved by the USDA as being truthful and accurate.

This is the *grade* shield you will sometimes see on *canned, frozen,* and *dried fruits* and *vegetables.* You may also see it on a few related products such as honey, jam, and jelly.

During periods of price control, grading may become mandatory, otherwise it is strictly voluntary. At the writing of this book, the products most apt to bear this mark are frozen vegetables, frozen orange juice, jam, and jelly.

Although the grade shown on the illustration is "U.S. Grade A (Fancy)," there are two other grades established by the government: "U.S. Grade B (Choice or Extra Standard)," and "U.S. Grade C (Standard)."

You may sometimes see these same grade designations used without the U.S. in front of them. If a producer used the grade this way in his label, his product is required by law to measure up to the Federal quality standard, even though it has not been officially graded.

According to the United States Department of Agriculture, at the writing of this book, most canned, frozen, and dried fruits and vegetables are packed according to the grade standards, whether or not it is indicated on the label, and priced according to their quality.

Grade A are the very nicest; *Grade B* are not required to be as uniform in size and color as Grade A products, or quite as tender or free from blemishes. *Grade* C products are fairly good quality, just as wholesome and nutritious as the higher grades and, of course, they usually are less expensive. The flavors, however, may lessen to the same degree as the percentages of partially ripened fruits and vegetables may be increased.

Store Brands Are Good Economy

How do you find the most economical canned goods without devoting your life to brand-name detecting? Try the store brands first. (Ask the market manager if you're not sure what they are.)

You can save up to 20 percent by buying store brands. If you don't like them, or there are cheaper ones with labels indicating they should be comparable, try the cheaper brands. Get in the habit of rinsing out cans that contained any new varieties you try so you can set them aside until your family has taste-tested the product. If your family liked what it tasted, jot down the pertinent information in a notebook or in a "brand name" column you could add to your Food Check and Shopping Lists. Use whatever method you find simplest . . . but don't trust your memory unless you have a much better one than most of us.

Convenience Foods vs. the Do-It-Yourself Kind

Which should you use?

Only you can answer this question, but we can give you some points to use as guidelines.

Keep Abreast of What's Happening to Convenience Food Prices

1. It's impossible to make a blanket decision about whether to buy ready-packaged foods or not. Frozen peas are almost always cheaper than buying fresh ones and shelling them. Frozen orange juice is often cheaper than buying fresh oranges and making your own. Instant coffee sometimes costs less per serving than the kind you make in a percolator.

2. Sauces calling for a multitude of parts of cans are cheaper to buy ready-made if the can remnants will spoil before they are used.

3. As of this writing, it costs considerably less to bake your own puddings, pastries, and cakes than to buy them ready-made. However, if you like what you can buy in a bakery just as well as what you can bake yourself, you may want to put a money value on your time and include it in the cost of the do-it-yourself method. Examine the prices on prepared cake mixes; you will probably find that it's just as cheap to use them as it is to start from scratch.

4. It's more economical and nutritious to add your own sugar and fresh, ripe fruit to cereals than to buy the packaged varieties that have them already added.

5. Expect the picture to change from month to month. Food processors are constantly searching for ways to sell ready-prepared foods at costs that can compete with the cost to the customer of raw ingredients. Since the packager starts with the advantage of wholesale raw ingredients, he is sometimes able to do this, in spite of the cost of labor, packaging, transportation, and merchandising.

Errors You Should Guard Against

1. We've all been amused at times by tricks of optical illusion. When those tricks take place on grocery counter shelves and we have to guess which bottle holds the most, a tall one with a wasp waist, or a squat, straight-sided one, it's not very amusing. Don't trust your eye. Read the writing on both bottles and compare the content weights.

If you always look for them, "Net Weight" are magic words that will keep you from buying a big box with less in it than is held by a smaller, but heavier, box containing a similar product. The "Net Weight" will help you select a less expensive loaf of bread that looks lighter than a loaf in a bigger package, but is actually heavier because the bigger package (but not the loaf) is loosely packed with lots of air between and around slices.

2. There is another kind of packaging you should be consciously aware of. That is the kind that makes you buy something you don't need or is not economical for you because it is packaged either very attractively or in a reusable container. There's nothing wrong with

buying a product in a cannister if (1) you need and want a cannister, (2) if the can will match your kitchen decor and, most important, (3) if the cost of the product in its fancy cannister is not greater than the combined cost of a plastic bag of the product and a cannister you pick out at a store whose business it is to sell cannisters.

3. A careless but costly mistake we frequently make is to note worthwhile sale prices on a number of canned and packaged goods when checking through our market's weekly food flyer. We list the items on our shopping lists, but we neglect to put down the advertised sale price. By the time we get to the store, we probably have forgotten what the advertised price was. So if we pick the items off the regular shelf instead of one the store may have set aside for sale-priced items and are charged regular, not sale, prices, we don't even notice.

4. Count your change and watch the cash register tape, not because you suspect the cashier, but because it is very difficult not to make an occasional mistake when ringing up many thousands of items each day.

5. Buy perishable foods last and then hurry them home into the storage space recommended in the next chapter. *Don't warm up freezer and refrigerator items in the car en route home.* Surround such things as frozen fish with cans of frozen juice. If you own a portable cooler, put it in the car when you expect to buy a supply of frozen foods for your freezer and bring them home in it.

4

HOW TO STORE AND OTHERWISE CARE FOR THE FOOD YOU BUY

Why Vitamin C Is Used as an Index to Retention of Other Vitamins: Nutritionists tell us that a vegetable cut or scraped with a dull knife will shed some of its Vitamin C. Same thing if a vegetable is roughly handled and bruised or otherwise damaged. So keep your knives sharp and watch yourself there, if you don't want a vitamin strike in the vegetable bin!

The reason you hear so much about what will and what won't destroy Vitamin C in comparison to the other vitamins doesn't mean they aren't so important or are too hardy to worry about. Indeed no!

The feeling among nutritionists seems to be that if sufficient precaution is taken to save something as perishable as Vitamin C, the other nutrients automatically will be protected too. It's happening in food processing plants; it can easily also happen in your kitchen.

Follow the food storage suggestions in this section of Pennysaver to conserve as much as possible of the valuable nutrients and flavors in all of your foods and to prevent loss from spoilage and waste.

Prepare Storage Space Before Going Shopping

While checking items on hand for your shopping list, organize and straighten your shelves. Don't wait until you come home from shopping laden with groceries. You don't want your perishables to stand around in a warm room, shedding their vitamins, waiting to be put away. If you never seem to have enough ready-made storage space, the following may suggest some possible solutions to your problem:

• Move sheets and towels out of a closet near the kitchen and utilize the shelves for storing canned goods.

• Hang pegboard on every empty kitchen wall and the backs of closet doors. Light won't deteriorate pots and pans the way it will packaged and canned foods so decorate your walls with your pots and pans and turn the dark cupboard interiors over to light-sensitive foods.

Storing Foods in the Freezer

Freezing Meats: The National Livestock and Meat Board recommends the following maximum periods for freezing fresh, cooked, and processed meats at zero degrees Fahrenheit or lower. It's a good idea to check your freezer with a thermometer periodically because if temperature rises above zero degrees, vitamin loss will increase.

FREEZER TIME LIMITS FOR MEAT, MEAT PRODUCTS AND COOKED DISHES

Fresh beef 6 to 12 months
Fresh veal 6 to 9 months
Fresh pork 3 to 6 months
Fresh lamb 6 to 9 months
Ground beef, veal and lamb 3 to 4 months
Ground pork 1 to 3 months
Variety meats 3 to 4 months
Luncheon meats never freeze them
Fresh pork sausage 60 days
Smoked whole ham 60 days
Ham slices 2 weeks
Corned beef 2 weeks
Leftover cooked meat 2 to 3 months
Precooked meat pies 3 months
Precooked Swiss steak 3 months
Precooked stews 3 to 4 months
Precooked meat dinners 2 to 6 months

BE SURE TO DATE FREEZER PACKAGES

The above chart points up the importance of dating everything that goes into a freezer. A date stamp will make this simple and quick to do.

The easiest place to stamp the date is on the freezer tape. As for how best to freeze meats, again the National Livestock and Meat Board tells it best. The same general instructions apply to poultry.

WRAPPING A PACKAGE FOR FREEZER

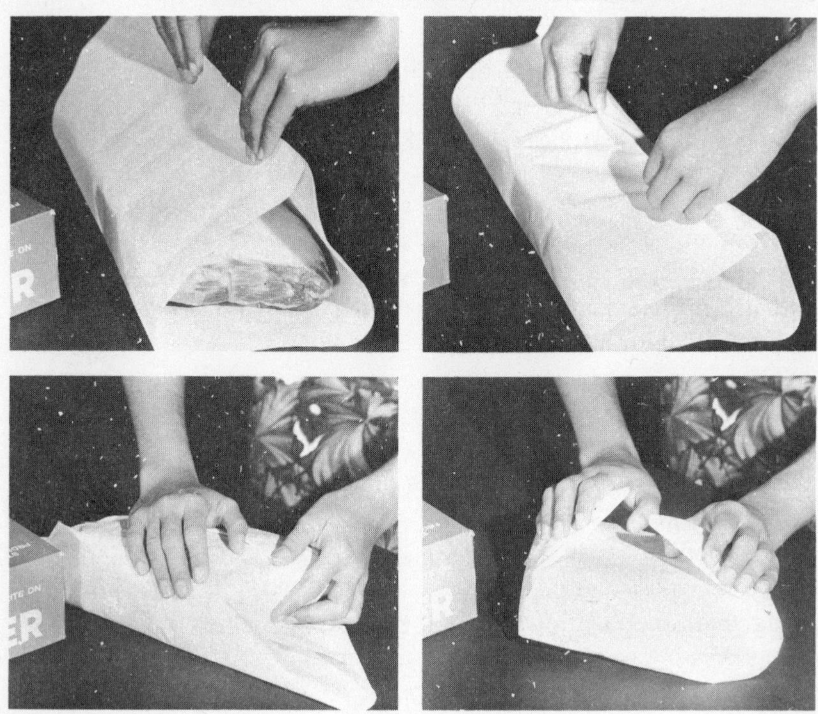

National Livestock and Meat Board

PREPARATION OF AND PACKAGING OF MEAT TO BE FROZEN

1. *Freeze meat while it is fresh and in top condition.*

2. *Select proper wrapping materials.* Choose a moisture- and vaporproof wrap, so that air will be sealed out and moisture locked in. Pliable wraps such as aluminum freezer foils and transparent moisture- and vaporproof wraps and thick, heavy-duty types of plastic bags are good for wrapping bulky, irregular-shaped meats since they may be molded to the meat. Also freezer papers and cartons coated with cellophane, polyethylene, or wax; laminated freezer paper; casserole dishes in which food has been cooked and in which it can be reheated. (Such casserole dishes must be manufactured for freezer use.)

3. *Prepare meat for freezing before wrapping.* Trim off excess fat and remove bones (rare is the supermarket that will do this for you) when practical to conserve freezer space. Do *not* salt. Wrap in family-size packages. When several chops, steaks, patties, etc., are to be packaged together, place double thickness of freezer wrap between them for easier separation while thawing.

4. *Wrap tightly, pressing out as much air as possible.* One of the best methods is shown in illustrations on page 34.

5. *Label properly.* See: "Keeping Track of What You Have in the Freezer."

6. *Freeze at once at minus ten degrees Fahrenheit or lower, if possible.* Allow air space between packages during initial freezing period. Do not overload freezer or the temperature of the meat before it freezes will raise the temperature of the freezer.

7. *Maintain freezer temperature at 0° F. or lower.*

Those are the freezing pointers to adhere to closely in order to get the most out of your meat-buying dollar. Those, and this one more thing: It is *not* recommended that defrosted meats be refrozen because there always is the possibility of deterioration setting in.

Freezing Poultry: To go in the freezer, choose *fresh-killed* poultry with fat well distributed and few skin blemishes. The same general rules as recommended by the National Livestock and Meat Board for packaging and freezing meat should be followed in freezing uncooked chicken or turkey, which, by the way, may be frozen for up to a year. Giblets may be frozen for three months. Uncooked duck and goose for six months.

As for cooked poultry of all kinds—chicken, turkey, duck, and goose—here is a United States Department of Agriculture timetable to guide you:

Freezer Time Limits for Cooked Poultry:

Slices or pieces covered with broth or gravy 6 months
Slices or pieces not covered with broth or gravy 1 month
Sandwiches 1 month
Casseroles, pies and other main dishes 6 months
Fried chicken 4 months

All timetables for keeping foods in the freezer assume that they are fresh, clean, and wholesome; that they have been prepared and stored under the most favorable conditions and that the storage temperature has been maintained at zero degrees or lower.

Meat slices covered with gravy can be frozen in the same manner as given for broths, gravies, and other liquids on page 36.

Freezing Fish: Fish that you freeze in a refrigerator's freezing compartment should not be kept for more than two weeks before using. But very fresh fish stored in a home freezer at temperatures ranging from minus 10° F. to zero can be kept for more than six months. Fat fish such as salmon and mackerel might still be highly edible up to eight months and lean fish up to a year, but we'd suggest ten months as a limit. Ten months also is a good cut-off date for shellfish. A word of caution: never refreeze packaged frozen fish that has started to defrost on the way home from market. Make such things your last purchase and hurry them home.

How to Thaw Frozen Fish

Both fish fillets and steaks may be cooked frozen, just as they come from the freezer, provided you allow more cooking time. However the best way to defrost fish, whether whole, drawn, steaked, or filleted, is to let it thaw in a refrigerator at about 40° F. Figure that a one-pound fillet thus will take about eighteen hours to become pliable enough to handle.

Frozen shellfish should be thoroughly defrosted in the refrigerator before cooking.

One cautionary word here. Never defrost fish by letting it stand outside the refrigerator at room temperature.

Freezing measured amounts of Broths, Gravies, Other Liquids, and Fats (Including Solids Frozen in Sauces): Strain liquids before freezing. Remove fat from larger containers after freezing.

For 1 (one) Tablespoon-size cubes:

Pour one cup of liquid into a 16-cube tray. When solid, remove to small plastic bag and store in freezer.

Tiny containers of various sorts can be saved for freezing dabs of steak sauce or nicely seasoned fat. Such things as coffee measures are good for a bit of fat. You can cover them with a bit of cellophane, wrap a piece of freezer tape around the container, and mark to identify the contents.

For 2 (two) Tablespoon-size cubes: Same as above. Most plastic measuring scoops for coffee hold exactly 2 Tbs. Each cube in a 16-section ice cube tray holding 2 cups of liquid would measure about 2 Tbs.

For ½ cup and over: Line an appropriately sized freezer dish with aluminum foil, letting foil extend beyond top of dish. Pour in measured amount of liquid (sauces, gravies, and small pieces of food being frozen in sauces or gravies can be handled in the same way), fold aluminum foil over top of container in such a way that it does not touch liquid, place in freezer until frozen solid. Remove frozen block and aluminum foil from container, carefully fold free ends of foil securely around frozen liquid. Fasten with freezer tape which should extend all the way around package and fasten on itself. (Some tapes will not adhere very well to cold foil or freezer paper.) Use heavy pencil, Magic Marker, or felt pen to mark date and identification of contents *on the freezer tape before it gets cold.*

Put small packages in a heavy plastic bag for added insulation and to keep them from getting scattered around the freezer.

Leave expansion space so containers don't burst. Maybe you've stuck a can of beer or soda into the freezer—just for a few minutes—to chill quickly, then forgot it. What happened? It expanded and exploded, and you had a frozen mess to clean up.

The same thing will happen to the liquid broths, gravies, and sauces you freeze unless you leave space for them to expand upward.

Leave about one-half inch of space in a one-pint bag; one inch in a quart bag. Low, broad, rigid containers such as casseroles need one-quarter inch for pints; one-half inch for quarts. Tall, narrow containers with a smaller diameter need more head space; roughly one-half inch for a pint and one inch for a quart.

Freezing Fruits and Vegetables: See "Should You Buy Fresh or Frozen or Canned Fruits and Vegetables?" page 184.

Cooking for the Freezer and the Future on Meat-Delivery Day

Chapter 1 of Section II discusses the advantages of buying meat from your butcher at quantity prices and having him cut it and package it in ways most convenient for storing in your home freezer for future cooking.

Here we call your attention to the advantages of cooking several meals at once when your freezer order is delivered.

Meat-delivery-day is beef broth making day: Plan on spending most of that day in the kitchen, storing, indexing, precooking what you can and, while all this is going on, making broth. Wash the bones and the scraps, put them in a pot, cover them with water and let it bubble away. Then, when you've finished all your other freezer chores, add onions, carrots, salt, pepper, and celery to the broth, let it boil some more, strain it, and store it.

Buying in bulk gives you the immediately noticeable advantage of economy. Cooking in bulk for the freezer has these other pluses:

Cooked foods often take up less room in the freezer than do foods that are raw, especially if the raw food is meat with the big bones in it.

The hours spent in the kitchen are lessened when you cook for more than one meal at a time.

You can save money not only on the bulk-purchased main ingredient, meat, but sometimes you save also on larger purchases of secondary ingredients that go into a recipe. Sometimes the saving is achieved because part of a container of something like sour cream or tomato paste doesn't go to waste.

Quality and Care of Freezer Packaging Materials

There are three good reasons for buying the heavy duty, more expensive types of plastic wrap, plastic bags, other containers, and aluminum foil:

(1) They are much easier to work with; (2) they provide better protection for the food they cover; (3) they cost less money in the long run because they don't tear easily.

Keep your freezer wrapping materials in a cool dry place where they are protected from dust and insects. Don't buy more than you can use before it dries out and becomes brittle.

Keeping Track of What You Have in the Freezer

It doesn't do any good to go to all the trouble of preparing seasonings, broths, and a second meal's main course for the freezer unless you can make easy use of these things. To do this, you must have some kind of system. If you have a large upright freezer and a good memory, this may mean nothing more than always putting certain types of foods in the same place. Unfortunately, most of us don't fit into this category.

The following suggestions may help:

1. Use different-colored marking pens for different types of meats.
2. If you need to write anything more than the date and one or two words on the freezer tape, use a label instead and tie it to the package with a piece of string. You can buy different-colored gummed labels, write what you want on them, fold them over the string and stick together, then tie the string around the package. Store in such a way that the labels can be lifted and read without removing packages from freezer. The different-colored labels can indicate different food classifications. But don't get carried away and devise too complicated a system.
3. Probably the easiest way of all is the way that sounds like the most work; that is to number everything larger than one-half cup, and keep a record of the numbered packages, showing date frozen and what they contain. The record can be kept in a notebook that is divided into separate sections for each category of food.

You'll have to remember, of course, to mark off the items you use.

Storing Food at Room Temperature and in the Refrigerator

The United States Department of Agriculture and *Spotlight on Food*, a publication prepared by the Oregon State University Extension Service, at Corvallis, Oregon, give us the following recommendations for storing foods at room temperature and in the refrigerator. Besides following these general recommendations, changing production and storage methods make it important that you also read package labels on all types of foods for individual, specific instructions.

"All foods depend on specific storage temperature and humidity to retain their quality. Temperatures in the home refrigerator should vary between about 38° F. to 42° F., and the food freezer should maintain 0° F. The ice cube compartments in many refrigerators are not cold enough (some run at 14° F. or 15° F. above zero) to maintain quality of frozen food for more than a few days. It's a good idea to check your refrigerator and freezer temperatures periodically with an ordinary thermometer, and adjust controls to maintain low enough temperatures.

"All meat should be promptly refrigerated. The transparent wrap on prepackaged meat, poultry, or fish is designed for refrigerator storage at home for 1 or 2 days.

"Meat or poultry wrapped in meat paper when brought from the store—or prepackaged roasts and steaks that may be stored in the refrigerator for 3 to 5 days—should be unwrapped, placed on a platter or tray, and loosely covered before refrigerating. Wrap and store fish separately from other foods. Poultry giblets should also be wrapped and stored separately.

"Use ground meat within one or two days, or freeze for longer use.

"Fish and poultry also have a short storage life—usually one or two days. [Freeze them, too, for longer keeping—Authors.]

"Keep cooked meat, poultry, and fish, and the gravy or broth made from them, in covered containers in the refrigerator. Use within 1 or 2 days.

"Cooked meats should be cooled quickly—preferably in a pan of cold water, then refrigerated promptly. [Author's note: Remove meat from any sauce and from the hot pot or pan in which it was cooked, place in a cool dish, and set the dish in ice water. Turn the meat over when the bottom is cool. Sauce can be cooled in the same way. Stirring it occasionally will speed chilling, as will dividing a large potful into smaller amounts. Chill in less than thirty minutes if possible. Always remove stuffings from birds before chilling and refrigerate separately.]

"*Cured and smoked meats*—ham, frankfurters, bacon, sausage—can be stored in their original containers in the refrigerator. Mild-cured hams are similar to fresh meats in keeping quality. Use whole hams within a week, half hams and slices within 3 to 5 days. For best flavor, use bacon, franks, and smoked sausages within a week."

Fats and Oils

"Refrigerate lard, butter, margarine, drippings, and opened containers of cooking and salad oils. You can store most firm vegetable shortenings (those that have been hydrogenated), covered, at room temperature. Refrigerate open jars of salad dressing; do not freeze."

Fresh Milk and Cream

"Keep containers covered and store in coldest part of refrigerator.

"Milk should not be exposed to light or left standing in a warm place. Exposure to sun impairs the flavor and the riboflavin content of milk."

Dried Milk

"Store *nonfat dry milk* in a closed container at a temperature of 75° F., or lower. Because of its higher milkfat content, *dry whole milk* does not keep as well as nonfat dry milk. Keep dry whole milk in a tightly closed container in the refrigerator. Refrigerate *reconstituted dry milk* as you would fresh fluid milk."

Cheeses

"Wrap tightly and keep in the refrigerator. Stored this way, hard cheeses will keep indefinitely. (Take out of refrigerator about ½ hour before serving for best flavor and texture.) Aroma needs to be released.

"Cottage cheese should be used within a few days, and other soft cheeses (such as cream cheeses) within two weeks."

Eggs

"Eggs lose quality quickly if not refrigerated. Buy eggs from refrigerated storage in retail stores and promptly place in refrigerator at home. For best flavor and cooking quality use eggs within 1 week. The original egg cartons are satisfactory for refrigerator storage.

"Leftover egg yolks can be placed in container with just enough cold water to cover. Leftover whites keep well in a tightly covered dish or jar in the refrigerator. (Use both within 1 or 2 days.)"

Vegetables

"The fresher vegetables are when eaten the better they are. With only a few exceptions vegetables keep best in the refrigerator. The exceptions—potatoes, sweet potatoes, dry onions, hard-rind squashes, eggplant, and rutabagas—keep well in cool rather than cold storage.

"The fresh vegetable and fruit compartment or crisper in your refrigerator performs better if it is *at least two-thirds full.* If crisper is less full than this, vegetables will keep better if they are first put into plastic bags. (This is also true if crisper does not have tight, well-fitting lid.)

"*Asparagus*—Discard tough parts of stalks. Store covered in refrigerator. [Do any trimming of this and other produce with a sharp knife—Authors.]

"*Beans, snap or wax*—Refrigerate covered.

"*Broccoli, cabbage, cauliflower, and Brussels sprouts*—Store in crisper or in plastic bags.

"*Carrots, beets, and radishes*—Remove root tips and tops and store covered in refrigerator.

"*Celery*—Separate stalks, scrub, drain, wrap tightly and store in crisper. (Celery will keep longer in the stalk, but is less convenient to use.)

"*Green peas and limas*—Leave in pods and store in refrigerator. Use within a day or two.

"*Lettuce and other salad greens*—Wash and thoroughly drain. Place in plastic bags in vegetable compartment. (Authors' note: There are plastic containers now available made especially for lettuce which work very well. Don't cut lettuce with a knife before storing as this may cause rust. Use your hands to remove the heart.)

"*Onions*—Store dry onions at room temperature, or slightly cooler. They sprout and decay at high temperature and high humidity. Allow for good circulation of air. Store green onions in plastic bag in refrigerator.

"*Parsley*—Wash, shake gently to remove excess water. Refrigerate in tightly covered jar. Fresh parsley will keep for weeks when stored in this manner.

"*Peanuts*—Keep peanuts in tightly covered containers in the refrigerator so they stay crisp and retain their flavor. Peanut butter, too, keeps best in the refrigerator. However, when cold it is difficult to spread, so remove from the refrigerator a short time before using to allow it to soften. (If the family is fond of peanut butter, it may be used so quickly that refrigeration is not necessary.)

"*Potatoes*—Store in a dark place with good ventilation and a temperature of 45 to 50 degrees. Light causes greening. High temperatures hasten sprouting and shriveling. Relative humidity should be 85% to 90%.

"Storing potatoes at refrigerator temperature causes some of the starch to change to sugar. If potatoes taste too sweet because of overly cold storage, their flavor may be improved by keeping them at room temperature for a week or two before using.

"*Sweet corn*—Store uncovered, in husks, in the refrigerator. Use as soon as possible.

"*Sweet potatoes, hard-rind squashes* (*uncut*), *eggplant, and rutabagas*—Store at cool room temperature around 60°. Temperatures below 50° may cause chilling injury.

"*Tomatoes*—Store ripe tomatoes uncovered in the refrigerator. Keep unripe tomatoes at room temperature away from direct sunlight until they ripen."

FRUITS

"*Apples*—Store ripe apples uncovered in the refrigerator. Unripe or hard apples are best held at cool room temperature (60° to 70°).

"*Apricots, avocados, grapes, pears, peaches, plums, and rhubarb*—Allow to ripen in open air at room temperature. Do not place in sun. When fruits are ripe, store uncovered in the refrigerator. Use within 3 to 5 days.

"*Bananas*—Store at room temperature—never in the refrigerator.

"*Berries and cherries*—Keep whole and uncovered in the refrigerator until ready to use. Washing and stemming these fruits before refrigerating causes loss of food value and increased spoilage. For best eating use within 1 or 2 days.

"*Citrus fruits, melons, and pineapples*—These fruits are best stored at cool room temperature (60° to 70°). Short-time holding in the refrigerator is not harmful. If citrus fruits are held too long at too-low temperatures the skin becomes pitted and the flesh discolors. Use fruits within a week for maximum quality.

"*Canned fruits and vegetables*—Unopened cans of fruits and vegetables should be stored in a moderately cool place away from heat. Avoid storage near steam pipes, radiators, furnaces, kitchen ranges, and refrigerator condensers.

"Canned foods will keep as long as nothing happens to the container to make it leak. Extremely long periods of storage at high temperatures may result in some loss in color, flavor, appearance, and nutritive value, but the foods will remain wholesome. However, a regular turnover about once a year is best. Fruit in glass jars should be stored in the dark. After opening, fruits should be covered and stored in the refrigerator. They can be safely stored in their original containers, although citrus juices, pineapple and tomatoes (yes, this is a fruit) develop an undesirable flavor if stored very long in the can.

"*Dried fruits*—Keep in tightly closed containers. Store at room temperature, except in warm, humid weather; then refrigerate.

"*Breads*—Bread should be stored in original wrapper in clean, well ventilated breadbox. It stays fresh longer at room temperature than in the refrigerator. However, in hot, humid weather the refrigerator will protect the bread against mold.

"Breads can be frozen in their original wrappers if storage is only for a week or so. For a longer time, tuck into a freezer bag or add an overwrap of freezer paper.

"*Coffee*—After it has been opened coffee ages rapidly, losing flavor, strength and aroma. The supply should be replenished regularly to insure freshness. Store coffee in a cool place; storing in the refrigerator preserves freshness for a longer time than room temperature storage."

How to Avoid Staphylococcus Food Poisoning

This is one of the Results of Improper Handling and Storage of Certain Types of Foods.

" 'Summertime, and the Living is Easy' is not true for those laid low with food poisoning. Extreme discomfort is experienced by people suffering from the most common type of food poisoning caused by the staphylococcus bacteria. When this organism grows in food it produces a poison called an enterotoxin which causes illness.

"Outbreaks of this kind of poisoning occur with greatest frequency in the summer—usually as a result of eating foods which have not had proper refrigeration. Fortunately, this poisoning can be prevented by the application of existing knowledge."

Foods Most Commonly Involved: "Custard and cream-filled bakery goods, ham, tongue, and poultry are the foods most often responsible for staph poisoning. Foods also frequently involved include other meats and meat products, fish and fish products, milk and milk products, cream sauces, salads, puddings and salad dressings. Usually the foods do not smell or appear spoiled in any way.

"Acidity hampers the growth of the staphylococcus, but if this acidity is reduced by added ingredients such as eggs or cream, even an acid food can become dangerous."

Prevention of Food Contamination: "The sources from which the staphylococcus enter foods are, for the most part, human or animal. The nasal passages of many persons are laden with the organisms. Boils and infected wounds may be sources. The human skin can be a carrier of these bacteria. Ordinarily, air is a carrier only when the organisms have been introduced there from human sources. Staphylococci can cause mastitis in cows, and the bacteria can form enterotoxin in milk.

"To avoid contamination, individuals with colds, sore throats, skin infection, and diarrhea should not handle food until they have recovered. Avoid sneezing and coughing near food. Use a clean spoon for tasting food. Hands should be thoroughly washed before handling any food or tableware.

"Purchase foods from markets which maintain high sanitation standards. Foods should be protected from flies, insects, and rodents. Wide use of cellophane or plastic wrappers is a boon to safeguarding foods."

Prevention of Outbreaks: "Unfortunately, prevention of contamination is not always possible because staphylococci are almost everywhere. Therefore, it is extremely important that food be kept so that the staphylococcus cannot grow to produce the harmful enterotoxin.

"The microorganisms grow and flourish when they are warm and moist. It has been reported that toxin is produced at an appreciable rate at temperatures between 50° and 115° F; and the production is best at 70° to 97° F. Most food poisoning outbreaks occur in the summer.

"Foods should be cooled rapidly. *Creamed dishes and other foods particularly favoring toxin growth should be cooled in the refrigerator.* In warm weather even cool foods should not be allowed to stand at room temperature for any length of time as this may invite food poisoning.

"Staphylococcus can be killed by heating to the boiling point. However, if toxins have developed before heating, these toxins may not be destroyed by boiling. The main thing is to refrigerate properly at 45°

or lower SO THE POISONOUS TOXINS HAVE NO CHANCE TO DEVELOP.

"If the food is to be served hot, it should be heated to a high temperature and kept hot.

"We might summarize by saying that staphylococcus food poisoning can best be prevented by cleanliness in all phases of food handling, by proper refrigeration of perishable foods, and by keeping hot foods hot until served."

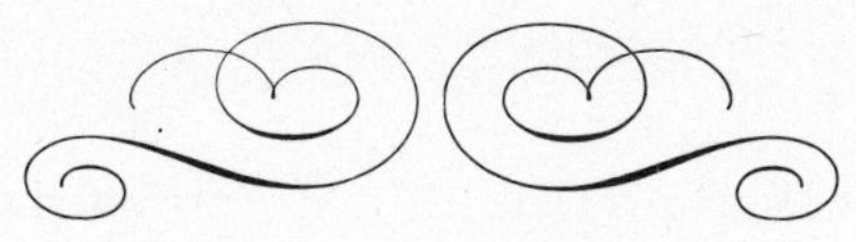

SECTION II

Recipes—and Helpful Specifics About Buying Economy Meats and Other Principal Ingredients

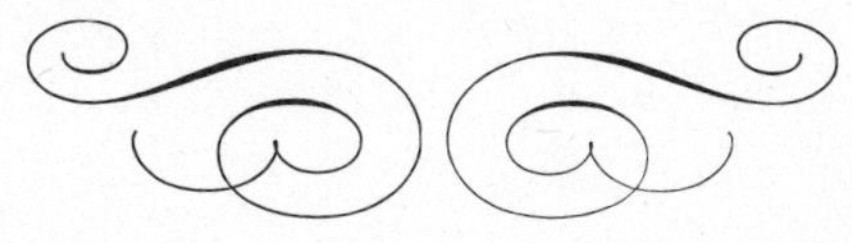

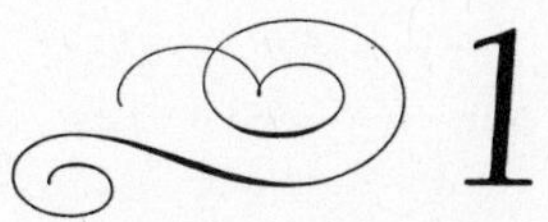

1

THINGS YOU SHOULD KNOW ABOUT BUYING MEAT

There are 173 retail cuts of all meats—beef, pork, veal, and lamb—on display in the nation's supermarkets. Not even the meat packers know for sure how many times that number is multiplied by the different regional names those 173 cuts are called. To confuse you further, the bone by which you may learn to identify a cut of meat is sometimes left in and sometimes cut out.

We don't know any magic that will reduce those 173 plus cuts to an easy-to-remember even dozen. But we have singled out some of the most confusing things about buying meat, tried to make them less confusing so as to give you a basis for understanding that can lead to economy—and more interesting ways of eating.

We have suggested some places a housewife with meat-buying problems can easily get advice; namely, a good newspaper food column, a good radio food program, and a reliable butcher. She might also want to check with her area United States Department of Agriculture Extension Service. One of the Extension Service's important functions is to conduct classes in Home Economics for housewives. Remember these people can help. Your taxes pay for these services, so you are shortchanging yourself if you don't take advantage of them.

National statistics give us the following breakdown of each dollar spent for food: 26¢ red meat, 7½¢ for poultry and eggs, and 2½¢ for fish; total, 36¢. Statistics about food change constantly. In spite of this, we feel the ones we are using in Pennysaver will give the reader valuable basic understanding.

Being informed about which meats vary in price with the seasons and when to expect these variations can indicate to a housewife when she might expect to be able to buy usually expensive cuts on sale, possibly to store in the family freezer, possibly just for a special treat. The following graph (based on New York City figures) does not necessarily reflect the national picture but it can serve as an indication to a housewife from another geographic area what fluctuations she might expect to find. Her neighborhood butcher or her County Extension Service could bring the picture into local focus for her.

MONTHS OF LOW, AVERAGE, AND HIGH RETAIL PRICES FOR DIFFERENT KINDS AND CUTS OF MEAT

New York City, 1961–1965 Average

(May, 1967 *Cornell Extension Bulletin 1184*)

KIND AND CUT OF MEAT	Average price	Average seasonal variation	Jan.	Feb.	Mar.	Apr.	May	June	July	Aug.	Sept.	Oct.	Nov.	Dec.
	Cents per pound													
BEEF														
Porterhouse steak	125.5	8.0	Near	Near	Near	Below	Below	Below	Below	Near	Above	Above	Near	Near
Round steak	114.8	5.8	Near	Near	Below	Near	Below	Below	Below	Near	Above	Above	Above	Above
Sirloin steak	103.0	10.4	Below	Below	Below	Below	Below	Below	Near	Above	Above	Above	Above	Near
Rib roast	83.0	4.8	Near	Near	Below	Near	Near	Below	Below	Near	Above	Near	Above	Above
Chuck, boneless	81.7	3.8	Above	Near	Above	Below	Below	Below	Below	Near	Near	Near	Near	Above
Chuck steak	60.5	7.8	Above	Above	Near	Near	Below	Below	Below	Near	Near	Near	Near	Near
Chopped beef	50.9	2.6	Below	Below	Below	Below	Below	Near	Near	Near	Above	Above	Above	Above
LAMB														
Loin chops	135.8	10.4	Below	Below	Below	Below	Below	Above	Above	Above	Above	Above	Near	Below
Shoulder chops	91.8	5.6	Below	Below	Below	Below	Below	Above	Above	Above	Above	Above	Near	Near
Leg	68.6	4.4	Below	Below	Below	Below	Above	Above	Above	Near	Above	Near	Near	Near
Shoulder	47.3	4.2	Below	Below	Below	Below	Near	Above	Above	Above	Above	Near	Near	Above
Breast and shank	35.9	7.5	Below	Below	Below	Below	Below	Above	Above	Above	Above	Above	Above	Above
PORK														
Loin chops	98.0	10.4	Below	Below	Below	Below	Below	Above	Above	Above	Above	Above	Above	Near
Bacon	75.0	8.4	Below	Below	Below	Below	Below	Near	Above	Near	Above	Above	Above	Above
Loin roast	68.0	8.8	Below	Below	Below	Below	Below	Near	Above	Above	Above	Above	Above	Above
Ham, ready-to-eat	66.0	4.4	Below	Near	Below	Below	Below	Near	Above	Above	Above	Near	Above	Above
Smoked calas	46.8	3.4	Near	Near	Below	Below	Below	Near	Near	Above	Near	Near	Above	Above
VEAL														
Cutlets	172.3	8.4	Near	Above	Near	Below	Below	Below	Below	Near	Above	Above	Near	Near
Liver	169.8	1.6	Near	Near	Near	Near	Near	Near	Near	Near	Near	Near	Near	Near
Loin chops	116.7	6.2	Above	Above	Above	Below	Below	Below	Below	Near	Above	Near	Near	Above
Leg and rump	78.3	4.2	Above	Above	Above	Below	Below	Below	Below	Near	Near	Near	Near	Near
OTHER MEAT														
Frankfurters	68.6	0.8	Near	Near	Near	Near	Near	Near	Near	Near	Near	Near	Near	Near

Retail prices, by months:

- [solid black] usually below yearly average.
- [hatched] usually near yearly average.
- [white] usually above yearly average.

The USDA Meat Inspection Stamp

To be economical, meat must be good as well as inexpensive; otherwise your health will suffer and you may have to pay expensive medical bills. Meat should come from healthy animals that have been raised, butchered, and otherwise processed under sanitary conditions. One of the best assurances we have that this has been the case is the stamp of the United States Department of Agriculture, "U.S. Inspected and Passed," on the meat we intend to buy. The stamp appears in a circle in purple vegetable ink on carcasses of animals that have been inspected by USDA agents. These agents must inspect not only the meat itself, but also the premises and assure themselves that both are absolutely healthy and sanitary, and place their inspection stamp on all meat that crosses state lines.

The Wholesome Meat Act, passed into law in December of 1967, requires that those plants doing business only within a single state must be inspected by a state inspection program with requirements that are at least equal to Federal requirements. These plants were given two, or in some cases three, years in which to make the necessary improvements in their facilities and comply. (The Wholesome Poultry Act of 1968 is patterned after the Wholesome Meat Act, with the same time limits for compliance.)

The USDA Meat Grade Stamp

The grade stamp means more on *beef* than on other meats which are butchered while young and tender.

Generally, since veal, lamb, and pork are slaughtered at an early age, the grade stamp is not as important for them as it is for beef.

It is the *grade* that indicates the difference between two beef steers that will result in a moderately priced cut from one animal being tender and juicy, while the very same cut of meat from another animal will be stringy and tough. Some of the things that determine such differences are age of an animal and how well-fed it was during its lifetime.

Grading is, for the most part, voluntary. If the packer requests it, after the USDA inspector has inspected and stamped his meat to show that it is wholesome, a Federal grader will grade and stamp it with one of the following grade marks which show the grade name on a shield.

Most USDA PRIME BEEF is sold to luxury markets, hotels and high-priced restaurants.

USDA CHOICE is the most tender and juicy of the beef commonly sold in retail stores.

USDA GOOD is relatively tender but has less fat marbling—therefore less juiciness and flavor than the two higher grades. If you are going to cook moderately priced cuts for a long time in a liquid, USDA GOOD is an economical buy.

USDA PRIME, CHOICE, and GOOD grades are probably the ones you will need to be most conversant with; however, you should know about the others, too.

USDA STANDARD: This grade is very lean and comes from young animals, so it's also fairly tender. But it lacks fat marbling and is therefore very mild in flavor. Most cuts will be somewhat dry unless prepared with moist heat.

USDA COMMERCIAL: Commercial grade beef is produced only from mature animals. Even though it is well marbled, it will require long, slow cooking with moist heat to make it tender.

USDA UTILITY, CUTTER and CANNER: These grades are used mostly to make ground beef or processed meat products. They are perfectly wholesome, but tough and dry.

The importance of knowing the grade, especially of beef, is to help you determine the cooking method. *Both the grade and the part of the animal a piece of meat is cut from* determine whether or not it will be tough and therefore cooked only in liquid or steam . . . and for a long time. (Some of the so-called "economy cuts" fall in this category).

Study the chart entitled "Wholesale Cuts of Beef and Their Bone Structure," page 64, and familiarize yourself with the names of the wholesale cuts: chuck, rib, short loin, sirloin, round, fore shank, brisket, short plate, flank. You will see when you look at the other carcass charts, that the wholesale cuts for them aren't too different. The economy cuts come from the same general part of the carcass on all the animals. They are generally the more wasteful, less desirable cuts.

Since beef is the meat in which it's most important that you match the cooking method to the grade as well as the cut, we've prepared the following list which we hope will help you do that.

Matching Cooking Methods to Beef Cut and Grade

• Cuts from the less-used muscles along the back—the rib and loin sections, will be tender in beef of the grades commonly sold at retail, and can be cooked in dry heat.

• Cuts from the more active muscles, such as the shoulder (chuck), bottom sirloin, and round are tougher. But these economical cuts are not as tough in Prime and Choice grades as they are in the lower ones. In Prime and Choice, some of these less expensive cuts can be cooked in dry heat.

• Meat from the very bottom of the animal—foreshank, brisket, plate, and flank—is usually best cooked in moist heat, no matter what the grade, unless it is ground.

• Small, economy cuts immediately adjacent to tender, expensive cuts are often tender, too. (They're "first cuts.")

If you know the difference in meat grades and the names of the wholesale cuts, and if you know how you want to cook the meat you plan to buy, you can ring the bell for the meat department manager at the supermarket and stand a good chance of successfully getting from him what you want. Don't feel embarrassed that you are not more knowledgeable about meat and the many names that each cut has. You are not alone in this.

If you always arrive at the supermarket during the rush hour when it's impossible to get within shouting distance of the meat department manager, and your reliable neighborhood butcher went out of business years ago, these lists, prepared by the National Livestock and Meat Board, should help:

Some Meat Cuts Suitable for Roasting: Beef Standing Rib, Beef Delmonico (Rib Eye), Beef Rolled Rump, Beef Sirloin Tip (High Quality), Veal Rolled Shoulder, Veal Rib Roast, Veal Shank Half of Leg, Veal Rolled Rump, Veal Arm Roast, Pork Boston Butt, Pork Blade Loin Roast, Pork Sirloin Roast, Pork Rolled Loin, Smoked Ham (Butt Half), Pork Rolled Leg, Lamb Rolled Shoulder, Lamb Leg, Sirloin off, Lamb Rib Roast.

(For most roasts, oven temperature should be set from 300° F. to 350°. Use a meat thermometer, place it in the heavy part of meat but do not let it touch the bone. Veal should be cooked well done, but not dried out—about 170° on your thermometer. Pork, for the sake of your health, should always be well done—185° F. for all roasts except loin which we are now told it is safe to cook to only 170° F. Find out if smoked ham is raw, partially, or fully cooked. Most people like lamb roasts cooked to a well done 175° F. but beef is very much a matter of personal taste, anywhere from 140° F. for rare to 170° for well done.)

Some Meat Cuts Suitable for Broiling, Pan-broiling, and Pan-frying: Beef Rib Steak, Beef Porterhouse Steak, Beef Sirloin Steak, Beef Delmonico (Rib Eye) Steaks, Beef Boneless Sirloin Steak, Beef Tenderloin Steak, Beef Patties, Beef Top Loin Steak, Sliced Bacon, Sliced Canadian Style Bacon, Smoked Ham (Center Slice), Pork Rib Chops, Smoked Pork Loin Chops, Lamb Rib Chops, Lamb Loin Chops, Lamb Sirloin Chops, Lamb Arm Chop, Lamb Saratoga Chops.

Other Meat Cuts Suitable for Pan-frying: Beef Cube Steak, Beef Round Steak, Veal Cube Steak, Veal Loin Chop, Veal Kidney Chop, Veal Rib Chop, Veal Sirloin Steak, Veal Round Steak, Veal Choplet, Mock Chicken Legs, Veal Patties, Porklet, Pork Tenderloin, Pork Leg Steak, Pork Sausage Patties, Pork Arm Steak, Pork Blade Steak, Lamb Arm and Blade Chops.

Some Meat Cuts Suitable for Braising: Beef Top Round Steak, Beef Bottom Round Steak, Beef Flank Steak, Beef Arm Pot Roast, Beef Blade Pot Roast, Beef English (Boston) Cut, Beef Short Ribs, Beef Shank Cross Cuts, Veal Arm Steak, Veal Blade Steak, Veal Brisket Pieces, Veal Blade Roast, Pork Loin and Rib Chops, Pork Butterfly Chops, Lamb Neck Slices, Lamb Shank, Lamb Riblets, Lamb Brisket Pieces.

The National Livestock and Meat Board has this to say about braising, a method of cookery with which not everyone is familiar:

"This method of cooking is suitable for less tender cuts of meat. Some tender cuts also are usually best if braised, including pork steaks and cutlets; veal chops, steaks and cutlets; and pork liver. Follow these steps for the best results in braising:

"1. Brown meat slowly on all sides in heavy utensil. Pour off drippings after browning. The browning develops flavor and color. Fat is usually added to prevent the meat from sticking as it browns. However, cuts with sufficient fat require no added fat unless they are coated with flour or crumbs. A slow brown stays on the meat better than a quick brown at a high temperature.

2. "Season with salt, pepper, herbs and spices, if desired. The meat should be seasoned after browning unless seasoning is added to the coating.

3. "Add a small amount of liquid, if necessary. Liquid is usually added to less tender cuts but may be omitted when cooking tender meat.

4. "Cover tightly. A tight-fitting lid holds in the steam needed for softening the connective tissue and making the meat tender.

5. "Cook at low temperature until tender. This means simmering, not boiling. It may be done on top of the range or in a slow oven (300° F. to 325° F.).

6. "Make sauce or gravy from the liquid in the pan, if desired. The gravy is a desirable part of many braised meat dishes." (Authors' note: The pan juices should be saved and used in some other way if not for gravy in order to conserve every bit of both food flavor and nutrition.)

Some Meat Cuts Suitable for Cooking in Liquid: Beef Heel of Round, Fresh Beef Brisket, Corned Beef, Beef Plate, Beef for Stew, Veal Heel of Round, Veal Foreshank, Veal Riblets, Veal for Stew, Salt Pork (seasoning), Smoked Ham Shank Portion, Smoked Picnic, Spareribs, Fresh Pork Hocks, Smoked Pork Hocks, Fresh Pig's Feet, Country Style Pork Backbones, Lamb for Stew.

The Best Approach to Quantity Meat Buying for the Freezer

There are many tantalizing ads for sides of beef, whole lambs, etc., that sound too good to be true; and they probably are just that; at least for the family with an average-sized freezer. If you know a lot about meat, its grades, its cuts and the waste involved in butchering (roughly 20–25 percent), and you have unlimited freezer space, you can probably both save money and eat well by buying a whole side of beef, particularly if you keep abreast of changing meat market conditions and stock your freezer just before the price starts an upward climb that will continue for several months.

If you don't fit into this category, and you know a reputable neighborhood butcher, your best bet is probably to arrange with him periodically to select a chuck (shoulder) of beef, plus whatever else your freezer can accommodate on which he can give you a good wholesale quantity price. He can remove most of the bone from the chuck. By using some of the bones and scrap for soup making and reduced broths for convenient freezer storing, you will cut down on the cutting waste.

The only way an independent butcher can afford to do this and give you a price comparable to supermarket prices is for you to let him fill this need for you more or less on a yearly basis, and at his convenience. It may take a few months for him to fit buying for you into his pattern of wholesale shopping and you will have to adapt yourself to planning ahead. You will have to know two weeks in advance when you will run out of freezer meat. You will have to organize your other freezer buying around this one large shipment so there is room for it. You will have to plan any freezer defrosting around it.

You may even have to break out of your cooking rut and try some new dishes in order to use up the balance of cuts you are not in the habit of preparing.

The shoulder area of beef is a very tasty, as well as an economical, section. There are different ways of butchering this meat. If your butcher will buy you a "Top Choice" (from the "Choice" available to him select the very best) and tailor it to your needs, you can substitute it for many of the much more expensive cuts of beef. Once your butcher understands the type of dishes you like to make, he will be able to cut suitable pieces from the chuck.

Following is a list of one of the ways Arthur Petry, a second-generation neighborhood butcher in Long Beach, N.Y., who has supplied us with chuck for many years, divides this section for our family freezer. (He adapts the way he does this to the season; winter more roast and stews: summer more hamburger and steaks.) When he gets an exceptionally nice animal, Arthur includes the areas shown on the Chart of Wholesale Cuts as: Chuck, Foreshank, and Brisket. His recommendations for the use of each cut and a reference to the Pennysaver Cookbook Recipe we actually made with it are included in the following list. Buying chuck this way will cost you a little more than buying it at the supermarket but it can be much more tender which means you will be able to cook more of the cuts in dry heat for shorter lengths of time. And this is a nutritional saving because meats cooked without liquid and for a short length of time retain a higher percentage of their nutrients than do tougher meats that must be cooked for a long time in liquid. There is also less shrinkage in the first method.

ONE OF THE WAYS BUTCHER ARTHUR PETRY DIVIDES A YOUNG, TENDER BEEF CHUCK (PLUS SOME OTHER SECTIONS) FOR OUR FAMILY FREEZER

The recipes listed will be found—in the same order as below—at the beginning of the Beef Recipes starting on page 65.

Meat Cuts	*Arthur Petry's recommended use*	*Pennysaver Recipe*
4½ lb. 2nd cut boneless brisket	Pot Roast or Braise	Oven Braised Brisket in Barbecue Sauce
4½ lb. 1st cut boneless brisket (sometimes called "Boston cut")	Pot Roast or Roast	Roast Brisket Cooked Without First Defrosting
5½ lb. boneless rolled rib	Roast or Pot	Chuck Roast of Beef and Vegetables in Tangy Wine Sauce
5⅓ lb. chuck boneless pot roast	Pot Roast	Sweet and Sour Pot Roast (with cabbage)
3½ lb. chuck short ribs (plus an extra 2½ lbs.)	Soup or Pot	Chuck Ribs With Barley-Mushroom Crust
2½ lb. London broil steaks	London broil	London Broil
4 club steaks	Club steaks	Chuck Club Steaks
10 "Chicken" or "chuck fillet" steaks	Broil or Fry	Chicken Fried Steaks
10 strips chuck (3 lbs.)	Stroganoff or Beef and Peppers	Beef Stroganoff With Mushrooms
8 steaks	Potting	Swiss Steak with Cherry Tomatoes (Basic instructions and marinades for broiling economy steaks are included here in recipes.)
2 3-lb. pkgs. boneless stew	Stew	Cubed Beef Stew With Egg Dumplings
Best of the bones and scrap	Soup Making	Making Broth from Scraps of Meat and Bones
10 2-lb. pkgs. chopped chuck (part of fat removed before chopping)	Miscellaneous	Beef and Bean Shepherd's Pies

Buying Meat For Your Freezer From the Supermarket

We realize that many of our readers no longer live within shopping distance of a "reliable neighborhood butcher." He probably went out of business while waiting for his customers to realize they don't get along quite as well in the baffling confusion of meat cuts without his know-how and advice about cooking methods. So now, in order to shop wisely at the supermarket counter, we must learn the things about meat that once we relied upon him to tell us.

You can and should take advantage of supermarket sales. Watch the supermarket ads for specials on the economy meats. (When buying meat in quantity for the freezer, it does pay to shop around sometimes.) Fill up your available freezer space with sale-priced pork, veal, and lamb shoulder roasts, breasts of lamb and veal, half-hams, poultry, and hamburger.

About Ground or Chopped Meat: Ground or chopped beef is one of the most economical and versatile of meats and frequently on sale at the supermarket. Its content is regulated by state and local laws and may vary greatly as to percentage of fat permitted and whether or not such things as muscle from the heart or tongue may be included.

It is not always easy to tell what meat is in hamburger or other forms of ground beef. The meat from older animals is darker than a young beef; but ground chuck is lighter in color than ground round. A light color may also be the result of excessive fat. There is now on the market a combination of different grinds called "meat loaf," which can add more variety to your ground meat recipes. Find out what your local regulations are concerning this meat and all forms of ground beef, so you know what to ask about it. You usually can have chuck or round steak ground to order, but this procedure doesn't go with special prices.

Ground Meat Loses Quality Rapidly

Any ground meat, no matter how fresh it may be, loses quality more rapidly and is more subject to bacterial growth than steaks, chops, and roasts because it has so much more surface exposed. Therefore, great care should be taken to package and store it quickly and properly.

When buying meat on sale at the supermarket you will have to take it as packaged. But you do not have to freeze it that way. In fact, you should not.

Consider the size of your family, the amount of meat it eats at a meal, the different recipes you might want to use. Some of the recipes undoubtedly will include other things such as vegetables, legumes, eggs, and bread crumbs and therefore will not require as much meat as other recipes. Then recut and repackage the meat accordingly.

It will pay you to own a good meat cleaver, butcher knife, and chopping block. You might even want to get a small meat saw. You will find suggestions under the individual meats in this section for ways of cutting up some of the economy cuts you might find at the supermarket that could be turned into two or three meals. *Be sure to keep all of your equipment, especially the block, very clean.*

When Is Bone-In or Bone-Out Best Economy? The chart on page 61 may be helpful in determining which of more than one meat offered is the best buy from the standpoint of which one costs the least per *edible serving,* rather than price per pound. Sometimes boneless meat, even though it costs considerably more per pound, costs less per edible serving than does a chunk of meat that is one-fourth to one-half bone.

How Much Meat to Buy

The American Meat Institute gives this general rule to follow in determining how much uncooked meat to buy per serving (families differ so much in their eating habits that it is impossible to make anything better than a very rough estimate):

BONELESS MEAT—as boneless round steak, cutlets, liver, stew meats, ground meat, and rolled roasts—allow ¼ pound per serving.

MEAT WITH AVERAGE AMOUNT OF BONE—as bone-in roasts, steaks, ham —allow ⅓ to ½ pound per serving.

MEAT WITH LARGER AMOUNT OF BONE—as short ribs, spareribs, pork hocks—allow ¾ to 1 pound per serving.*

This chart was prepared by Ohio State Extension Service using information from Cornell University to help shoppers determine which of more than one meat offered is the best buy from the standpoint of which one costs the least per *edible serving,* rather than price per pound.

* From American Meat Institute Booklet, *Ideas with Meat.*

MEAT

Retail Cut	Servings Per Pound	Price Per Pound											
		29	39	49	59	69	79	89	99	109	119	129	139
		Cost Per Serving											
Beef													
Sirloin Steak	2½	12	16	20	24	28	32	36	40	44	48	52	56
Porterhouse, T-bone Rib Steak	2	15	20	25	30	35	40	45	50	55	60	65	70
Round Steak	3½	8	11	14	17	20	23	25	28	31	34	37	40
Chuck Roast, bone-in	2	15	20	25	30	35	40	45	50	55	60	65	70
Rib Roast, boneless	2½	12	16	20	24	28	32	36	40	44	48	52	56
Rib Roast, bone-in	2	15	20	25	30	35	40	45	50	55	60	65	70
Rump, Sirloin Roast	3	10	13	16	20	23	26	30	33	36	40	43	46
Ground Beef	4	7	10	12	15	17	20	22	25	27	30	32	35
Short Ribs	2	15	20	25	30	35	40	45	50	55	60	65	70
Heart, Liver, Kidney	5	6	8	10	12	14	16	18	20	22	24	26	28
Frankfurters	4	7	10	12	15	17	20	22	25	27	30	32	35
Stew Meat, boneless	5	6	8	10	12	14	16	18	20	22	24	26	28
Lamb													
Loin, Rib, Shoulder Chops	3	10	13	16	20	23	26	30	33	36	40	43	46
Breast, Shank	2	15	20	25	30	35	40	45	50	55	60	65	70
Shoulder Roast	2½	12	16	20	24	28	32	36	40	44	48	52	56
Leg of Lamb	3	10	13	16	20	23	26	30	33	36	40	43	46
Pork—Fresh													
Center Cut or Rib Chops	4	7	10	12	15	17	20	22	25	27	30	32	35
Loin or Rib Roast	2½	12	16	20	24	28	32	36	40	44	48	52	56
Boston butt, bone-in	3	10	13	16	20	23	26	30	33	36	40	43	46
Blade Steak	3	10	13	16	20	23	26	30	33	36	40	43	46
Spare Ribs	1⅓	22	29	37	44	52	59	67	74	82	89	97	104
Pork—Cured													
Picnic, bone-in	2	15	20	25	30	35	40	45	50	55	60	65	70
Ham—Fully Cooked													
bone-in	3½	8	11	14	17	20	23	25	28	31	34	37	40
boneless and canned	5	6	8	10	12	14	16	18	20	22	24	26	28
shankless	4¼	7	9	12	14	16	19	21	23	26	28	30	33
center slice	5	6	8	10	12	14	16	18	20	22	24	26	28
Poultry													
Broiler, ready-to-cook	1⅓	22	29	37	44	52	59	67	74	82	89	97	104
legs, thighs	3	10	13	16	20	23	26	30	33	36	40	43	46
breasts	4	7	10	12	15	17	20	22	25	27	30	32	35
Turkey, ready-to-cook													
under 12 lbs.	1	29	39	49	59	69	79	89	99	109	119	129	139
12 lbs. and over	1⅓	22	29	37	44	52	59	67	74	82	89	97	104

2

ABOUT THE RECIPES

There are recipes here for steaks, chops, roasts, stews, chickens, and turkey—whole or in parts, whole fish and fish fillets, fruits and vegetables and salads, soups, sauces and desserts.

There are recipes here that combine top quality, expensive meats with the inexpensive alternate protein called "legumes" (actually, they are the seed of the legume, a plant with a seed pod opening on two sides)—peas, beans, lentils, and peanuts.

There are recipes designed to stretch a small quantity of meat by adding bread crumbs, eggs, and vegetables, and combining them to make loaves, pies, stews, and stuffed vegetables.

There are recipes that, by adding just a little of the more expensive ingredients, turn everyday fare into company dishes.

In Grandma's time, some of these recipes might have been put in a section called *Cooking with Leftovers*. They employ a type of food magic that made everyone want to go to Grandma's house and today attracts us to *gourmet* French, Italian, Chinese, or other restaurants whose chefs were trained in the Old World tradition of substituting loving care and imagination for the money they did not have.

How to Use the Creative Art of Substitution in Planning Economical Meat Dishes

The combination recipes in this book can be changed by a little creative cookery to adapt to your budget and your stock on hand. You must, of course, give consideration to taste compatibility, moisture, fat content, and cooking time of substituted or added ingredients.

1. The amount of beans might be increased and the meat decreased.

2. Leftover cooked meat might be substituted for raw. Consider whether or not to change cooking time of recipe.

3. An inexpensive meat that you got on sale may sometimes be substituted for a more expensive one . . . particularly in recipes calling for ground meats.

4. *Very young* leftover lamb meat or veal can be substituted for chicken and turkey meat in some of the recipes. And vice versa.

5. Cooked, ground veal often can be substituted for cooked ground beef but you might want to add a little more seasoning to the dish. Consider taste carefully before substituting cooked ground beef for veal. The recipe may have been designed for a delicately flavored meat.

6. Very lean, delicately flavored pork can be substituted much more frequently now that the fat content has been greatly reduced in pork. Consider flavor compatibility carefully, however.

7. One delicately flavored, white-fleshed fish can almost always be substituted for another. When substituting shellfish for fin fish, be very sure not to overcook it or cook at a high heat unless you enjoy chewing rubber.

8. When substituting skim for whole milk in making a recipe, the U. S. Department of Agriculture bulletin, *Family Fare,* recommends the addition of 2½ tsps. butter or margarine per cup of skim milk. The results are usually better than plain skim milk in a recipe calling for whole milk.

9. Two egg yolks can be substituted for 1 whole egg in baking or thickening. Seven-eighths cup vegetable or animal shortening plus ½ tsp. salt can be substituted for 1 cup butter or margarine in baking.

As examples of substitution possibilities, we have made a note on some of the beef recipes.

CHART OF BEEF CARCASS SHOWING WHOLESALE AND RETAIL CUTS OF BEEF AND WHERE THEY COME FROM

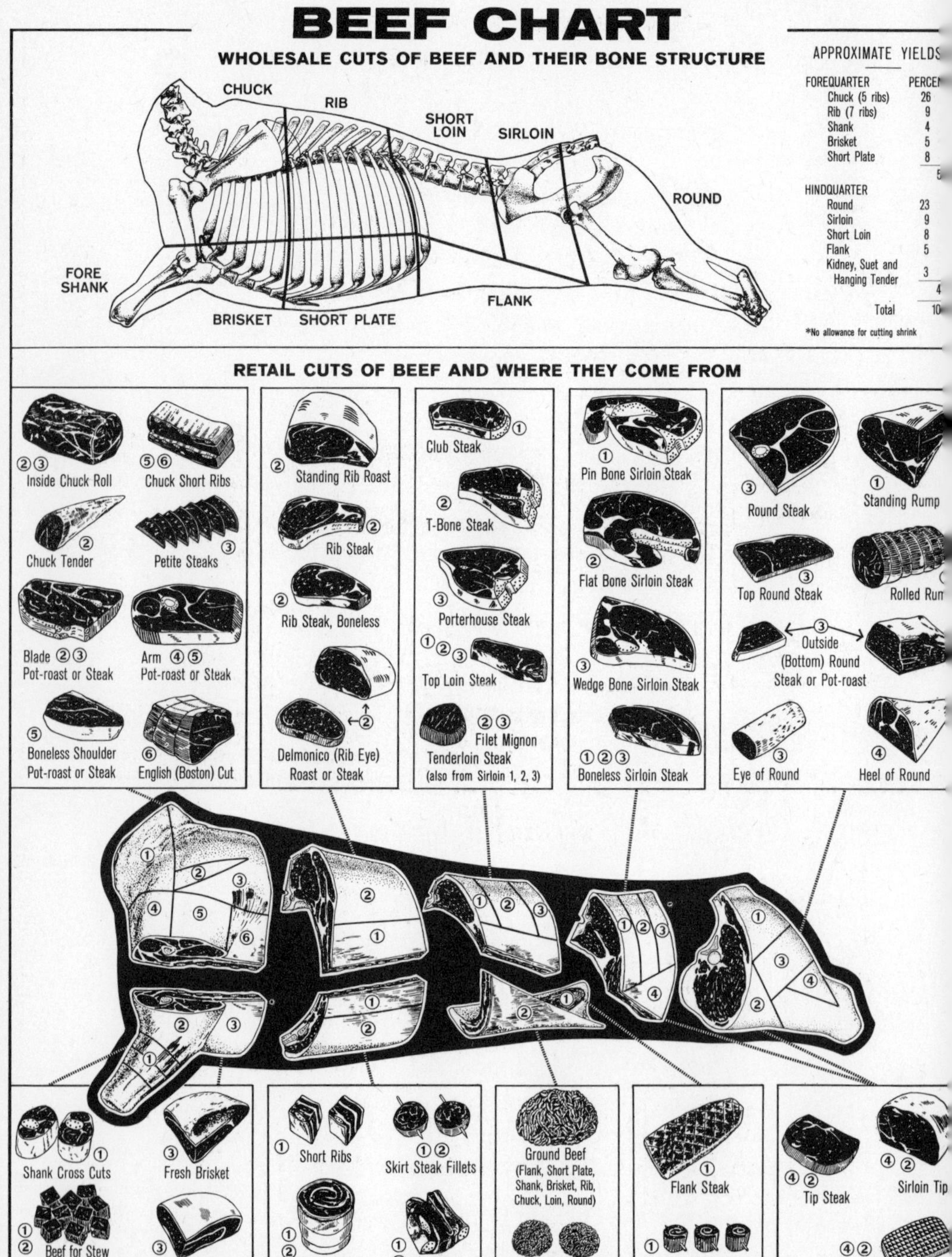

From *Lessons in Meat* published by National Livestock and Meat Board.

3

BEEF AND BEEF RECIPES

Beef Chuck Recipes Illustrating How We Cooked Meat Prepared and Delivered by Our Neighborhood Butcher.

(See page 58 for details of buying.)

Oven Braised Brisket in Barbecue Sauce

1 4½-lb. brisket of beef, second cut
1 1-lb. 12-oz. can tomatoes
1 6-oz. can tomato paste
⅛ tsp. pepper
1 tsp. salt
1 Tb. wine vinegar
1 Tb. brown sugar
½ tsp. thyme
½ tsp. dry mustard
¼ tsp. liquid smoke
½ tsp. monosodium glutamate
4 to 6 ripe olives, pitted and chopped

Cut excess fat from brisket and lay it in a roasting pan that is not very much bigger or deeper than the piece of meat itself. Combine remaining ingredients and pour over and around meat. Cover securely with a tight-fitting lid or aluminum foil. If there is any danger of sauce spilling over while meat cooks, set on a sheet of foil extending 1½ inches beyond edges of pan. Turn oven to 300° F. and bake for 3 to 3½ hours or until meat is very tender. (USDA GOOD grade may take a little longer than USDA CHOICE. Test for doneness with fork.) After meat has been cooking 2 hours, uncover, and turn it over. Recover and continue cooking. When meat is done, pour sauce into a bowl, let stand until most of fat rises to top (you can hasten chilling by setting in a bowl of ice and water), skim off, and reheat sauce. Slice meat against the grain and serve with sauce. Serves 8 to 12.

Leftovers: Cold brisket slices well for sandwiches or combination dishes.

Roast Brisket

Cooked without first defrosting

4½ lbs. brisket of chuck, *first* cut
(sometimes called "English" or "Boston" cut)
Salt and pepper to taste (optional)

Put meat, frozen, in a shallow roasting pan without liquid or seasoning of any kind. Cook, uncovered, in 200° F. oven for 3¼ hours. It will come out lightly browned and juicy, with almost no grease or juice in pan, medium-well done to rare. Eat unseasoned or add salt and pepper to taste. Makes 14 to 16 servings, hot or cold roast beef.

Note: This method will be nice only if young, tender chuck is used. Be sure to slice across the grain.

Chuck Roast of Beef and Vegetables in Tangy Wine Sauce

1 Tb. oil
1 5½-lb. boneless rolled chuck roast
1 tsp. Kikkoman Soy Sauce
1 tsp. dry, ground mushrooms
¼ cup red wine
1 cup water
3 medium carrots, thinly sliced
3 medium potatoes, thinly sliced
1 stalk of celery, sliced crosswise
3 medium onions, thinly sliced
4 Tbs. flour

Heat oil in heavy skillet, add roast, and brown on all sides. Rub Kikkoman Sauce and ground mushrooms over meat, place in roasting pan, add wine and water, and bake at 300° F. for 2 hours.

Remove meat and gravy from pan. Spread carrot and potato slices over bottom of pan, cover with celery and onion, place meat on top of the vegetables and pour gravy over all. If necessary, add water to cover layer of carrots and potatoes. Put roaster lid or aluminum foil over pan and bake in 350° F. oven for 1 hour. Put roast on a platter and keep warm. Dip 4 Tbs. fat from gravy in roasting pan into skillet and stir in flour. Pour gravy from vegetables and, if necessary, add water to make 2 cups. Add slowly to flour mixture in skillet and cook, stirring constantly, until thickened.

While gravy cooks, spread vegetables over preheated, lightly buttered broiler pan, turn broiler on high and cook for about 10 minutes or until vegetables are brown and crisp. Serve with sliced meat over which hot gravy has been poured. Serves 10 to 12.

Sweet and Sour Pot Roast

Cooked Either Before or After Defrosting

1 5⅓-lb. boneless chuck pot roast (rolled and tied)
8 cups cold water, or almost to cover
1 small envelope beef broth mix
(or substitute one bouillon cube)
1 clove garlic
⅛ tsp. pepper
¼ tsp. celery salt
1 tsp. salt
2 bay leaves
2 peppercorns
1 1-lb. 12-oz. can tomatoes
1 8-oz. can Spanish-style tomato sauce
2 Tbs. brown sugar
2 Tbs. lemon juice
6 serving-size wedges of cabbage
½ cup gingersnaps, crumbled

Put meat in a large, heavy pot. Add water, broth mix, garlic, pepper, celery salt, salt, bay leaves, and peppercorns. Simmer for 1 hour, uncovered—or until broth has a nice flavor. (If you are using meat that has not been defrosted, add 1 hour to this simmering time. Start with cold water and turn meat several times.) Dip out 4 cups of broth, set aside to cool, and then refrigerate or freeze for use in dishes calling for meat broth. See: "Freezing Measured Amounts of Broth, etc." Add balance of ingredients except lemon juice, cabbage, and gingersnaps and bring to a simmer. Cover loosely (don't quite set the lid on straight), and cook for 2 hours more. Remove meat and set aside to cool. If you have time to chill it in the refrigerator before slicing, it will be much nicer. Reheat only the slices you are going to serve in the sauce. Stir lemon juice in, remove 1 cup of this sauce and set aside to cool. Add 1 cup water and cabbage wedges to pot and cook, covered, until tender. Remove cabbage with slotted spoon, add crumbled gingersnaps and cook, stirring frequently, until sauce is smooth. Return cabbage and meat slices to pot to heat. Serve, using sauce as gravy. Serves 16.

Leftovers

SAUCE POLONAISE: To 1 cup of sweet and sour tomato-beef sauce removed before cabbage was added to pot, add ¼ cup finely crumbled gingersnaps and ¼ cup seedless raisins. Freeze and use with poached fish. Add ½ to 1 cup poaching liquid to sauce and, if necessary, thicken with cornstarch.

Chuck Ribs with Barley-Mushroom Crust

6 lbs. chuck short ribs
1½ cups water
¼ cup sherry wine
2 11-oz. cans Rokeach Barley-Mushroom Soup

Brown ribs in heavy skillet and discard fat. Place ribs in shallow oven casserole, fat side up, add water and cook at 325° F. for 2 hours or until meat is tender. Skim excess fat from gravy in pan and discard. Add wine and, if pan is almost dry, ½ cup of water.

Spread undiluted soup over tops of ribs keeping as much of it as possible from falling into bottom of pan. Turn heat to 400° F. and cook 20 to 30 minutes or until top of meat is brown and crusty. Serves 4 to 6, depending on meatiness of ribs.

London Broil (Chuck)

2½ lbs. London Broil (1½ to 2 inches thick)

Marinate steak for several hours (if frozen, overnight) in the refrigerator in the following marinade:

3 Tbs. cooking sherry
1½ tsp. Worcestershire Sauce
1 tsp. parsley flakes
1 Tb. butter (to be added later)

Preheat broiler and cook steak, about 3 to 5 inches from source of heat, 10 to 12 minutes to a side for medium rare; 12 to 15 to a side for medium well done. When turning steak, baste with marinade remaining in dish in which steak was refrigerated.

Put steak on preheated platter and keep warm while you quickly heat sauce from bottom of broiler pan in a small skillet or saucepan. Add 1 Tb. butter to sauce and boil for one minute. Slice meat to serve, spooning just a little of the sauce over each piece. Let each person add additional salt and pepper if he wants it. Serves 8 to 10.

Note: Extra slices of this steak are nice heated in the frying pan and served with eggs for breakfast. It slices nicely cold for sandwiches.

Variation: Use the following marinade; cook same as above:

2 Tbs. olive oil
2 Tbs. wine vinegar
1 clove garlic, minced
⅛ tsp. pepper
¼ tsp. salt

Chuck Club Steaks in Wine Sauce

2 Tbs. butter
2 Tbs. cooking oil
2 cloves garlic, cut in half
4 chuck club steaks (2 lbs.) ¾ to 1 inch thick
(from "Top Choice" meat)
Salt and pepper to taste
½ cup red wine

Put butter, oil, and garlic in one very large skillet or divide between two smaller ones. Heat, stirring pieces of garlic until sizzling hot but not smoking. Discard garlic and add steaks to pan. Cook meat 4 minutes to a side for medium-rare steaks; about 6 minutes to a side for medium-well done. Put steaks on heated plates and salt and pepper them. Very quickly, so steaks don't get cold, add wine to oil in pan and boil, stirring constantly, until it is reduced to about half and thickened slightly. Spoon this sauce over steaks and serve at once.

Chicken Fried Chuck Steaks

½ cup flour
½ tsp. salt, or to taste
⅛ tsp. pepper
4 "chicken steaks" or "chuck fillets" (1-to-1¼-lb. small chuck steaks cut ½ to ¾ inch thick)
1 Tb. cooking oil
1 Tb. butter or margarine

Mix flour, salt and pepper together. Dredge steaks with flour. Heat cooking oil and butter or margarine in heavy skillet. When small bubbles begin to appear, spread oils evenly over skillet and add 2 steaks—don't crowd more into the pan or steaks will be soggy and gray instead of crisp and golden. Fry 5 or 6 minutes to a side at a moderate heat that is hot enough to keep oil moving but not smoking. Remove steaks to a preheated serving dish and cook the remaining two—or use a second skillet and cook all the steak at one time. Serve at once. Serves 4.

Chuck Beef Stroganoff with Mushrooms

Freeze Half, Eat Half

3 lbs. beef chuck strips partially cut for Stroganoff
1 Tb. oil
1 Tb. butter
1 tsp. salt
⅛ tsp. pepper
½ cup sliced onions
1 cup sliced mushrooms
1 Tb. oil
1 Tb. butter
2 Tbs. flour
1½ cups beef broth
1 cup sour cream

Cut meat into 2 x ½ x ¼-inch pieces. Sauté in 1 Tb. oil combined with 1 Tb. butter until steak is nicely browned on outside and medium well done. Don't crowd in skillet—do a few pieces at a time. Sprinkle with salt and pepper. In another skillet, sauté onions and mushrooms together in 1 Tb. oil combined with 1 Tb. butter. Remove meat, mushrooms, and onions from skillet with slotted spoon. Combine oil in one pan, brown 2 Tb. flour in it, cooking for 2 minutes. Heat 1½ cups beef broth, pour into flour mixture, stir with a wire whisk and cook until sauce is smooth and thickened. Add meat, mushrooms, and onions to sauce in skillet and heat for about 1 minute. Turn off heat, stir in sour cream, and serve ½ at once with rice, noodles, or toast. Serves 4 to 6.

Freeze Half: Defrost before reheating. Put in top of double boiler and heat, stirring frequently. Turn off heat and serve at once before it quite reaches simmering heat. Handle with great care or cream will curdle.

Swiss Steak with Cherry Tomatoes

¾ cup flour
1 tsp. salt
½ tsp. chili powder (optional)
2½ lbs. chuck potting steak (8 steaks, ¾ inch thick)
2 Tbs. cooking oil
2 cups beef broth, your own (or substitute canned broth)
1 cup water
1 large onion, sliced
1 green pepper, finely sliced
16 to 24 cherry tomatoes
1 10½-oz. can cream of mushroom soup, undiluted

Combine flour, salt, and chili powder. Dredge steaks in the flour mixture, pounding it in with a mallet. Heat cooking oil in large heavy pot and brown steaks lightly on both sides. Do not let oil burn. Add beef broth, water, and onion. Cover pot and cook on very low heat for 1½ to 2 hours or until meat is very tender. Add green pepper and cherry tomatoes for last ½ hour of cooking. With a slotted spoon, remove meat and tomatoes and set aside where they will keep warm. Add undiluted mushroom soup to the gravy and stir until smooth and hot. Serve meat on a preheated platter, garnish with cherry tomatoes, and pass the gravy in a gravy boat. Serves 8.

Basic Economy Cut Steak Broiled in a Marinade

2-to-2½-lb. steak, 1 to 1½ inches thick, marinated in one of the Basic Steak Marinades for Broiling Steaks in next recipe.

Broil in preheated broiler, about 3 inches from source of heat, for the following length of time—with heat regulator turned to Broil:

RARE	8 to 10 minutes to a side
MEDIUM RARE	10 to 12 minutes to a side
MEDIUM WELL	12 to 15 minutes to a side

Different ovens cook differently and different people have different ideas about what is and is not rare, so all anyone can really give you is a suggested time to use. If this meat is too rare for you, increase the cooking time, but remember this:

Economy cut steaks are more apt to be tough if cooked beyond the medium-well stage than are some of the more expensive steaks. So serve the outside edge pieces to those who like their meat well done, the center of the steak to those who like their steak medium or rare.

Place cooked steak on a preheated platter, pour marinade out of broiler pan into measuring pitcher. You can serve it with steak or not, as you like. Either pour over steak as is or put in a heavy skillet, add ¼ cup of wine, boil down until it is reduced and slightly thickened, and pour over steak. If meat was very fat, spoon excess fat off before pouring marinade over steak or into skillet.

Note: We don't recommend broiling this type of steak until it is well done. But if you do, the heat in many broilers should be reduced from Broil to about 550° F., or the pan lowered to 5 inches below source of heat.

Basic Steak Marinades for Broiling Steaks

2 to 2½ lbs. steak, 1 to 2 inches thick
2 Tbs. olive oil or 2 Tbs. cooking oil;
  or 1 Tb. olive oil and 1 Tb. cooking oil, combined
½ tsp. salt
⅛ tsp. pepper

Combine the Above and Add 1 or More of the Following:

⅛ to ¼ tsp. garlic powder
1 small clove garlic, finely minced
⅛ to ½ tsp. onion powder
1 Tb. soy sauce
1 Tb. teriyaki sauce
2 Tbs. wine vinegar
2 to 4 Tbs. wine
¼ tsp. ground ginger
1 tsp. molasses
⅛ tsp. Worcestershire sauce
¼ tsp. liquid smoke

Marinate steak in mixture for 30 minutes to 24 hours.
Note: Reduce amounts for smaller steaks.

Cubed Beef Stew with Egg Dumplings

This is cooked for convenience with frozen meat that has not been defrosted. Vegetables are peeled after cooking for extra flavor and nutrition.

3 lbs. lean chuck of beef stewing meat, frozen
5 medium potatoes, scrubbed, skins left on
4 medium carrots, scrubbed, skins left on
2 medium onions, peeled and chopped
2 pinches garlic powder
2 pinches pepper
¼ tsp. celery powder
2 10½-oz. cans cream of mushroom soup (optional)

Put frozen stew meat in shallow metal roasting pan and place, uncovered, in 200° F. oven. Cook for 45 to 60 minutes or until meat pieces can be easily broken apart and spread over bottom of pan. Turn heat to 350° F. and continue cooking for ½ hour. Transfer to large, heavy stew pot and cover completely with water. Add vegetables and seasonings, bring to a boil, turn down to a high simmer, and cook for 30 minutes or until potatoes and carrots are just tender. Remove carrots and potatoes. Continue cooking meat. Cool vegetables, then peel and cut them into ½- to ¾-inch cubes. Continue cooking beef until tender, 30 to 60 minutes.

Skim off any excess of fat from top of stew broth, add cream of mushroom soup to the pot, stir until well blended and bring to a simmer. Return vegetables to pot, stir for a few minutes until reheated, cover pot, turn off heat, and let stand while you make dumplings.

DUMPLINGS

Use egg dumplings if you need to increase family's protein. Eggs are less expensive—by the pound—than meat. However, the stew is very good without any dumplings.

2 cups all-purpose flour
2 tsps. baking powder
1 tsp. salt
2 eggs, well beaten
⅔ cup water

Sift dry ingredients together, stir in egg and water. Drop by teaspoonful onto stew (try to rest dumplings on meat and vegetables so they don't sink into liquid and become soggy. If there is too much liquid in stew to do this, you can set a rack over it and cook dumplings on top of liquid in steam.) Cover pot tightly and simmer 15 minutes without removing cover. Serves 12.

Extra Portions: Before making dumplings, take out extra stew that will not be needed for that meal. Immediately cool and refrigerate for 2nd day eating. If possible, don't leave the extra stew standing around until after dinner at room temperature. Doing so will sacrifice flavor and nutrition and invite bacterial growth.

Variation: Add 1-lb. 12-oz. can tomatoes, eliminate 2 cans of cream of mushroom soup. Use flour thickener. See general thickening instructions in "Soups and Sauces."

For Stew Gravy with a Richer Flavor: Add 1 or 2 envelopes of beef bouillon or 1 pkg. mushroom soup mix powder. Taste as you add.

Note: See Stuffed Zucchini for using 1 cup leftover stew.

Making Broth from Scraps of Meat and Bones

1 lb. or more of meat scraps. If you don't have any, use a little of your stew meat.
Bones that came with your delivery of chuck
2 large onions
2 large carrots, scrubbed
2 large, outside stalks of celery, leaves on
4 or more quarts of water
Salt and pepper to taste

Put all of above, except seasonings, in one or two large soup pots and boil for a minimum of 3 hours, longer if possible. Occasionally skim off scum that forms on top. After first 2 hours, add a little salt and pepper. Before using broth, taste and add more water if necessary. Strain through lint-free (much-washed) toweling or several thicknesses of cheesecloth. Make soup for immediate use of some (cut up carrots, celery, and onions and include). Reduce the balance further and freeze for use in soups, sauces, gravies.

Beef and Bean Shepherd's Pies

3 Tbs. cooking oil
1 cup chopped onion
1 cup chopped celery
2 Tbs. finely minced celery leaf (from inside stalk)
2 lbs. ground chuck, from which most of fat was removed before grinding
1 tsp. salt

2 6-oz. cans tomato paste
1 1-lb. 5-oz. can red kidney beans
Instant mashed potatoes for 6 to 8
Milk and butter necessary to make the potatoes according to package instructions

Heat cooking oil to sizzling in heavy skillet and add chopped onion, chopped celery, and minced celery leaves. Cook, stirring frequently, until onions and celery start to soften, then remove with a slotted spoon and set aside. Add ground chuck to pan (if necessary divide into two pans), and cook over medium heat, stirring almost constantly, just until all pink disappears. Add salt, tomato paste, and red kidney beans to pan and stir. Pour into 6 to 8 lightly greased individual casseroles. Make instant mashed potatoes and spoon or squeeze through a decorator tube around edges of meat pies. Bake in 325° F. oven until potatoes are lightly browned. Serves 6 to 8.

Variation: Add lightly sautéed green pepper to meat mixture. Add sautéed fresh or canned mushrooms.

Substitutions: Increase proportion of beans to beef; substitute very lean ground lamb or ground veal for beef.

Beef Cakes with Apple and Sauerkraut

2 lbs. ground chuck of beef
1 tsp. salt
1 medium onion, grated
2 small, somewhat tart apples, peeled, cored, and finely chopped
1 large stalk of celery, grated
1 cup sauerkraut, chopped, and water run through it for about 10 seconds
1 cup mashed potato flakes
¼ cup meat broth
½ cup milk
1 6-oz can tomato paste
2 eggs, lightly beaten
1 to 2 Tbs. cooking oil for frying

Combine first 6 ingredients and mix well. Mix potato flakes with meat broth and milk. Add potato mixture, tomato paste, and eggs to first mixture and stir until well blended. Form into small patties. Heat 1 Tb. oil in skillet until hot but not smoking and fry patties without crowding in pan. Clean pan between batches or use 2 skillets. Cook until nicely browned on both sides.

Variation:

GROUND MEAT LOAF WITH APPLES AND SAUERKRAUT One half of mixture may be put into greased loaf pan, cooked, and frozen for future use. Bake for 1 hour at 350° F. or until lightly browned.

Use Leftovers for Gourmet Omelet: Break one or two cakes or a slice of meat loaf into small pieces, heat in half butter and half cooking oil in a heavy skillet, pour egg seasoned with salt and pepper and lightly beaten with a little water over the meat and cook until eggs are done the way you like them.

Substitutions: Ground veal or very lean pork from which all fat had been removed before it was ground could be substituted for beef.

Chili Con Carne

¼ cup oil
2 large onions, diced
1 large green pepper, seeded and diced
3 stalks celery, cut in ⅛- to ¼-inch slices
2 lbs. chopped beef
1 2-lb. 9-oz. can red beans, preferably Ann Page
3 8-oz. cans tomato paste
3 cups water
2 tsps. salt
½ tsp. crushed red pepper, or to taste
2 Tbs. chili powder, or to taste
Paprika for garnish

Heat oil in large heavy pot, add onions, green pepper, and celery, and sauté until onions acquire a slightly golden color. Use wooden spoon to stir. Break chopped beef into small lumps, add to vegetables, and sauté until lightly browned, stirring often. Add all remaining ingredients except paprika, stir well to mix thoroughly with meat and vegetables, bring to a boil, and then slowly simmer for a half hour. Ladle into individual serving bowls, sprinkle with paprika and serve with oyster crackers. Makes about 14 servings.

Mild Spanish Rice

2 slices bacon, cut in small pieces
2 medium onions, chopped
2 small green peppers, chopped
2 medium stalks celery, chopped
2 lbs. chopped lean chuck
1 tsp. salt
1 1-lb. 12-oz. can tomatoes
1 8-oz. can Spanish-style tomato sauce
2 6-oz. cans tomato paste
½ cup water
1 pinch garlic powder
1 tsp. oregano
2 cups rice cooked according to package instructions
Grated Parmesan cheese

Start bacon frying in large heavy pot. Add onions, green pepper, and celery, and cook for about 5 minutes with the bacon. Add meat and 1 tsp. of salt and cook on medium heat, stirring frequently, until all pink color has disappeared. Add canned tomatoes, sauce, and paste. Wash paste cans out with the half cup of water, add to the pot and stir. Stir in garlic powder and oregano. Simmer uncovered, stirring frequently, for one hour. Serve over cooked rice and pass grated Parmesan cheese for those who want to sprinkle it over sauce. Serves 8.

Leftover Rice and Sauce: Mix together, add some black olives if you have them, put in buttered casserole, top with slices of cheese and bake, uncovered, in 350° F. oven for 40 minutes or until heated through. Cheese should be melted and lightly browned.

Pepper Steak

Use Leftover Steak and Steak Sauce

When you have half a pound or more of nicely seasoned steak left over, try turning it into Pepper Steak this easy way. Rinse all the remains of the sauce out of the broiler pan and off the rack with ½ cup of hot water combined with ½ cup of wine. Save liquid.

Leftover steak (about ½ lb.)
1 Tb. butter
1 Tb. cooking oil
1 medium onion, sliced
2 medium green peppers cut in strips
1 medium stalk celery, sliced across
1 Tb. cornstarch
Liquid from broiler pan
1 Tb. soy sauce
½ cup your own beef or chicken broth (or substitute 1 small envelope beef broth powder or 1 bouillon cube mixed with water)

Cut leftover steak in small strips, about 2 inches x ½ inch by whatever thickness your original steak was cut. Heat butter and cooking oil in a heavy skillet. When small bubbles are beginning to appear, add sliced vegetables, a few pieces at a time so as not to cool the pan, and lightly sauté. They should be crisply done, not mushy. Remove vegetables from pan. Mix cornstarch with liquid from steak broiler pan, soy sauce, and broth. When cornstarch is dissolved, stir into pan, cook on medium heat, continuing to stir, until sauce has thickened. The sauce will taste better if you continue cooking it on low heat for 5 or 10 minutes longer. Add sautéed vegetables and meat slices to sauce 2 or 3 minutes before you serve it over rice. Serves 2 to 4.

Stuffed Peppers

8 medium green peppers
1 large onion, chopped
1 clove garlic, finely chopped
2 tbs. cooking oil
½ tsp. salt
¼ tsp. chili powder
1 lb. lean chopped chuck
1 1-lb. 5-oz. can red kidney beans
1 cup cooked rice
2 6-oz. cans tomato paste
1 cup seedless raisins
1 egg, lightly beaten

Cut tops from green peppers, clean seeds and pulp from inside, wash, put in large kettle, cover with warm water, bring to a boil, and cook 1 minute. Remove peppers with slotted spoon, invert and let drain.

In heavy skillet, lightly sauté chopped onion and garlic in cooking oil until they are beginning to get soft. Don't let them brown. Remove from skillet with slotted spoon and set aside. Mix salt and chili powder into ground chuck and cook in skillet, stirring constantly, just until pink all disappears. Combine with balance of ingredients, mix, and use as stuffing to fill green peppers. Set peppers in shallow roasting pan (they should fit snugly so none of them falls over). Pour ½ cup water into bottom of pan and cook in 350° F. oven for 45 minutes. Check now and then to see if pan is dry. If it is, add a little more water. Serves 6 to 8.

Variation: Cover pepper tops with slices of cheese last 20 minutes of cooking.

Substitutions: Use chopped veal or very lean chopped lamb for beef.

CHART OF LAMB CARCASS SHOWING WHOLESALE AND RETAIL CUTS OF LAMB AND WHERE THEY COME FROM

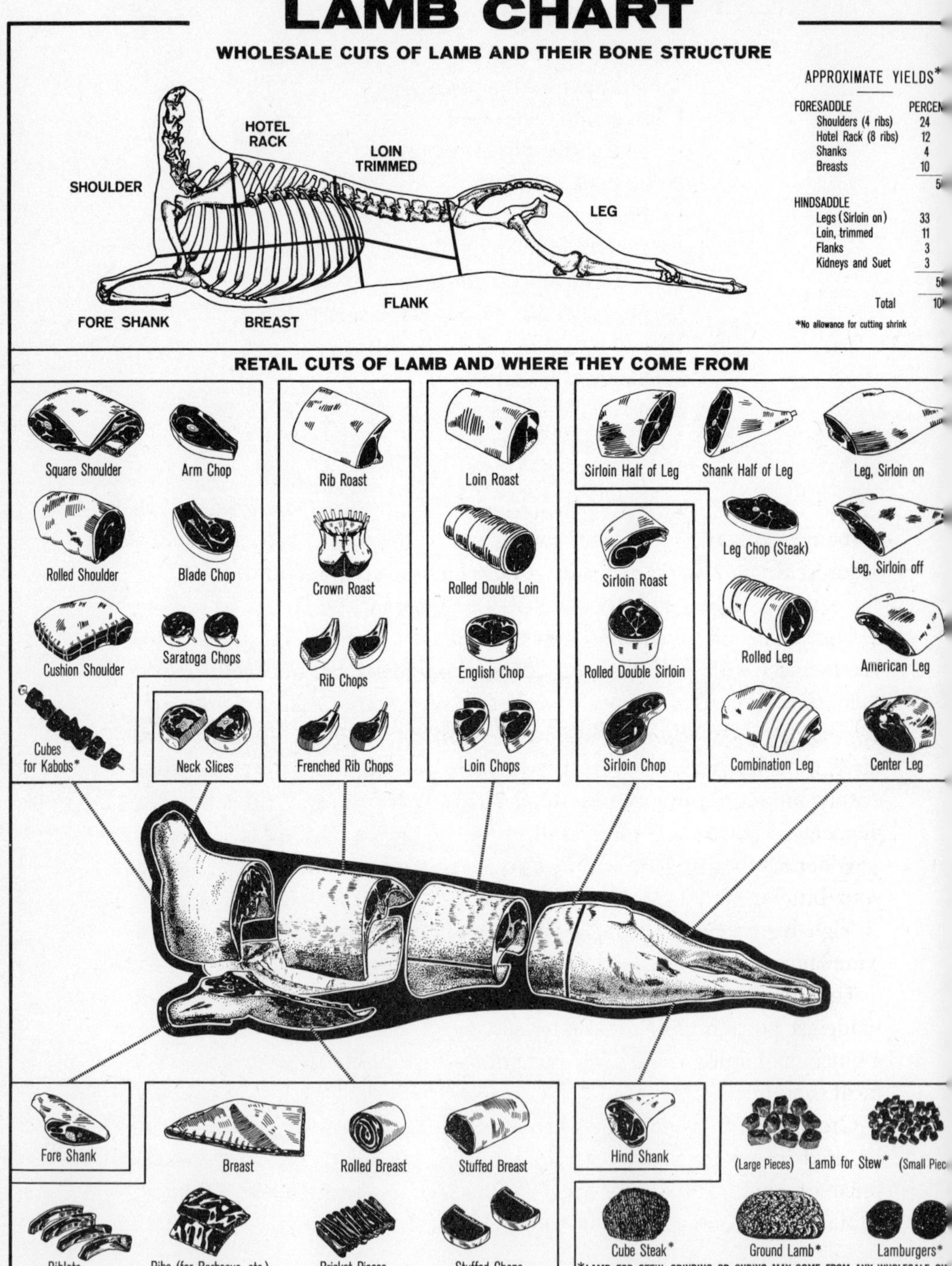

From *Lessons in Meat* published by National Livestock and Meat Board.

4 LAMB AND LAMB RECIPES

The Economical Way to Buy Lamb

Although some cuts of lamb are expensive, there are often wonderful specials on the "economy" cuts—the shoulder, the breast and, one of the best of all if properly cooked, lamb shanks.

The Lamb Shanks Braised with Rice and Vegetables recipe that you'll find a few pages farther on in the Pennysaver we think makes this economy cut even more flavorful than an expensive leg of lamb. So, too, with shoulder chops when they come from young lambs. Broiling is a perfect and easy way to cook shoulder chops, and they are good crisply browned with no seasoning at all, nothing more than salt and pepper, or dressed up in any kind of sauce you want to put on them.

When lamb is in good supply and at its cheapest, buy a nice leg from your butcher and have him cut some steaks off the end, leaving just enough leg for one or two days' eating. Try marinating the steaks in a wine sauce, then broil them over charcoal.

Your butcher also can cut cubes for making "shish kabob" from the tenderest portion of the shoulder section of your lambs. Marinating in a sauce containing citrus fruit juice or vinegar will help to tenderize the meat even further.

Ground lamb is sometimes economical, since the tougher pieces can be used in making it. If you are having it ground to order, check the price of the meat to be used. (See: Lamb, Lentil, and Eggplant Moussaka for one interesting way to use ground lamb.)

Shoulder Lamb Chops Broiled in Lemon Barbecue Sauce

6 large shoulder lamb chops
¼ cup undiluted frozen lemonade
¼ cup catsup
1 tsp. mustard
1 medium lemon, sliced into 12 thin circles

Place chops 2 to 3 inches from source of heat in preheated broiler pan and cook at 500° F. for 20 minutes. Mix lemonade, catsup, and mustard together and spread half of it over chops. Cook for 5 minutes, respread sauce, and continue cooking for another 5 minutes, checking to be sure sauce—which has a high sugar content—does not burn.

Turn chops and cook for 5 minutes, then spread with remainder of sauce and place 2 slices of lemon on each chop. Broil 5 to 7 minutes more, or until chops are nicely browned, and serve. Serves 4 to 6.

Lamb Shanks Braised with Rice and Vegetables

6 lamb shanks, one per person
1 small onion
1 tsp. salt
⅛ tsp. pepper
2 large carrots, unpeeled
2 cups onion slices
2 stalks celery, sliced
Instant rice for 6
1 10½-oz. can cream of mushroom soup, undiluted

Put lamb shanks in a large pot, add small onion, water to cover, salt, pepper, and carrots. Bring to a boil, turn down to a simmer, and continue cooking for 30 minutes. Skim as much of the fat as you can from top of liquid. Lightly grease shallow baking pan and arrange onion and celery slices over bottom. Cover with the lamb shanks, in a single layer. Pour one cup of broth from pot over the shanks and bake for 30 minutes at 350° F.

While shanks are baking, boil broth remaining in pot until it is reduced to approximately 3 cups (you should have about 1 cup more than amount of liquid instant rice package calls for to make 6 rice servings). When shanks have baked for 30 minutes, remove baking pan from oven and take out shanks. Combine rice, lamb broth, and undiluted mushroom soup and pour over onions and celery in bottom of baking pan. Top with shanks—other side up from the way they had been—return to oven and bake for another 30 minutes, or until tops of shanks are crisply browned and rice is no longer runny. Serves 6.

Leftovers: Remove bones, dice meat and vegetables, put in individual casseroles, cover with piecrust topping, and bake until crust is done. If lamb mixture is dry, add undiluted cream of celery or mushroom soup.

Acorn Squash Stuffed with Leftover Lamb

3 medium acorn squash
1 Tb. butter or margarine
Salt to taste

Cut squash in half and remove seeds. Rub inside with butter and sprinkle lightly with salt. Place squash halves, cavity up, in baking pan containing about ½ inch of water (replenish water if necessary to keep squash from sticking or burning on bottom), cover with lid or foil and bake 50 minutes—or until tender—in 350° F. oven. (Cooking time may vary considerably in cooking squash.)

Scoop out most of pulp, add more butter and salt to taste, mash with fork, and replace in shells.

STUFFING

3 slices bacon, cut into small pieces
1 onion, chopped
2 stalks celery, finely chopped
4 slices white bread, crisply toasted
½ to 1 cup leftover ground lamb, cooked
1 cup leftover creamed vegetables or 1 10½-oz. can undiluted mushroom soup
6 Tbs. bread crumbs
2 Tbs. butter for dotting

Start bacon frying, add onion and celery, and cook until lightly browned. Cut toast into small pieces and stir into mixture until it absorbs all bacon grease. Stir in lamb and creamed vegetables and spoon mixture into squash cavities on top of mashed squash. Sprinkle with bread crumbs, dot with butter, and bake in 375° F. oven for 20 minutes or until crumbs are lightly browned. Serves 6.

Lamb, Lentil, and Eggplant Moussaka

1 tsp. olive oil
¾ lb. chopped lamb
1 tsp. butter or margarine
½ cup onions, chopped
2 cloves garlic, chopped
2 14½-oz. cans tomatoes
1 6-oz. can tomato paste
1 tsp. oregano
1 qt. water
½ tsp. salt
½ lb. lentils
2 medium eggplant
¼ cup olive oil
¼ cup flour
½ tsp. salt
1 cup Ricotta cheese

Heat 1 tsp. olive oil in heavy skillet until it sizzles. Add lamb and cook, stirring constantly, until pink color is almost gone. Press out fat with slotted spoon, pour off and discard. Heat 1 tsp. butter in a clean skillet until it sizzles, add onions and garlic and cook until very lightly browned. Add lamb, canned tomatoes, tomato paste, and oregano. Stir together and simmer gently for 10 minutes.

Bring water to a boil, add salt and lentils, and cook at a slow boil until all water disappears or until lentils are soft. Add more water if necessary. When lentils are soft, drain off any excess water, and combine them with lamb mixture. Set aside.

Peel eggplant and cut in slices ¼ to ½ inch thick. Heat olive oil, dredge eggplant in flour to which salt has been added, and fry until lightly browned, about 5 minutes to a side.

Place eggplant in buttered casserole in alternating layers with lamb and lentil mixture. Top with Ricotta cheese and bake in 350° F. oven for 1 hour. Serves 4 to 6.

CHART OF PORK CARCASS SHOWING WHOLESALE AND RETAIL CUTS OF PORK AND WHERE THEY COME FROM

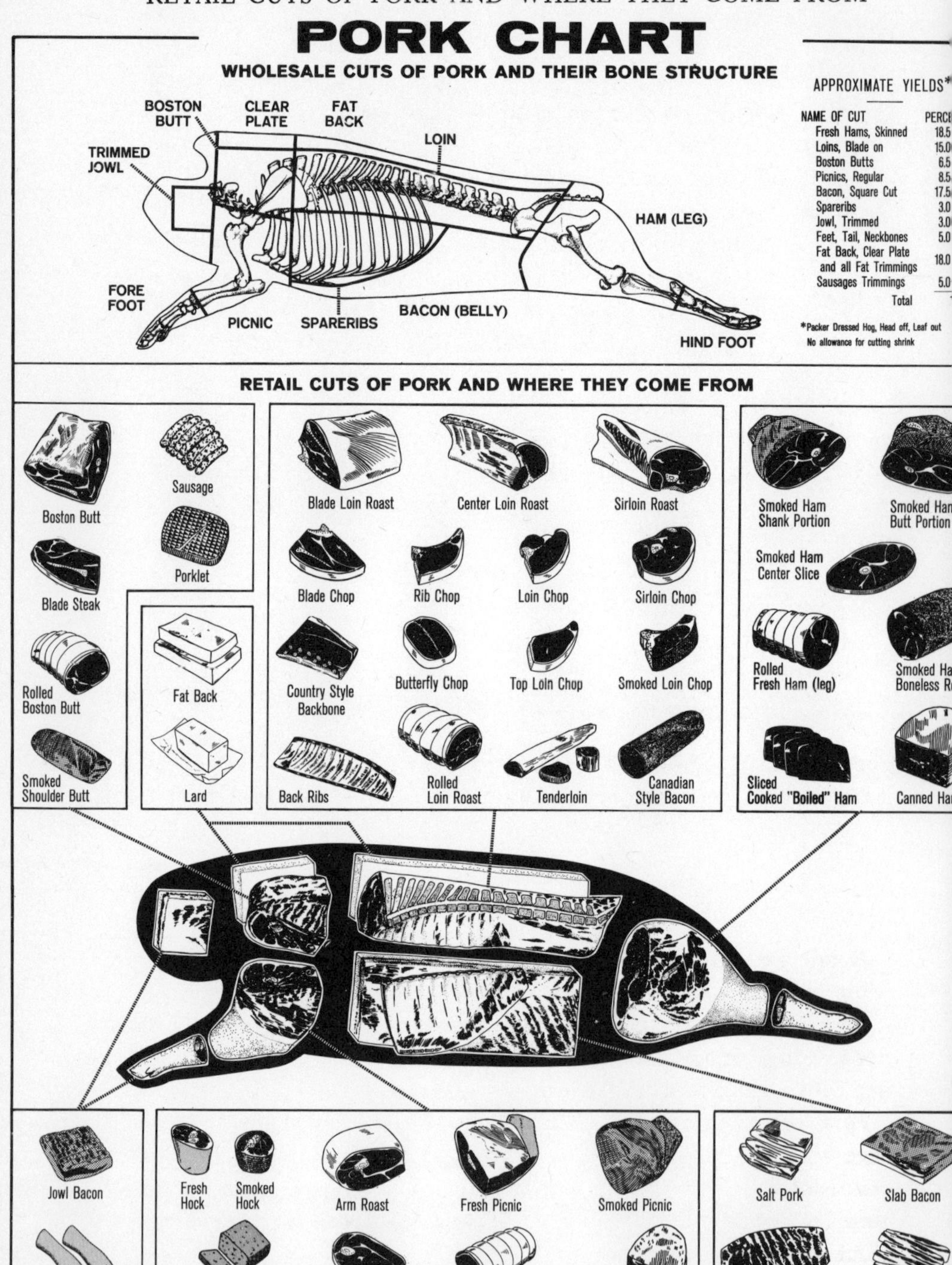

From *Lessons in Meat*, published by National Livestock and Meat Board.

5
PORK AND PORK RECIPES

Pork is especially important to the nutrition-conscious housewife because it is a valuable food source of thiamin.

Selecting Good Pork

Retail grades for pork are seldom used, since it is usually marketed when very young, and therefore tender.

Pork bones should be porous with red centers; the meat should be fine-textured, smooth and velvety, of a delicate rose or grayish-pink color and with a large proportion of lean.

Pork isn't so fat anymore. Pork is no longer the excessively fat meat it once was. The National Livestock and Meat Board says that while 3½ ounces of yesterday's cooked pork contained 30.7 gms. of fat, today, the same serving would contain only 13.1 gms. Of course, the percentage of fat varies in different cuts.

Economy Cuts

The Boston butt (top part of shoulder) deserves more attention than it gets for two reasons; besides being the leanest of all pork cuts (it can be as high as 84 percent lean), it is economical in price. The following illustration shows how you might, yourself, divide the whole fresh pork shoulder butt into three separate and different dishes; pork roast, pork steaks, and cubed pork for grinding or cooking in casserole dishes.

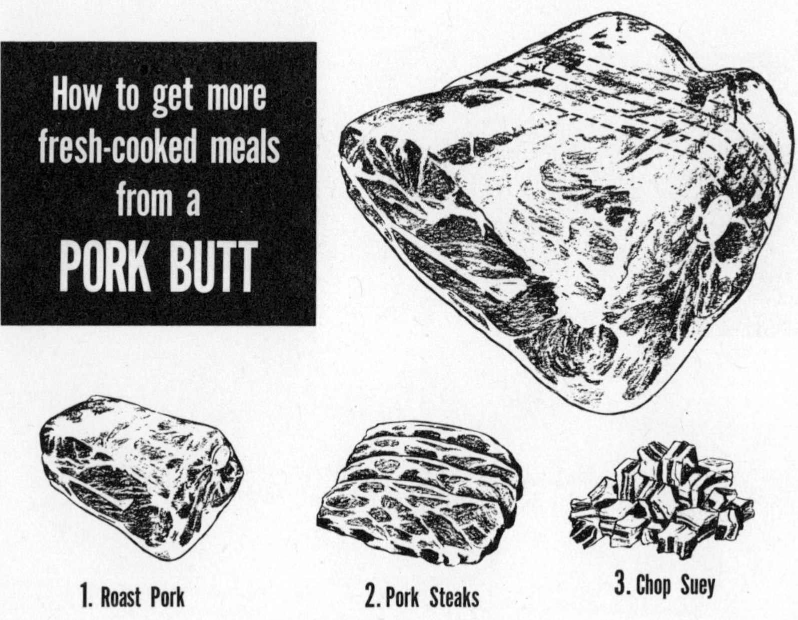

Fresh pork shoulder butt or "Boston butt." Average weight range, 5 to 7 pounds.

1. Roast Pork. Cut along bone, as shown, to divide pork butt into pieces. Use the piece with the bone as your smaller pork roast.

2. Pork Steaks. The remaining piece is boneless. Use a sharp knife to slice from it several half-inch thick pork steaks for braising.

3. Chop Suey. As you get to the small end of the boneless piece, cut the remaining meat into small cubes for chop suey or a similar meat-stretching dish.

Illustration from *Ideas with Meat,* published by American Meat Institute.

Ham hocks also are economical in price. So, sometimes, is the shank end of whole ham. The market may sell the very end of the ham shank for 49¢ a lb., at the same time as it sells the almost boneless steaks it cut off those shank ends for 99¢ a lb. If it sells the whole ham shank half for 57¢ per lb., this would be your best buy, although your first impulse would probably be to get some good cheap 49¢ meat. You could, without much difficulty, cut up the half ham for three completely different dishes in the following manner:

Full shank half of ham. Usually available in sizes from 5 to 9 pounds.

1. Boiled Dinner. Have butcher saw off a generous shank end. Use as the basis of a "boiled" dinner with carrots, onions and wedges of cabbage.

2. Baked Ham. Divide the large remaining piece into two equal parts as shown. Bake the piece with the bone. Slices will be small but tender.

3. Boneless Slices. The rest of the ham is boneless and easily sliced for two more meals. Broil the first, larger slices. Cook the smaller end slices with scalloped potatoes.

Illustration from *Ideas with Meat*, published by American Meat Institute.

National habit gives preference to chops, ham, bacon, and spareribs, so it will pay you to find out when pork is cheapest in your area and purchase these more expensive cuts at that time. Remember, however, that pork prices are influenced by the same vagaries as other foods. An overabundance one year may cause such a drop in price that raisers will cut production sharply . . . with a resultant sharp increase the year immediately following.

Boiled New England Dinner with Ham Shank

3 or 4 lbs. bone end cut from a shank half of ham
1 bay leaf
1 clove of garlic
2 peppercorns (optional)
½ large head of cabbage cut in 6 wedges
1 tsp. caraway seeds
4 to 6 small potatoes (new potatoes if available), peeled
4 to 6 small carrots, scraped
4 to 6 small, white onions, peeled
¼ lb.—or less—string beans, broken in half

Wash ham, cut off rind and most of fat, put in large pot and cover with water. Add bay leaf, clove of garlic, and peppercorns. Bring to a boil and simmer for 1 hour. (If ham is precooked variety, simmer for ½ hour.) Remove clove of garlic and discard. Remove ham, cut meat from bone, reserve bone for making split pea soup, and return meat to pot.

Put cabbage in a separate pot, add 2 cups of ham broth and caraway seeds, bring to a boil, turn down to simmer. Cover and cook until tender.

Add the remaining vegetables to ham pot and simmer for ½ hour or until all vegetables are tender.

Serve meat and vegetables on a large, preheated serving platter. Add cabbage wedges. Serve mustard. Serves 4 to 6.

Notes:

1. Cut up any leftover vegetables, add broth in which cabbage was cooked, and serve as a soup the next night.

2. Strain broth in which ham was cooked, add ham bone, and see Split Pea Soup With Ham instructions.

Roast Pork Stuffed with Sauerkraut and Fruit

1 1-lb. 11-oz. can of sauerkraut
12 raw dried prunes
12 raw dried apricots
1 4½-lb. shoulder of pork, boned and prepared with pocket for stuffing
½ cup cranberry jelly
½ cup orange marmalade

Pour three cans of water through the sauerkraut and squeeze most of water out with your hands. Mix sauerkraut with fruit, stuff into pork, and skewer shut. You can also tie with cords for extra security against your stuffing forcing its way out while cooking. Put in shallow roasting pan, on a rack, push meat thermometer into thickest part of meat, avoiding the stuffing. Do not add any water to pan. Roast in 325° F. preheated oven for about 3 hours, until meat thermometer registers about 183°. Mix cranberry jelly and marmalade together and brush about half of it over roast. Continue basting with the glaze until it is used up. When roast registers 185°, it is done. If outside of meat is not brown enough, turn heat up to 375° F. for a few minutes, but watch it closely or the glaze may burn.

If meat is fat, pour accumulation of grease out of pan after first 2 hours of cooking. If grease in pan starts to smoke, add water, but no more than ½ cup at a time or it will create too much steam. Serves 6 to 8.

Pork Cutlets with Apple

10 thinly sliced (Italian style) pork cutlets. (Ask butcher to cut them in same way as veal cutlets and pound them.)
¼ tsp. salt
6 medium red cooking apples, cored and thickly sliced—skins on
4 Tbs. lemon juice
4 Tbs. honey

Lay 5 cutlets in bottom of large shallow casserole, sprinkle with salt, and cover with half of apple slices. Mix lemon juice and honey and pour half of it over cutlets and apples. Top with remaining cutlets, then remaining apple slices and remaining juice and honey mixture over all.

Bake for 45 minutes, uncovered in 400° F. oven, or until meat is well done. Baste 3 or 4 times with juice in pan. When done, juice and honey should be thickened enough to make a sauce to spoon over cutlets, which should be nicely browned. Serves 6.

Pork and Veal Meatballs

1 lb. lean ground pork
½ lb. veal or very lean beef, ground
½ tsp. black pepper
1 tsp. salt
1 Tb. potato flour
1 Tb. finely crushed cracker crumbs
½ cup milk
½ cup chopped cooked prunes
2 to 4 Tbs. cooking oil
1 to 2 Tbs. butter

Combine all ingredients except oil and butter and form into small balls. Heat 2 Tbs. oil and 1 of butter in heavy skillet until it sizzles but is not smoking. Add meatballs (cook in two batches if necessary to avoid crowding them or they won't brown nicely) and cook on medium heat, turning as each side browns. When all sides are brown, test one to be sure pork is cooked all the way through the meatballs. Serves 6.

CHART OF VEAL CARCASS SHOWING WHOLESALE AND RETAIL CUTS OF VEAL AND WHERE THEY COME FROM

VEAL CHART

WHOLESALE CUTS OF VEAL AND THEIR BONE STRUCTURE

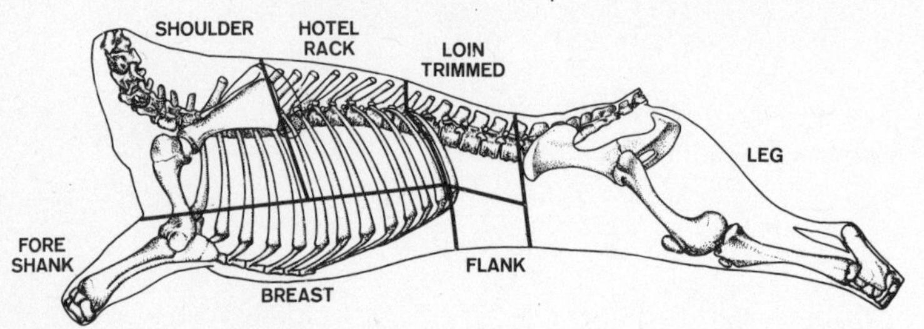

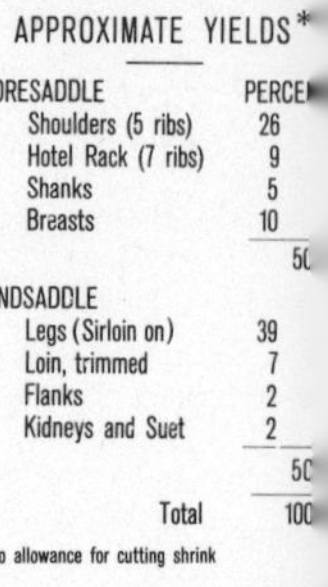

APPROXIMATE YIELDS*

	PERCE
FORESADDLE	
Shoulders (5 ribs)	26
Hotel Rack (7 ribs)	9
Shanks	5
Breasts	10
	50
HINDSADDLE	
Legs (Sirloin on)	39
Loin, trimmed	7
Flanks	2
Kidneys and Suet	2
	50
Total	100

*No allowance for cutting shrink

RETAIL CUTS OF VEAL AND WHERE THEY COME FROM

Arm Roast
Blade Roast
Arm Steak
Blade Steak
olled Shoulder
Neck
rge Pieces) Veal for Stew* (Small Pieces)

Rib Roast
Crown Roast
Rib Chop
Frenched Rib Chop

Loin Roast
Rolled Stuffed Loin
Loin Chop
Kidney Chop

Sirloin Roast
Sirloin Steak
Rolled Double Sirloin
Cube Steak*

Standing Rump
Shank Half of Leg
Rolled Leg
Center Leg
Cutlets, Boneless
Round Steak
Rolled Cutlets (Birds)
Heel of Round

Fore Shank

Breast
Stuffed Breast
Riblets
Brisket Rolls
Brisket Pieces
Stuffed Chops

Rolled Cube Steaks (Birds)*
Ground Veal*
Mock Chicken Legs*
City Chicken*
Patties*
Choplets*

*VEAL FOR STEW, GRINDING OR CUBING MAY COME FROM ANY WHOLESALE CUT

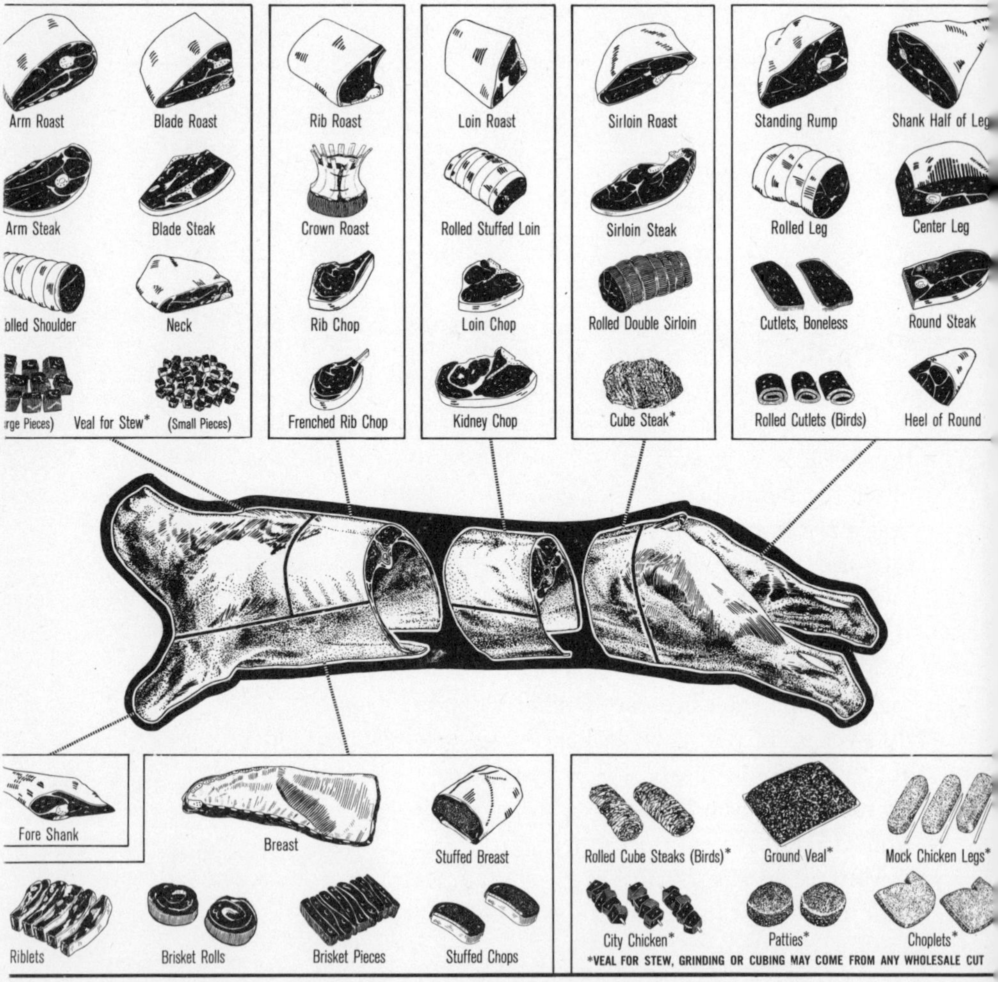

From *Lessons in Meat*, published by National Livestock and Meat Board.

6

VEAL AND VEAL RECIPES

Some Economical Ways to Buy and Cook Veal

As we pointed out earlier, veal is a very expensive meat, primarily because it is butchered before it has time to develop enough weight to offset the initial high cost of growing it. There are, however, veal cuts that are less expensive than others. These are similar to those that are economical in the other animals; shoulder, foreshank, and breast.

The so-called variety meats—liver, heart, tongue, brains, sweetbreads, tripe, and kidney—that come from veal are often the nicest and most delicately flavored. Their economical prices make them well worth trying, and once you become familiar with their unusual flavors, you will discover some very good eating. Because the flavors of these meats are apt to be more delicate if they come from veal than from other meats, try them first, even though they will also be more expensive if they come from veal rather than from other meats. (See "Variety Meats.")

Most of us are familiar with stuffed breast of veal, which, with a little attention, can become a special or "gourmet" dish.

Since veal is butchered so young, a larger percentage of the carcass should be tender than is the case with older beef. These areas include the shoulder, leg, and breast.

Veal is not quite as easy to cook to perfection as is beef. Though the meat is tender, it lacks the marbling of fat that helps make beef juicy. It needs to have more fat added in the cooking methods and is not suitable for broiling—the driest and least fatty method of cooking there is. Veal has a good deal of connective tissue and needs to be cooked until well done, at a low temperature, if it is to be tender and flavorful.

Substituting Other Meats in Veal Recipes

There are many wonderful recipes for which it has become traditional to use only veal, but, now that pork has become leaner and chicken and turkey breasts have become inexpensive, these meats can be substituted for expensive veal cutlets in some of them.

Veal and Pepper Rolled Roast

2 Tbs. butter.
1 Tb. olive oil
3 large scallions, sliced and including 2 or 3 inches of green stem
6 medium mushrooms, sliced
5 frying peppers, cleaned and cut into 4 lengthwise strips each
½ tsp. salt
⅛ tsp. pepper
⅛ tsp. thyme
⅛ tsp. paprika
⅛ tsp. garlic powder
1 5-lb. boned shoulder of veal

Melt butter and olive oil in heavy skillet. Add scallions, mushrooms, and peppers and lightly sauté. Rub seasonings into roast. Spread sautéed vegetables over roast, roll up, tie, and roast for 3 hours in 300° F. oven.

After 2 hours, add water, ½ cup at a time to bottom of pan if it becomes dry and juices start to become a dark brown. Baste meat occasionally with juices. When cooked and nicely browned from basting, remove meat from pan and add enough water to juices to make a nice-tasting gravy. Heat and ladle over sliced meat. Serves 8 to 10.

Breast of Veal with Blue Plum Stuffing

1 6-oz. pkg. white and wild rice with herbs and seasonings
4 slices bacon, fried and cut in small pieces
2 Tbs. melted bacon fat
1 cup coarsely crumbled toasted whole wheat crumbs
1 cup soft white bread crumbs
1 1-lb. 14-oz. can whole purple plums in extra heavy syrup, drained and juice reserved and 5 plums set aside
1 4½-to-5-lb. breast of veal with pocket cut in it
1 cup water
½ cup Rhine wine
1 Tb. butter
2 Tbs. Damson plum preserves

Cook wild and white rice as directed, but turn off after 20, not 25, minutes. Add bacon pieces, 2 Tbs. melted bacon fat, bread crumbs, and all but 5 purple plums. Stuff into veal pocket and skewer cavity shut. Pour juice from canned plums over and around meat and add 5 reserved plums. Bake in 350° F. oven for 30 minutes. Add one cup of water and wine and cook for an additional 60 minutes, basting occasionally but alternate the pan juice with melted butter. Spread 2 Tbs. Damson plum preserves over top and cook 15 minutes, basting 2 or 3 times. Serve in slices. Serves 8.

Veal and Lentil (Leftovers) Gourmet Combination

2 Tbs. butter
1 Tb. cooking oil
2 stalks of celery, sliced
1 green pepper, cleaned and sliced
1 medium onion, sliced
½ cup cooked chestnuts, sliced
1 cup of rice
1 to 1½ cups leftover veal, cut in bite-size pieces
1 to 2 cups leftover lentils cooked with ham bone (see Split Pea Soup with Ham)
1 can (about 10¾ oz.) beef gravy

Heat butter and cooking oil in heavy skillet until sizzling but not smoking. Add sliced celery, green pepper, onions, and sliced chestnuts, and lightly sauté until vegetables are crisply done. Prepare rice according to package instructions. Heat leftover veal and lentils with beef gravy. Serve over the rice and top with sautéed vegetables and chestnuts. Serves 4.

7

FISH—ONE OF THE MOST IMPORTANT ECONOMIES

Fish is one of the most nutrition-packed of all foods; therefore one of the most economical foods from a health standpoint. But it also can be economical from the standpoint of price per pound of meat if you practice this rule:

Always buy the fish that is caught nearest to where you live and always buy it at the peak of its season in those local waters.

How do you know what fish this is?

You can ask the man who waits on you at the fish market (even at the supermarket, there is usually someone actually handling the fish for you who can answer your questions), ask a friend who is a sports fisherman, look in your newspaper fishing column, or listen to your radio reports on what fish are currently being caught the most by sportsmen where you live.

And that, you can be sure, is the fish that the commercial fishermen will be catching the most of too because that's the fish that's in season in the waters nearest you, therefore that's the fish that's most plentiful —the fish that's most economical to buy.

The Various Forms in Which Fish are Sold

1. *Whole or round:* meaning just as they come from the water.
2. *Drawn:* meaning the entrails have been removed.
3. *Dressed:* meaning not only the innards but also scales and usually the fins, tail, and head have been removed.
4. *Chunked:* a dressed fish cut into several pieces; usually a cross section.
5. *Steaks:* dressed fish cut crosswise into steaks about three quarters to one inch thick.
6. *Fillets:* the sides of a whole fish cut lengthwise away from the backbone. They're practically boneless and the skin may be on or off.

What to Look for in Determining Freshness:

You're on your own when you go to market to buy fresh fish because the federal government neither grades them nor stamps them as to freshness and quality. At the writing of this book, there are no laws such as the 1967 Wholesome Meat Act or the 1968 Wholesome Poultry Act covering the sale of fish; however, legislation has been proposed. Whether it finally does or does not become law, you'll be wise to look for the following signs when you go to market:

1. Whole, drawn, and dressed fish-flesh should be firmly elastic to the touch and not separating from the bone; odor should be fresh and mild, not what we call "fishy"; eyes should be bright, clear and full; gills should be red and free from slime; skin should be shiny with its color unfaded.
2. Chunks, steaks and fillets—flesh should be fresh-cut in appearance, the color should resemble that of freshly dressed fish and it should be firm in texture without traces of browning about the edges and without a dried-out look; odor should be fresh and mild; if they're wrapped, the wrapping should be a moisture- and vaporproof material and there should be little or no air space between the fish and the wrapping.

You're quite a bit better off when it comes to buying packaged fish than when you purchase fresh fish because here the government lends more of a hand. Specifically what Uncle Sam does is make inspectors available to commercial processors. All they need do is ask and one will be assigned to their plant to see to it that the finished package meets government standards. Processors who avail themselves of this service then may print on their package that it has been manufactured or processed under government supervision and the label may bear the official grade or inspection shield of the United States Department of Interior (USDI). *Examine packaged fish for USDI inspection stamp below.*

Determining Which is the Most Economical Form of Fish to Buy

Though fillets will be priced much higher than whole or dressed fish, they are sometimes more economical to buy because you get more eating for your money:

Fillets are 100 percent edible.
Steaks are 85 percent edible.
Dressed fish is only 45 percent edible.
Whole fish is even less edible than dressed, roughly 33 percent.

Therefore, if the price per pound of fillets is no more than three times as much as that of whole fish, it's just as economical, or more so, to buy the fillets. And much easier to prepare.

If fillets are no more than twice as expensive as dressed fish, the fillets are a better buy.

But if the price per pound for fillets is more than 15 percent higher than the price per pound for fish steaks, then the fish steaks are more economical . . . unless they are from a very bony fish and your family is not expert at removing the meat and discards a lot of it along with the bone.

For the cook who has had no experience preparing fish; for the family that has had no experience picking the delicate flesh away from the bone, fillets are the best buy.

You usually won't have to figure all these things out for yourself if you read a good newspaper food column regularly. Such a columnist has access to all the background information and he or she gets paid to analyze it for you and present it in understandable form as best buys of the day or week.

How Much Fin Fish Makes a Serving:

Whole—1 pound per person
Dressed or Chunked—½ pound per person
Fillets or Steaks—⅓ pound per person

Those are the amounts of fin fish generally recommended that you buy in order to serve three ounces of boneless, cooked fish flesh to each person. This recommendation is a basic guide because only you know your family's ages, sizes, and appetites.

We don't recommend that you buy large quantities of whole fish to stock your freezer, even when the price is good. Whole fish takes up too much freezer space for the percentage of edible meat on it. Very good fillets, all packaged, labeled, and frozen, can usually be purchased at your supermarket for less than you can buy the same fillet even when that fish is in season, and freeze it yourself. Of course, if you have one favorite fish such as salmon, and you know you are buying it fresh-caught, that's different. By all means freeze it, and in whatever form you enjoy eating it.

Except for the special favorites, then, the whole fish that goes in your freezer should be the fish you catch yourself or that a neighbor gives you after a successful fishing expedition.

Preparing Your Fish Catch for Freezing

As for how to prepare yours (or your neighbor's) catch for freezing, it's best to leave the fish whole until ready for cooking. Simply remove its innards as soon after death as possible, wipe away the blood with a barely dampened cloth, wrap it as you would meat, label it, and store it. Water should be used in the cleaning only after you have defrosted the fish and it's about to be cooked. The best possible way to make use of whole fresh fish you don't want to cook within a day or two is to turn it easily into fish broth and flaked fish for convenient freezer storage and a myriad of uses.

Freeze Dibs and Dabs of Fish for Making Bouillabaisse and Other Delicacies: We do urge though that a little bit of all the fish that you catch, buy, or have given to you go into the freezer for including in a score or more of delicacies that you might not otherwise ever be able to afford to serve. (Freeze it immediately.)

Bouillabaisse is one such so-called gourmet dish. The cost can be prohibitive if all the ingredients must be purchased at once. Especially when you consider that you may have to buy a pound of this or a pound of that although all you need is perhaps a quarter pound or an eighth of a pound and often even less.

Two or three large shrimp saved from a package of individually frozen ones can be broken into bits to season and color a white sauce or gelatin salad.

Shellfish

What to Look for When Buying Shellfish, Lobster, Crayfish, and Crab

Different sections of the country have different species of both crabs and lobsters and, when buying them alive, the general rule to follow is to buy the ones that are native to the waters nearest you because they're most apt to be fresh. If frozen, it makes no difference where they were bred; for example, lobster tails come from Africa and king crab from Alaska.

Live lobsters and crabs should show movement in their legs, and lobster tails should curl under their bodies when the lobster is picked up. Both lobsters and crabs should be bright red and without disagreeable odor when cooked. Live, they should be in their natural color. For lobster that is a dark bluish green. Crabs range from several shades of brown to blue.

FORMS IN WHICH SHELLFISH ARE MARKETED

Lobsters cooked in the shell also are marketed. They should be bright red and their tails should spring back into a curl after you try holding them straight.

Lift the lid under their body section slightly and sniff crabs. If you detect a disagreeable odor, the crab is not to be eaten.

SHRIMP: This highly popular delicacy is sold in a variety of ways:

1. Fresh and whole with their heads left on.
2. Fresh or frozen: headless, shelled and unshelled.
3. Fresh or frozen: cooked, peeled, and deveined.
4. Frozen: peeled, deveined, and breaded with crumbs or cornmeal.
5. Canned in their natural juices.

The meat of fresh shrimp is firm, with a mild, pleasant odor. The shell color may vary from light pink to tan or a gray-green. All shells, however, should turn pink when the shrimp is cooked and the meat should acquire an opaque white to reddish tint.

Shrimp are sold according to size. Generally they are graded by marketing names that are the key to the number of headless shrimp there are to the pound. So-called jumbo shrimp run about fifteen to the pound; the smallest shrimp run about sixty to the pound. The large ones cost more but require less time to peel and devein.

SCALLOPS: There are only two kinds: bay and sea scallops. The former are small, the latter are big. But, big or small, fresh or thawed after freezing, the meat should have a sweetish odor. Packaged scallops should be practically free of liquid. The color of fresh scallops varies from light cream to delicate pink.

Only the eye, or muscle, of the scallop is marketed. The bay scallop, since its eye is only about a half-inch in diameter is sold whole; the sea scallop, whose eye may run up to eight inches in diameter, is cut up to resemble bay scallops. But both are good to the taste and the health-giving values are equal.

They are available all year round in the nation's markets, but they're at their best from November to April.

CLAMS AND OYSTERS: Clams taste like clams, oysters taste like oysters, no matter where in the country they are harvested, no matter what their size or shape may be. And, no matter where they're grown and no matter what they're called, they all taste good either eaten raw, baked in a pie, or cooked in a stew.

They're sold in these three basic ways:

1. In shells: They must be alive. The shells must be tightly closed. If a shell is open the clam or oyster may be taking a breath. So tap the shell. If it doesn't close, the clam or oyster is dead and not to be eaten. They'll keep alive for several days if refrigerated at 32° F.

2. *Shucked:* The meat has been removed from the shell for you; it should be plump and creamy in color; the liquid should be clear. If purchased frozen they should not be defrosted until you plan to use them. They should never be refrozen.

3. *Canned:* Food processors now package them in a great variety of ways from minced to in-the-shell.

How Much Shellfish to Buy for Six People

Live lobster or crayfish: 4 to 6 pounds
Cooked lobster meat: ¾ pound
Live hardshell crabs: 6 to 12 pounds or 18 to 36 crabs
Cooked crab meat: 1 pound
Cooked Dungeness crabs: 4 to 6 pounds or 3 to 6 crabs
Oysters and clams in shell: 3 dozen
Oysters and clams shucked: 1 quart
Scallops: 1 pound
Headless shrimp: 1½ pounds
Cooked shrimp: ¾ pound

These quantities are a general guide only and are based on the assumption that they will be used in combination with other things. For specific quantities, see specific recipes.

Fish Recipes

Two simple secrets for making fish taste good demonstrate the two cardinal rules to follow in making sure that fish is at its most-flavorful best when set upon the table. The first is that it be as fresh as possible when cooked. The second is that it not be overcooked. Fish that's being cooked should never be timed with a clock.

Use a fork instead. It keeps better time.

If, for example, a recipe says a fish should be cooked for 30 minutes start testing it for doneness with a fork at 15. Fish should never be cooked beyond the point when the protein coagulates and the flesh loses its translucent appearance and turns a milky white. Check by poking the tines of a fork gently into the thickest part of a piece of fish. If the natural divisions flake apart easily, the fish is done.

The main determining factor, other than the method of cooking, is the thickness of the fish you're cooking. No one but you, and certainly not a recipe printed in a book, can possibly know if the fish in or on your stove is short and fat or long and lean. So, no matter how much cooking time a fish recipe may call for, start testing with a fork at half that time and the flavor of the fish you serve your family will increase immeasurably.

Another thing to remember if you want you and your family to enjoy the wonderful taste of fish is this . . .

Properly cooked fish does *not* have an unpleasant odor. The canard that all fish smells that way comes about because (1) the fish that's being cooked isn't as fresh as it should be; (2) the fish is being overcooked; and/or (3) the fat in which it's being cooked was allowed to smoke.

That's where the unpleasant odors come from, and all of them can be avoided. Once you become accustomed to the odor of fresh fish—and by that we mean properly frozen fish, too—being cooked, you'll find that the smell of fish cooking is just as appetite-tingling as the smells of other foods.

Basic Broths Made from Whole Fish Either Caught or Purchased on Sale in Quantity

4½ to 5 lbs. white-meat fish
8 cups water
2 whole onions
2 whole carrots
2 stalks celery
2 cups white wine
2 peppercorns
1 tsp. salt (Add more to taste after you finish cooking. Don't overdo it as some of the dishes with which you may be combining broth probably will be salty.)

Add all ingredients to a large pot, cover, bring liquids to a boil and turn down to a gentle simmer. After 5 minutes, test with a fork to see if the flesh flakes easily away from the bone. If not, continue cooking, but check every minute, as it should not be overcooked. When done, carefully remove fish from pot, lay on a plate and cut a boneless fillet from one side; turn and cut another fillet from the other side. Hold fish fillet over a bowl and remove skin. At this point the fish flesh will fall apart into tender flakes. Refrigerate the fish flakes until broth is finished, then freeze flakes in small packages for use in any flake fish recipes. Place in foil-lined freezer dishes with a little strained broth, and freeze. When solid, remove foil wrapped package from dish, rewrap and label. Throw fish carcass back into broth pot and continue cooking for another ½ hour.

Wash off vegetables, chop and reserve for making Fish Broth and Vegetable Soup. Taste broth. If it is not strong enough, or if you want to reduce it for space-saving freezer storage, continue simmering. When it is the strength you want, add more salt if necessary, strain through three layers of cheesecloth, cool and freeze. (See "Freezing Measured Amounts of Broths.")

Variations:

BEER INSTEAD OF WINE IN BROTH: Substitute beer for wine in basic broth recipe, but cut recipe in half first time you try it.

DARK-FLESHED FISH: Substitute dark-fleshed fish such as striped bass, bluefish, mackerel in basic broth recipe. Change white wine to red wine. Leave the skin on the fillets and freeze meat as fillets, instead of flaked fish. Use in recipes calling for cooked fish, or cut down the cooking time as much as possible. Sample recipe: Fried Mackerel in Red Wine.

Basic Recipe for Frying Fish Fillets or Shellfish

1½ lbs. fish fillets (⅜ to ½ inch thick), whole shrimp—shelled and deveined—scallops, or small chunks of lobster or crab meat
1 cup flour
1 tsp. salt
⅛ tsp. white pepper
2 Tbs. butter or margarine
4 Tbs. cooking oil

Wash fish or shellfish by dipping in cold, salted water. Dry thoroughly on absorbent paper or lint-free towel. Mix seasonings into flour and dredge fish with the mixture. (If you prefer, you can put flour mixture in a heavy paper bag and shake a few pieces of fish in the bag at a time to coat with flour.) Heat butter and oil in one very large or two smaller heavy skillets until sizzling hot but not smoking. Add fish, being sure not to crowd. Shake pans occasionally to keep fish from sticking. When golden brown on one side, turn each piece over and cook until golden brown on the other side. This process should not take more than a total of 5 minutes. Poke fish gently with fork tines. It is done if flakes fall apart easily when tested this way. Serve at once with lemon wedges and/or Easy Tartar Sauce. Serves 4 to 6.

Fish Fillets or Shellfish Fried in a Batter

1½ lbs. fish fillets (⅜ to ½ inch thick), whole shrimp—shelled and deveined—scallops, or small chunks of lobster or crab meat
1 cup flour
1 tsp. salt
⅛ tsp. white pepper
2 eggs, lightly beaten
¼ cup milk
2 cups dry bread crumbs
2 Tbs. butter or margarine
4 Tbs. cooking oil

Wash fish or shellfish by dipping in cold, salted water. Dry thoroughly on absorbent paper or lint-free towel. Mix seasonings into flour and dredge fish with mixture. (If you prefer, you can put flour mixture in a heavy paper bag and shake a few pieces of fish in the bag at a time to coat with flour. Combine beaten egg and milk, dip each piece of floured fish or shellfish into the egg mixture, then into bread crumbs, coating completely, and lay on waxed paper to dry. Let stand for at least 5 minutes. (You can let stand overnight, covered with wax paper, in the refrigerator if you want to prepare ahead.)

Heat butter or margarine and cooking oil in one large heavy skillet or 2 smaller ones until sizzling but not smoking. Add fish, being careful not to crowd it. Shake pans occasionally to keep fish batter from sticking. When golden brown on one side, turn each piece over and cook until golden brown on the other side. This process should not take more than a total of 5 minutes for both sides. It is done when flakes fall apart easily when gently poked with fork tines.

Fish That One Kid Called Candy

We know that that is quite a name for a recipe but, still, it's the best way we know of describing it. Our daughter, who does not particularly like fish, took her first taste of it and exclaimed, "Oh, boy! It tastes like candy!" Try it on your kids and hear what they say.

2 lbs. flounder fillets, about ¼ inch thick
Bread crumbs to cover, no substitutes
Butter
Milk

Place fillets on wire rack in shallow broiler pan and generously sprinkle with bread crumbs. Dot liberally with butter. Pour enough cold milk into pan to not quite reach the rack. Preheat broiler to 550° F. Slide pan into broiler, making sure fish is 3 to 4 inches below heat. In 5 minutes at the most the fillets will be beautifully brown on the top and nicely steamed on the bottom. But, to make sure that they're not overdone, test at about 3 minutes with a fork. If the flesh flakes easily, the fish that tastes like candy is done. Serves 4 to 6.

Variation: Use water instead of milk.

Wine-Marinade Fillets with Leftover Creamed Vegetables

Enough leftover cooked creamed vegetables to line small baking pan
3 lbs. fish fillets
1 cup white wine
Salt and pepper to taste

Remove vegetables from freezer and defrost. Place fillets in glass bowl with wine and marinate 1 or 2 hours in refrigerator, turning once or twice. Line bottom of small baking pan at least ¼ to ½ inch thick with leftover vegetables. Place fish fillets side by side on top of vegetables, pour wine in which they marinated over all and bake in preheated 350° F. oven for 20 minutes, but start testing with a fork at about 10. When the fish flakes easily and the vegetables are eating hot, it's time to serve. Serves 6 to 8.

Broiled Split Fish in Mustard-Dill Cream

4 whole fish, split for broiling, ¾ to 1 lb. each
2 tsps. mustard, or to taste
½ tsp. dill weed
¼ tsp. salt
1/16 tsp. pepper
½ pint sour cream

Preheat broiler (don't use a wire rack), lay split fish, skin down, in lightly greased pan, and place 2 to 3 inches from source of heat and broil at 550° F. Do not turn. Cook for 5 minutes, then combine all other ingredients and spread over fish. Continue broiling from 3 to 7 minutes or until fish flakes easily with a fork. Do not overcook. Serve at once on preheated plates. Serves 4 to 6.

Portuguese Baked Fish

1 3-to-5-lb. dressed fish
4 Tbs. olive oil or margarine
¼ cup white wine
Salt and pepper to taste
6 small onions, sliced
3 medium tomatoes, sliced
3 medium potatoes, cooked, peeled, and cubed
¼ cup white wine

Place fish in baking pan and brush with oil mixed with ¼ cup wine; sprinkle with salt and pepper. Arrange onions, tomatoes, and potatoes around it, and add remaining ¼ cup wine.

Bake in a 350° F. oven for 40 minutes or until fish flakes easily when tested with a fork. Add water if necessary. Serve in the baking pan with its own sauce. Serves 6 to 8.

Baked Fish Smothered in Wild Rice with Mushrooms and Water Chestnuts

2 Tbs. butter or margarine
1 can (about 5 oz.) water chestnuts thinly sliced and then cut into pieces
1 cup sliced fresh mushrooms
1 large stalk celery, thinly sliced
1 large onion, minced
1 6-oz. pkg. long-grain white with wild rice mixture
1 10½-oz. can condensed cream of mushroom soup, undiluted
1 3-to-5-lb. fish (bass or any that's in season)
2 Tbs. butter or margarine
1 tsp. salt
Lemon wedges
Parsley sprigs for garnish

Melt. 2 Tbs. butter or margarine in skillet, add chestnuts, mushrooms, celery and onion, and start to sauté. Start cooking rice according to package directions. When chestnut mixture is tender, add to rice. Stir and continue cooking until rice is done, adding more water if necessary, but no more than will be absorbed by the time rice is tender. When done, stir undiluted mushroom soup in and set aside.

Rub fish inside and out with remaining 2 Tbs. butter or margarine, sprinkle cavity very lightly with salt, and stuff with part of rice mixture. Place fish in smallest-possible, well-greased baking pan and smother with remainder of rice mixture. Preheat oven to 350° F. Bake 30 minutes or until fish flakes easily when tested with a fork at its fattest point. Transfer to platter, garnish with lemon and parsley. Serves 6 to 8.

Bouillabaisse—Made from Dibs and Dabs of Frozen Fish

2 to 2½ lbs. assorted fish pieces and shellfish saved up in freezer
⅛ cup olive oil
⅛ cup butter
½ cup chopped onion
½ cup chopped celery
1 clove garlic, chopped fine
4 cups fish broth (your own frozen or substitute canned)
3 cups canned tomatoes
¼ tsp. thyme
1 bay leaf, crushed
½ tsp. saffron
1 large loaf French bread

Defrost pieces of fish and shellfish and frozen broth overnight in refrigerator. Cut fish into small pieces and remove as much of the bone as possible. Combine oil and butter in large pot and, when butter is melted, add onion, celery, and garlic, and sauté until onion is golden. Add fish, fish broth, tomatoes, thyme, bay leaf and saffron. Cover, bring to a boil, and simmer for 20 minutes, adding shellfish last 5 minutes. Meantime slice bread in 3 pieces lengthwise and then into thirds and toast the 9 pieces in oven. Place 1 slice toast in each soup bowl, top with the bouillabaisse, making sure that fish is evenly divided, decorate with the leftover shellfish and serve. Serves 6 to 8.

Note: Canned clams and canned shrimp may be added last 5 minutes of cooking if you think your bouillabaisse needs enriching or if you had no shellfish to begin with.

For a real party look, bring bouillabaisse to table in a tureen and serve as above.

Leftover Fish Newburg

2 Tbs. butter or margarine
½ cup fresh mushrooms
4 Tbs. butter or margarine
5 Tbs. flour
1½ cups milk, hot
2 egg yolks
½ tsp. Worcestershire sauce
1 tsp. salt, optional
1 tsp. lemon juice
3 Tbs. cooking sherry
2 cups leftover cooked fish, drained and flaked

Melt 2 Tbs. butter or margarine in skillet, add mushrooms, and stir-fry the mushrooms about 10 minutes or until lightly browned. Remove from heat and set aside.

Melt 4 Tbs. butter or margarine in heavy saucepan, stir in the flour, and cook together for 2 minutes. Using a wire whisk, stir as you pour the hot milk in all at once. Cook over medium heat until thickened, stirring constantly.

Add a little of the milk-and-flour mixture to the egg yolks, stirring until thoroughly mixed, and then blend gently back into the saucepan. Add Worcestershire sauce, salt, lemon juice, sherry, fish, and mushrooms. Mix well and cook for 2 minutes, stirring constantly, over low heat. Serve over rice. Serves 4.

Gefüllte Fish

Made-at-home gefüllte fish—which broadly translated from the Yiddish means stuffed fish—is a fast-fading art form in the United States. Generations once or twice removed from Old World ties are content to leave the work to the commercial food processors who have put their versions—some good, some so-so, but none of them bad—within easy reach of every housewife's shopping cart.

There is another way, though, of cutting down on the not-too-great labor that goes into the making of gefüllte fish and that is to prepare not one, but two meals at once. Gefüllte fish is the first meal. Or if you'd rather, serve it as a first-course appetizer, or just make each piece toothpick-spearing size and include them in your next canapés-and-cocktail party.

Meal Number Two, and whether you have it the next day or the next month is dependent upon the available space in your freezer, is Gefüllte Fish Stew.

Here they are:

Grandma Lena's Gefüllte Fish

4 lbs. dressed carp, or any dark-meat fish
2 lbs. any white fish, preferably a mixture
4 stalks celery
2 large onions
Salt and pepper to taste
4 eggs, beaten
Water
2 lbs. carrots, sliced
Grated horseradish, red or white, to taste

Carefully remove skin and large bones from carp and set aside.

Cut carp into workable pieces and put through fine-blade food grinder along with white fish, celery, and onions, emptying the grindings into a large mixing bowl. Run through grinder a second time if necessary to assure a fine grind. Add salt, pepper, and beaten eggs. Mix well.

With your hands roll mixture into baking potato-shaped ovals, about 3 inches long and 1½ inches in diameter. Wrap each oval in a piece of fish skin and fasten with wooden toothpicks. Place fish bones in large stewpot, cover with water and place the ovals gently on top of the bones. Add sliced carrots, bring water to a boil, turn down heat, and gently simmer about 30 minutes. Cool fish enough to handle, then carefully remove skin and discard. Remove bones from broth with slotted spoon and discard.

Now divide broth, carrots, and fish ovals in half; one half for use now, the other for stew on another day. Place the second half in an all-purpose covered casserole dish and, when cool enough, store away in your freezer. Then, getting back to the first half, return the fish to the broth-and-carrot mixture, place in refrigerator, and chill until liquid forms a jelly. Serve cold with grated horseradish. Serves 8 to 10.

Note: Cold, as an appetizer, is the most popular way of eating gefüllte fish. But, if you want it as a hot main course, simply eliminate chilling, reheat to serving temperature, and serve with vegetables.

Grandma Lena's Leftover Gefüllte Fish Stew

Leftover gefüllte fish from freezer, including carrots
2 lbs. medium potatoes, peeled and quartered
⅛ lb. (½ stick) butter or margarine
Salt and pepper to taste
2 Tbs. fish broth, about
Parsley for garnish

Remove casserole from freezer and allow contents to thaw. Cook potatoes in separate pot as you always cook them. When gefüllte fish is ready for the fire, place on low heat, add potatoes, and gently simmer until hot. Then transfer half the potatoes and carrots to a mixing bowl, add butter, salt, pepper, and broth from the casserole as needed, and mash. Return the mixture to casserole. Stir in gently, taking care not to break the fish ovals, and serve when hot, garnishing with parsley. Serves 8.

Oyster-Stuffed Baked Potatoes

3 large baking potatoes
3 Tbs. butter, about
6 Tbs. milk, about
Salt and pepper to taste
6 shucked oysters, drained
¼ cup buttered bread crumbs
3 Tbs. grated cheese, about

Scrub potatoes clean with cold water and bake in 450° F. oven for 1 hour or until done. Remove from oven, slice in half lengthwise, and scoop pulp into a bowl. Add butter, milk, salt and pepper, and mash.

Stuff each potato jacket half with mashed potato, and press an oyster gently into each. Cover with bread crumbs, sprinkle amply with grated cheese, and bake in 350° F. oven 10 to 15 minutes or until cheese is melted and crumbs are brown. Serves 6.

Note: Be sure to eat the skins. They're good for you.

Variations: Substitute any flaked cooked fish, canned tuna, canned salmon, scallops, shrimp, or clams for the oysters.

Salmon Loaf

2 cups canned salmon, flaked
1 cup chicken or fish stock
1 cup light cream or canned milk
2 cups day-old bread finely crumbed
½ tsp. salt, or to taste
Pepper to taste
3 egg yolks
3 egg whites, beaten

Thoroughly mix all ingredients except egg whites. Fold in beaten whites, stir a few strokes but not enough to change consistency of whites. Pour into lightly buttered casserole, 2½ to 3 inches deep, and bake in 350° F. oven for 50 minutes, or until loaf is lightly browned and firm in center. Serves 4 to 6.

Shrimp and Chicken Parmesan in Casserole

2 Tbs. milk
Salt and pepper to taste
1 egg, beaten
1 lb. raw shrimp, shelled, deveined, and washed
1 lb. cooked white chicken meat, cut in small cubes
1 cup cracker crumbs
4 Tbs. butter or margarine
1 lb. Mozzarella cheese, sliced
2 15-oz. cans Buitoni Marinara Sauce

Stir milk, salt and pepper into beaten egg. Dip shrimp and chicken chunks into mixture, dredge with cracker crumbs, and fry in butter until golden brown. Remove with slotted spoon onto absorbent paper.

Place half of shrimp and chicken in bottom of a lightly greased casserole, cover with half of sliced Mozzarella cheese, and cover the Mozzarella with half the Marinara Sauce. Repeat layers. Bake in 350° F. oven 30 minutes. Serves 6 to 8.

Note: Save 1 cup for a shrimp and chicken Parmesan omelet. Keep in refrigerator for one day, or put in airtight container and freeze for future use.

8 POULTRY AND POULTRY RECIPES

A scientific revolution has been taking place in the poultry industry for a number of years with the result that young, tender chicken has been taken out of the Sunday Dinner Only class and turned into one of the most economical meats available to the consumer.

Plump, flavorsome turkey, once considered a luxury eaten only at Thanksgiving and Christmastime, can now be purchased the year round. While not yet as economical as chicken, it's moving in that direction. Several times a year now you're likely to pick up the paper and see ads for turkey at bargain prices. Now and then, parts of turkeys are available at very reasonable prices.

We suggest ways to take advantage of turkey sales a little later on under "Buying and Preparing Whole Turkeys for the Freezer."

What to Look for in Buying Poultry

1. A short, plump body, rather than a long, lean one.
2. Skin free of bruises, pinfeathers, and discoloration.
3. Undamaged packaging, especially if frozen.

4. Chicken and turkey, to be tender, should have a good fat covering. You can see it through the skin and there will be layers of fat at the cavity openings.

5. For assurance of best quality buy U.S. Grade A poultry.

6. Read the label. Poultry described as *mature, hen, stewing, yearling, fowl* or just plain *old* will be tough and will have to be braised or cooked in liquid until tender. Poultry labeled *fryer* or *broiler, roaster* or *young* is usually tender and you can purchase it for preparing almost any recipe you want.

7. Look for the USDA Poultry Inspection and Grade stamps, shown below. (Poultry grades are *not* an indication of degree of tenderness.)

USDA Poultry Inspection and Grade Marks

All poultry sold across state lines must be checked for wholesomeness by a United States Department of Agriculture inspector and bear his mark, a circle similar to that placed on meat. Prepared poultry food products to be sold across state lines must be prepared under inspection of the USDA and also bear this mark.

The Wholesome Poultry Act of 1968 requires that those plants doing business only within a single state must be inspected by a state inspection program with requirements that are at least equal to Federal requirements. Such plants were given two, or in some cases three, years in which to make the necessary improvements and comply.

The USDA grade mark is in the form of a shield and indicates whether poultry is U.S. Grade A (the finest quality), Grade B, or Grade C. Grading is a voluntary program which is available to processors and others who request it. Poultry must be USDA-inspected and approved for wholesomeness before it can be Federally graded. The U.S. grades for poultry are based on meatiness, freedom from defects, and general appearance. The Grade shield and/or inspection circle usually appears on the wrapper, wing tag, giblet wrap, package insert, or label.

When grading is done in cooperation with a state, the official grade shield may include the words "Federal-State Graded."

Amount of Chicken to Buy
(a very general estimate)

For braising, frying, roasting, stewing: ½ lb. ready-to-cook weight per serving

For broiling: ¼ to ½ chicken per person

Is It Really Cheaper to Buy Whole Chickens and Cut Them Up Yourself? There is a general belief that you save a considerable amount of money if you buy whole chickens and do the cutting up yourself. It doesn't take very long and it's not a difficult task as the illustrations in this section show. Most times it saves you money, but sometimes it doesn't. It's not always easy to figure which way is best, but the following comparison schedule will help.

	Price per pound									
When 1- to 2-lb. broilers are selling at:	.25	.27	.29	.31	.33	.35	.37	.39	.41	.43
Legs and thighs are an equal buy at:	.57	.61	.66	.70	.75	.79	.84	.88	.93	.97
Breasts are an equal buy at:	.76	.82	.88	.94	1.00	1.06	1.12	1.18	1.24	1.30
Approximate cost per serving of each of above:	.19½	.21	.22½	.24	.25½	.27	.28½	.30	.31½	.33

Figures from Oregon State University Extension Service's *Spotlight on Food.*

Buying and Preparing Whole Chickens for the Freezer

To conserve your freezer space in the best way possible, buy four to six chickens in the young tender class at a time. Take them home, cut them up as shown in illustrations which follow* and then prepare a supply of chicken broth and the precooked makings for a variety of chicken dishes in one session.

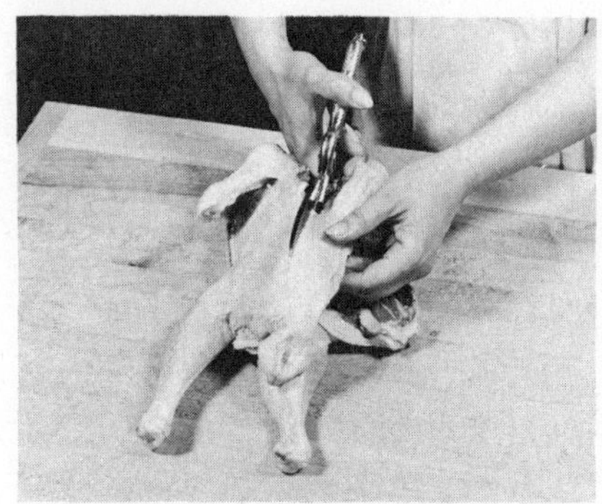

1. Remove neck-and-back strip by cutting from neck to tail along both sides of the backbone.

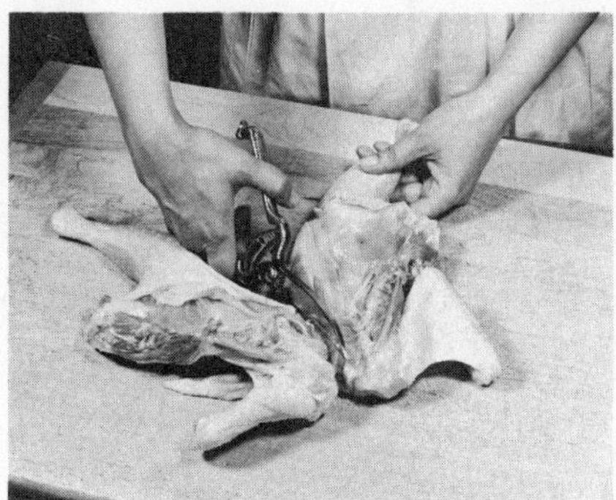

2. Turn bird on its breast. Cut in two along the breastbone.

* Courtesy of United States Department of Agriculture, Office of Information.

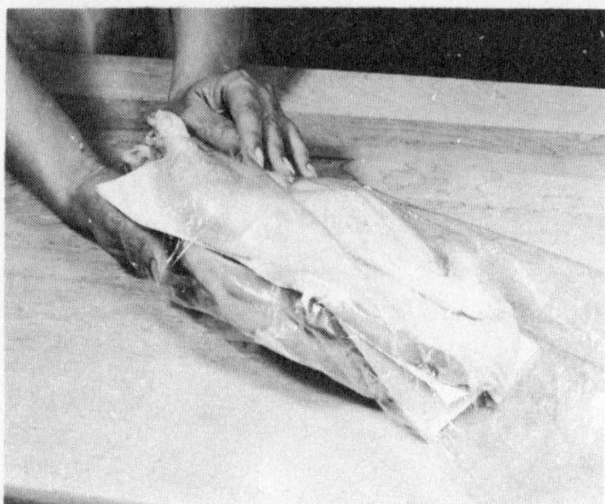

3. If halves are packaged together, place a double fold of freezer paper between them.

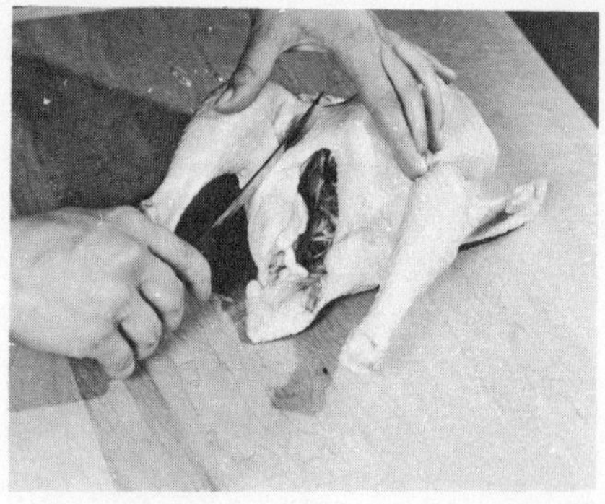

4. Cut skin between thighs and body of the bird.

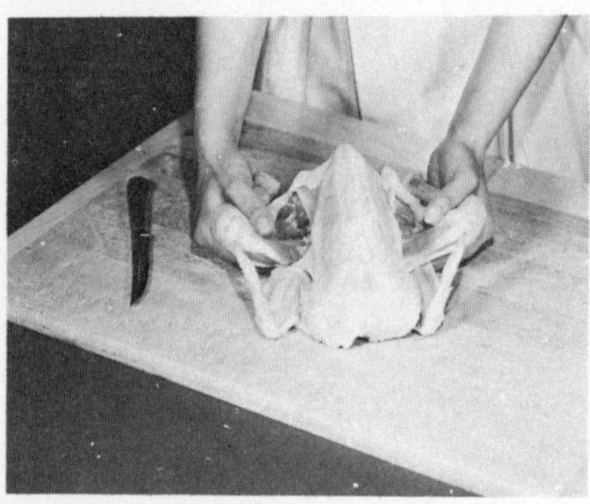

5. Grasp a leg of the bird in each hand and lift the bird from the table, bending its legs back as you lift. Bend legs until hip joints are free.

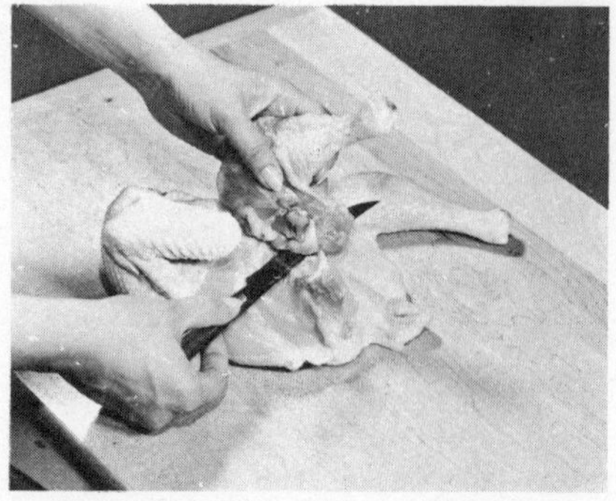

6. Remove leg-and-thigh piece from one side of the body by cutting from back to front as close as possible to the bones in the back of the bird.

7. Locate the knee joint by squeezing thigh and leg together. Cut through this joint to separate thigh and leg.

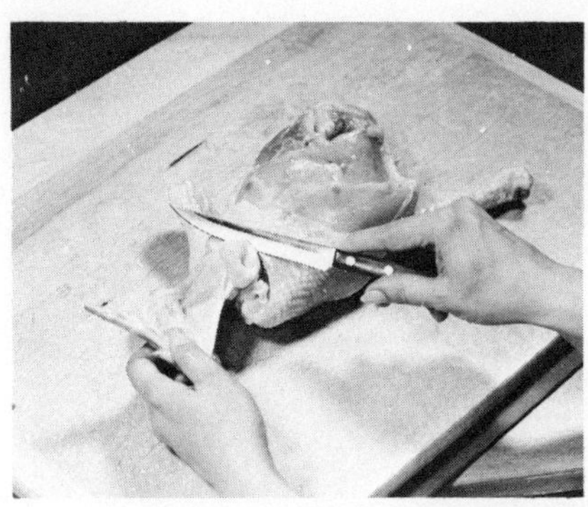

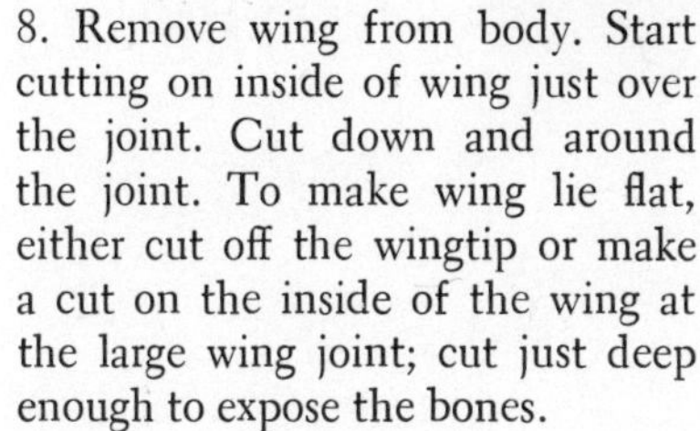

8. Remove wing from body. Start cutting on inside of wing just over the joint. Cut down and around the joint. To make wing lie flat, either cut off the wingtip or make a cut on the inside of the wing at the large wing joint; cut just deep enough to expose the bones.

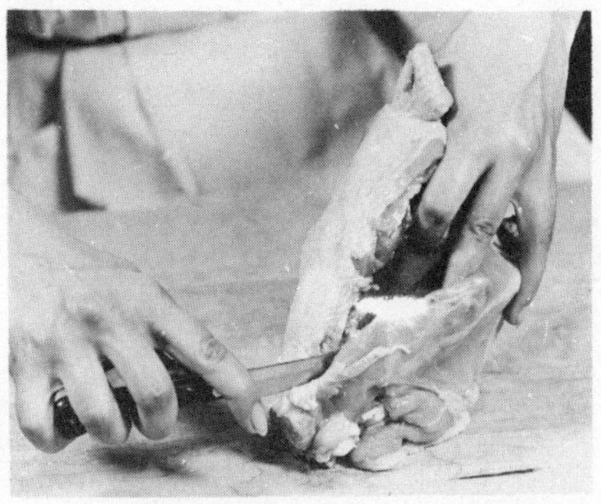

9. Divide the body by placing bird on neck end and cutting through the meat from back to tail along the end of the ribs. Then cut along each side of the backbone through the rib joints, then between backbone and flat bone at the side of the back. Cut the skin that attaches neck-and-back strip to the breast.

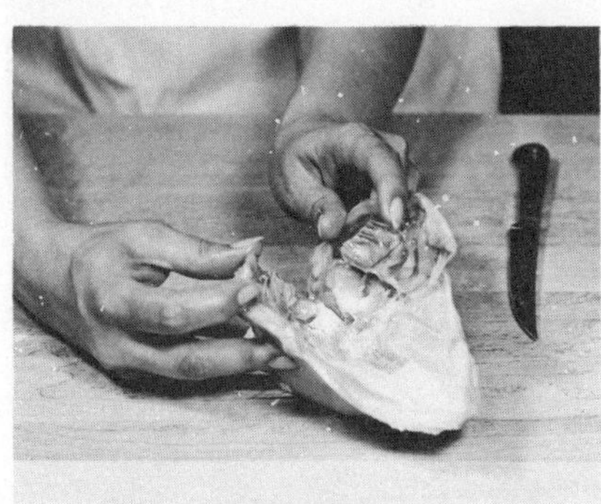

10. Place the breast, skin side down, on the cutting board. Cut through the white cartilage at the V of the neck as shown.

11. Grasp the breast piece firmly in both hands. Bend each side of the breast back and push up with the fingers to snap out the breastbone. Cut the breast in half lengthwise.

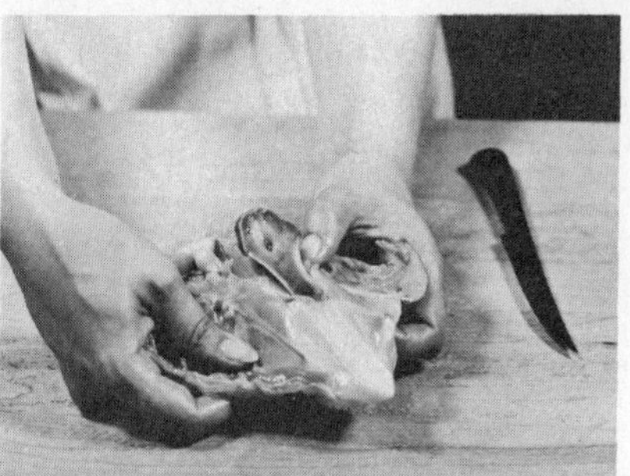

12. The disjointed chicken. Meaty pieces at left (legs, thighs, wings, breast halves). Bony pieces at right (wingtips, back strip, back, and neck).

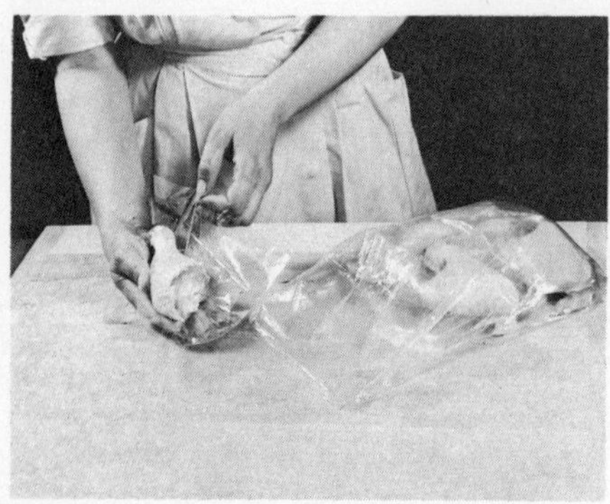

13. Wrapping for freezing.

14. Packaging large slices of roast turkey.

15. Adding broth to small pieces of turkey packed for freezing.

16. Cool cooked food immediately by placing pan on ice or in iced water. Then package and freeze cooled food promptly.

This will enable you to keep a supply of cubes and blocks—from 2 Tbs. to 1-cup size—of basic chicken broth in your freezer. ("Freezing Measured Amounts of Broths" gives instructions for packaging them.) It will cost you almost nothing to prepare and it will add immeasurably to the flavor of many, many dishes. You can prepare a little or a lot at one time; depending on what is easiest for you and you can reduce it to ½ or ¼ volume if you are short of freezer space. While making the broth, you can cook some of the chicken, making it easier to package in compact shapes and freeze.

Defrosting Fresh-Frozen Chicken

Fresh-frozen chickens defrost nicely as a rule simply by leaving them in the refrigerator overnight. The running water method of defrosting chicken more quickly is safe if the proper procedure is followed.

Put the chicken (preferably while still in wrapping) in a pot and let *cold water* run into the pot. The iciness of the frozen part of the chicken will keep the water surrounding the outer, defrosted part of the chicken good and cold. Remove from the water and get ready for the oven immediately when defrosted, and while still icy cold.

Defrosting Other Birds

Domestic duck can be defrosted in the same way as chicken. Check the label on any other birds or ask your poultry butcher's advice. See Turkey Recipes for defrosting instructions.

Timing Poultry for Doneness

Timetables for roasting poultry vary greatly because of the many factors affecting how long it takes a bird to reach the desired degree of doneness. The easiest way is to use a thermometer and let the cooking time given in each individual recipe serve as a rough guide. Insert the thermometer into the thick part of thigh, next to where it joins the body but not touching the bone; poultry should be done when thermometer registers 185° F. Since, from the standpoint of safety and health, poultry *should not be eaten rare,* you can double-check by testing to see if the drumstick moves up and down easily and the leg joint gives readily.

Also heed any package or other wrapping instructions.

General Instructions for Stuffing Poultry

Wash bird inside and out. Dry and stuff immediately. Loosely fill body and neck cavities, skewer body cavity closed. If there is a tough band of skin at tail, tuck ends of drumsticks under it. Otherwise tie or skewer legs together close to body. Skewer skin at end of neck opening to bird's back and tie a string around wings to hold them against the back.

Poultry should not be stuffed until just before going in the oven and the stuffing should be removed from cavity of cooked bird before it is stored in the refrigerator. Neither the stuffing nor the bird should be allowed to stand around at room temperature any longer than is absolutely necessary.

We mention elsewhere in the book (but it is important enough to repeat here), that cooked meats (it makes no difference whether poultry or red meats), stuffing and gravies should be chilled quickly by setting in a bowl and placing the bowl in a pan of ice water. As the ice melts, replenish it. Remove stuffings and chill them in a separate bowl. Cutting a large bird into several pieces also speeds the chilling process along. Cover and place immediately in the refrigerator, just as soon as the contents of each bowl is cool.

Chicken Recipes for Cooking Chicken Purchased in Quantity for the Freezer While also Making a Supply of Basic Chicken Broth

Before starting, plan your preparations so that chicken for each package can be chilled quickly and put into the freezer.

It sometimes helps decide just what recipes you will prepare and what will go in each if you spread the cut up chicken pieces out on the kitchen table and regroup them according to recipe. If you make a list of just what part and how many go where, it will make it easy to handle the cooked chicken quickly.

The next step would be to put the parts in the refrigerator while you prepare any sauces, wash your vegetables, choose your freezer containers, tear off suitably sized strips of freezer paper, and lay out freezer tape and marking pencils.

You can use any shape of freezer container that is most convenient, but keep this in mind: single layers of chicken in a sauce will defrost more quickly, or reheat in the oven more quickly without being defrosted first, than will that packaged in a deep container. Inexpensive aluminum piepans or shallow cake pans, which you either buy or save when you buy a pie or cake, make excellent freezer containers for chicken parts frozen in a sauce. You can transfer them from freezer to refrigerator to oven, too, without using another dish.

The recipes listed below are meant to suggest suitable ways to use some of the chicken parts, but you need not restrict yourself to them.

Basic Chicken Broth

Do not add seasonings that might conflict with dishes in which broth will be used at a later date.

4½ to 5 lbs. chicken which you have cut up into serving-size pieces—do not include liver—and which is *small, tender,* and *young.* (After you have done this a time or two and streamlined the procedure, you might use two or three large pots and prepare 6 to 8 lbs. at one time. Poultry and sauces are too perishable to handle more than that.)
8 cups water
2 tsps. salt
2 whole carrots (scrubbed but not peeled)
2 stalks celery, from the outside with leaves left on
1 large, whole onion (stick toothpicks through it to keep it from falling apart)

Place all ingredients in large pot, cover and bring to a boil. Turn down to simmer and continue cooking for 15 to 20 minutes, or until chicken is just done. Do not overcook.

Remove drumsticks, thighs, wings, necks, and breasts and cool them enough to handle, meanwhile continuing to simmer the vegetables and chicken backs. (As parts cool, refrigerate those you are not working with.)

DRUMSTICKS AND THIGHS: Pull bones out, slitting meat if necessary, and package for freezer. Pour a little chicken broth over meat unless you package it in a sauce. See Chicken Parts Baked in Sour Cream Sauce with Mushrooms and Wine, page 136, and Chicken Baked in Tomato Sauce, page 136.

WINGS AND NECKS: Prepare for freezing plain or in sauce. See Chicken Wings and Necks in Barbecue Sauce, or put back in cooking broth to make it richer.

(For dinner on this busy day you may want to serve chicken broth and any boiled chicken parts you don't want to freeze.)

BREASTS: Remove bones and cut meat in slices that can be used as is —after heating in a sauce—or chopped to use in one of the recipes calling for chopped or diced cooked chicken meat. If you don't freeze this meat in a sauce, pour a little broth over it before closing the container. Put bones back in the broth. See Poultry Balls in a Nest of Spinach for one way such meat can be used at a future date.

Now, with all the bones and possibly the wings and necks back in the broth, continue cooking for ½ hour. Remove vegetables, chicken parts, and bones. Taste soup. If it is the way you like chicken broth to taste, strain, cool, and freeze, either as it is or first reduce to ½ or ¼. See "Freezing Measured Amounts of Broth," page 36. If broth is too weak, continue simmering. Before freezing, skim off most of the fat and freeze in separate, small containers to use in cooking. (It adds to the flavor of omelets and sautéed vegetables.)

Remove all bits of meat from chicken bones and rinse off carrots and celery by placing very briefly beneath running, cool water. Peel carrots, discard celery leaves, chop both vegetables and set aside with bits of meat to make Creamed Chicken with Vegetables and Rice, page 137. Set aside bits of chicken skin and cut up larger pieces to make Greiven, see page 140.

LIVER: Chopped Chicken Liver Spread can be prepared, then frozen, or the livers can be frozen raw and prepared after defrosting. It will depend on how much time you have when you are preparing and freezing your initial chicken purchase which way you should handle the livers.

Wrap, label, freeze, and enter each dish in your freezer index as you complete it.

Stuffed Chicken in Easy Orange Sauce

2 2½-lb. chickens (eat one; freeze one)
½ lb. lean bacon, chopped
½ cup chopped onion
¼ cup margarine
2½ cups your own crisply toasted bread crumbs
¼ tsp. sage
¼ tsp. celery salt
½ tsp. salt
¾ cup chicken broth (your own if you have it)
1 egg, lightly beaten
1 6-oz. can undiluted frozen orange juice (optional; the chickens can be cooked plain or basted with a little butter)

Wash and dry chickens. Start bacon cooking in heavy skillet. When most of fat is rendered out but bacon has not started becoming crisp, add chopped onion and cook until onion starts to get soft. Turn off heat, add margarine and let it melt. Put crumbs in a large mixing bowl, sprinkle seasonings over them, and mix well. Combine chicken broth and beaten egg, and mix thoroughly into bread crumbs. Add bacon, onion, and margarine mixture; mix and divide stuffing in half. Stuff one chicken with one half, put other half in a buttered baking pan.

Put stuffed chicken, backside up, in a shallow roaster, bake 30 minutes (in 325° F. oven). Add unstuffed chicken, bake 30 minutes longer. Turn chickens over, put pan of stuffing in oven and continue baking another 30 minutes. Baste top of stuffing loaf with any juices that have run out of chickens. Spread ½ can of thawed orange juice over the two chickens. Continue cooking for another 30 minutes, basting chickens with the balance of orange juice until it is all used up, then use sauce from bottom of pan. Add 1 cup of water to pan. If juices start turning brown, add a little more water.

Serve stuffed chicken; freeze unstuffed chicken and pan of stuffing for future use. Cut unstuffed chicken into serving pieces, arrange in single layer in shallow freezer dish in which it can be reheated. Spoon some pan sauce over it before wrapping and freezing. Each chicken serves 4.

To defrost and reheat stuffing loaf and unstuffed chicken: Defrost overnight in refrigerator. Put in 300° F. oven and heat through. Spread 1 Tb. butter over top of loaf. Baste chicken with sauce in pan in which it was frozen.

Willie Boldizar's Chicken Paprikash

2 2-lb. chickens, washed and cut into serving pieces
½ cup flour
1 tsp. salt
1 tsp. paprika
1 Tb. butter
2 Tbs. cooking oil
1 large onion, sliced very fine
½ green pepper, sliced very fine
1½ cups water
3 Tbs. butter
4 Tbs. flour
⅔ cup milk
1 tsp. paprika
½ pint sour cream

Dredge chicken in mixture of flour, salt, and 1 tsp. paprika. Heat butter and oil in large skillet. When just beginning to sizzle (don't let it smoke) add chicken, a few pieces at a time so pan is not crowded, and brown very lightly on both sides. Remove chicken with a slotted spoon and lightly fry onion and green pepper slices. Transfer onion, green pepper, and oil from skillet to a large, heavy pot, add chicken and water, and simmer 30 minutes or until chicken is tender.

Melt 3 Tbs. butter in skillet in which chicken was browned. Add flour and cook the flour in the butter for 2 or 3 minutes, stirring constantly. Heat milk to just under boiling, add one cup of liquid from chicken pot, pour into skillet, and beat with a wire whisk until flour blends into sauce. Boil, continuing to stir until sauce reaches desired thickness. Add remaining spoonful of paprika and remaining liquid from chicken pot. Bring to a boil, blend thoroughly, then turn off heat. Stir a small amount of hot gravy into sour cream, gradually adding at least a cup of the hot sauce. Then gradually stir the cream mixture into the gravy. (Cream will curdle if the temperature is changed too quickly or if it becomes very hot.) Pour gravy over chicken. Serve with cooked noodles. Serves 8.

Note: Freeze leftover pieces of chicken in the leftover gravy, or . . . Make Chicken Cutlets with Paprika Sauce from leftovers.

Oven Fried Chicken

Dipped in Buttermilk and Bread Crumbs

1 3-lb. chicken with a nice coating of fat, washed, dried, and cut into serving pieces.
¾ cup cultured buttermilk
1 cup bread crumbs
1 tsp. salt
⅛ tsp. pepper
5 Tbs. liquid cooking oil

Dip each piece of chicken into buttermilk, shake off excess, and coat with bread crumbs into which salt and pepper have been mixed. Let chicken dry, spread out, for 5 to 10 minutes. Spread 2 Tbs. cooking oil over bottom of large, shallow pan. Spread chicken pieces over pan in single layer so that they don't touch each other. Drizzle remainder of oil over them and put in oven preheated to 400° F. After 25 minutes, use spatula and carefully turn chicken pieces over. Continue cooking 10 minutes, then remove pan from oven and pour off fat. Carefully loosen all pieces from pan, using a spatula, return to oven, turn off heat, and leave until ready to serve. Chicken can stand in pan for 5 or 10 minutes in warm oven without losing crispness. Serves 6.

Note: Uncooked chicken prepared this way can be wrapped in wax paper packages—in single layers—and stored overnight in refrigerator for use the next day. It can also be wrapped in freezer paper and frozen.

Chicken Wings and Necks in Barbecue Sauce

Hot Hors d'Oeuvres

You can save and freeze these parts when you buy several chickens, or you can buy a package of necks and one of wings when these parts are on sale, or you can cook these parts and freeze them in the sauce when Cooking Chicken Purchased in Quantity for the Freezer; see page 129.

6 small chicken necks
12 small chicken wings
2 Tbs. soy sauce
2 Tbs. pineapple juice
1 tsp. honey
1 Tb. lemon juice
1 Tb. prepared mustard
¼ cup catsup
¼ cup white wine

Put necks and wings in a dish. Combine all other ingredients, pour over chicken and refrigerate overnight. If necks and wings are frozen, separate them as soon as they will come apart and spread out in the sauce, coating each piece.

Put in shallow baking pan and bake in 350° F. oven for 1 to 1½ hours, or until tender and well done. If chicken is cooked, frozen in the sauce and undefrosted, decrease temperature to 200° F. for first half hour.

If sauce gets thick or starts to burn, add water.

Serve to eat in fingers, separated into small pieces, in heated sauce . . . with plenty of napkins. Makes 48 hors d'oeuvres.

Baked Chicken Parts in Sour Cream Sauce with Mushrooms and Wine

2 Tbs. soft butter
8 cooked chicken parts (legs, etc.)
Salt and pepper to taste
1 Tb. cooking oil
1 Tb. butter or margarine
1 cup sliced mushrooms
½ cup sliced sweet onions (use shallots if you have them)
½ cup chicken broth
¼ cup white wine
1 cup sour cream

Rub soft butter over both sides of chicken parts, salt and pepper to taste, and lay parts in a single layer in a shallow baking pan. Put in preheated 400° F. oven and cook for 30 minutes. Use spatula to turn over after first 15 minutes. Heat cooking oil and butter or margarine together in large, heavy skillet until small bubbles begin to form. Sauté mushrooms and onions together.

Heat chicken broth and wine in saucepan. Turn off heat and add sour cream gradually, stirring until well blended. Arrange chicken on heat resistant serving platter, pour sauce over it, and top with onions and mushrooms. Place platter in broiler, 3 or 4 inches from 500° F. heat, and broil just until sauce browns very slightly. Serve at once. Serves 4 to 6.

Chicken Baked in Tomato Sauce

8 cooked pieces of chicken (legs, thighs, etc.)
2 cups tomato sauce
½ cup your own chicken broth

Place pieces of chicken in single layer in bottom of shallow pan Cover with tomato sauce mixed with chicken broth and bake in 350° F.

oven for 1 hour. Turn chicken over once and baste with sauce whenever tops of chicken pieces become dry. Serves 4 to 6.

To Bake While Frozen in Foil-covered Dish: Put in 250° F. oven for 20 minutes. Turn heat to 350° F. and continue cooking for 20 minutes. Uncover and cook for 20 minutes more or until chicken is heated through and sauce is nice consistency. Baste with sauce.

Creamed Chicken with Vegetables and Rice

2 10½-oz. cans cream of mushroom soup, undiluted
½ cup chicken broth
2 Tbs. white wine
1 pinch marjoram
1 pinch white pepper
½ to 1 cup cooked chicken meat, chopped
2 carrots, cooked, peeled, and chopped
2 stalks celery, cooked and chopped
¼ cup sour cream
1 cup brown rice, cooked according to directions on package

Combine cream of mushroom soup, chicken broth, wine, marjoram, and pepper in saucepan or top of double boiler and heat until simmering hot. Stir in chicken meat, carrots, and celery. When sauce is again simmering hot, turn off heat, stir in sour cream, and serve over rice. Serves 4.

Note: This recipe can be made from the chicken and vegetables used in preparing Basic Chicken Broth. The bits of chicken skin can be fried until crunchy and sprinkled over creamed chicken as an unusual garnish. See Greiven.

Note about Brown Rice: Fewer nutrients have been milled away in brown than in white rice. It has a richer flavor than white rice, but it takes a little longer to cook. For best results, the instructions on the package should be followed.

Poultry Balls in a Nest of Spinach

2 cups chopped cooked turkey or chicken or a mixture of both
½ cup soft bread crumbs, finely crumbled
1 egg, lightly beaten
Salt and pepper to taste (don't overdo it if meat is already seasoned)
¼ cup grated onion
2 Tbs. grated celery
2 Tbs. cooking oil
1 to 2 10-oz. boxes frozen chopped spinach
4 Tbs. flour
4 Tbs. butter or margarine
1 cup milk
½ cup your own chicken broth (canned broth may be substituted)
¼ cup heavy cream (optional)

Combine first 6 ingredients, thoroughly mix, and form into balls not more than 1½ inches in diameter. Heat cooking oil in heavy skillet and fry meatballs until lightly browned all over. Don't let oil get hot enough to smoke. Prepare spinach according to package instructions.

Mix 4 Tbs. flour into 4 Tbs. butter or margarine in a skillet and cook for 2 or 3 minutes, stirring constantly. Heat milk and broth almost to simmering point, add all at once to flour and butter mixture, and beat with a wire whisk until smooth. Bring to a boil and stir until thickened. Turn off heat and stir in cream. Serve meatballs in small nests of spinach and pour gravy over them. Serves 4 to 6.

Chopped Chicken Liver Spread

Save livers and freeze when you buy low cost chickens; combined with relatively low-cost eggs, this makes a reasonably priced spread.

2 Tbs. cooking oil
½ lb. chicken livers
½ cup finely minced onion
½ tsp. salt
⅛ tsp. pepper
4 hard-cooked eggs

Heat oil in heavy skillet and fry livers until lightly browned on both sides. Remove with slotted spoon and fry onion in the pan. Mash liver and onion together—if they are hard to handle, put them through meat grinder together—and season with salt and pepper. Mash hard-cooked eggs, stir into liver mixture, and put in a serving bowl or mound on lettuce leaves on a small plate. Serve on crackers as an appetizer. Try a little in an omelet.

Note: A little milk poured over livers while they defrost overnight in refrigerator will give them an especially sweet flavor. Pour milk off, and thoroughly dry livers before frying.

If you don't have a supply of frozen chicken livers saved, you can combine chicken livers with beef liver, if it is less expensive. Be sure it is young and sweet. Liver is such a nutritional economy, it's not wise to risk turning your family into liver haters by serving them one dish that is too strong!

Hot Chicken Liver Hors d'Oeuvres in Mustard Sauce

1 lb. chicken livers
1 cup flour
1 tsp. salt
⅛ tsp. pepper
2 Tbs. butter or margarine
1 Tb. cooking oil

Wash and thoroughly dry chicken livers and cut into quarters. Season flour with salt and pepper and dredge livers with it. Heat butter and cooking oil in a large, heavy skillet. When very hot but not smoking, add livers, one at a time, and cook until nicely browned and crisp on both sides. Don't crowd in pan. Serve on warm platter with mustard sauce for dipping and toothpicks for spearing. Serves 8 to 10 as hors d'oeuvres; serves 4 as meat course of dinner.

MUSTARD SAUCE DIP

2 Tbs. mustard
3 Tbs. catsup
4 Tbs. canned cream of mushroom soup, undiluted. (Left-over cream sauce or cream gravy can be substituted.)

Combine all ingredients and mix together until blended.

Note: When you buy chicken, freeze livers until you have enough to make this recipe. Put them in small, one-layer packages for quick defrosting to stretch a dinner for unexpected guests.

Greiven

Crisp Fried Chicken Skin

Cut chicken fat and skin into small pieces.

Fry together in medium hot pan until oil is rendered out of fat and nothing is left but crisp, crunchy bits and the liquid fat. Pour off fat and chill in refrigerator or freeze for cooking. Drain browned bits of skin on absorbent paper and eat as a snack or serve as a garnish as you would crumbled bacon. Try it over creamed chicken dishes such as Creamed Chicken with Vegetables and Rice.

Chopped Chicken (or Turkey) Cutlets

Can be made from leftover Chicken Paprikash

¼ tsp. grated nutmeg
1½ cups chopped or ground chicken or turkey meat. (Other cooked meat, or white tuna fish can be combined with chicken or turkey meat to make enough.)
¼ cup melted butter, not hot
½ cup flour
1 large egg, lightly beaten
1½ cups toasted bread crumbs
1 Tb. dried parsley
2 Tbs. butter
1 Tb. cooking oil

Sprinkle nutmeg over chopped chicken meat. Pour melted butter over it and work into the meat with your fingers, thoroughly mixing the nutmeg as you do so. Shape mixture into 6 to 8 cutlet shapes, about ½-inch thick. Put in the freezer to chill and become firm—15 to 20 minutes. Dip each cutlet in flour, then egg, then bread crumbs, into which dried parsley has been mixed. Let dry for at least 5 minutes (you can refrigerate overnight in wax paper packages if you like).

Heat 2 Tbs. butter and 1 Tb. cooking oil in large, heavy skillet. Add cutlets and fry until light golden brown on each side. Don't crowd in the pan and don't let the oil smoke. Serve plain or with any cream style sauce of your choice. If made from leftover Chicken Paprikash, paprikash sauce can be stretched by adding more sour cream and a little more paprika . . . or by adding undiluted canned creamed chicken or mushroom soup.

Buying and Preparing Whole Turkeys for the Freezer

You'll note that the bigger turkeys usually cost less per pound than the small ones. Besides which, there is a larger percentage of meat compared to bone on the big birds. Chances are there's not room in your freezer, though, for even one big turkey much less two or three.

What to do about it then? Simple. If the supermarket's prices on fresh-killed birds are low, chances are that your neighborhood butcher's prices also are low. So the thing to do is buy a large fresh-killed bird—a seventeen or eighteen pounder—and have him cut it in two, slicing along the center of the breastbone from neck to tail.

Have him leave one half intact while removing the wing, drumstick, thigh, and a few thin slices of breast meat from the second half. Then have him cut that half in two. Package and freeze the half that was cut up, wrapping the separate parts in separate packages, marking them and making a record of what's in each.

Sliced turkey breast meat (as well as pork) can be substituted for expensive veal cutlets in some recipes. See Pennysaver recipe for Breaded Turkey Breasts Cutlets.

The two bony chunks, the wing, leg and thigh, can be roasted either plain or in a sauce or, before freezing, they can be made into broth and boiled meat for salads and creamed dishes and loaves. (Follow recipe for Basic Chicken Broth.)

Stuff and cook the turkey half that you left intact. See Roast Half Turkey for cooking instructions.

We don't particularly recommend you buy more than one large turkey at a time, but, if you're crazy for turkey, the price is irresistible, and you have freezer space, there's nothing like keeping a whole turkey there for any-time-of-the-year entertaining. Ask your butcher to suggest ways he might saw up a second bird for you to make a variety of dishes possible. He just might even be willing to bone one for you, but don't be surprised if he refuses. It takes time. We think it best to buy frozen turkeys one at a time and use them within a month or two.

*The Poultry and Egg National Board Gives These Two Defrosting Timetables for Fresh-Frozen Turkey:**

IF YOU COOK IT LATER TODAY . . .

1. Leave turkey in original wrap.
2. Thaw in running water or water that is changed frequently.

* Turkey that was freshly killed and otherwise in topnotch condition immediately prior to being frozen.

Thawing Time
5–9 pounds 3–4 hours
Over 9 pounds 4–7 hours

3. Cook or refrigerate thawed turkey immediately.

If You Cook It Day After Tomorrow . . .
1. Leave in original wrap and place on tray or drip pan.
2. Thaw in refrigerator. (Turkeys over 12 pounds may take up to 3 days.)

Do Not
. . . . allow thawed bird to stand at room temperature. (Refrigerate thawed turkey or cook immediately.)
. . . . stuff bird until ready to cook.
. . . . thaw commercially stuffed birds.

Roasting Turkey

Thoroughly wash bird inside and out and dry. Then, after stuffing and skewering or sewing your bird:

Place turkey breast down for first ⅓ cooking time, then turn over for balance of cooking time. (There is some disagreement over whether or not turkey needs to be turned over during roasting time. The answer lies partly in your oven; if it's well-insulated and cooks evenly, and you don't care whether or not the center of the back is a deep brown, lay the bird on its back and don't turn it over.)

Lay turkey on a double thickness of heavy-duty aluminum foil that rests on top of rack in bottom of a shallow roasting pan. Use large sheets of foil and let them extend well over all sides of the pan, but crumple them loosely so they don't interfere with heat circulation and cooking. The reason for the excess of foil is so that you can pull sections of it up as needed to cover any spot on the turkey that has browned ahead of other spots: wings, drumstick, stuffed neck. Punch holes in bottom of foil with a fork so grease will run down into the roasting pan instead of collecting in foil. (Use of foil in pan is optional. You can use small pieces instead just to cover parts browning too rapidly.)

Turkey is in the oven for such a long period that it is seldom necessary to baste in order for it to have a brown skin. If you do want to baste, try to allow some room around the edge of the bird for getting at juices without moving it. Use a rack that is either smaller than the pan or has a corner cut out to give you access to juices. You can use either a spoon or a basting bulb for basting. If the juices in pan start to turn brown, add some water, but not more than a cup at a time or you will create too much steam. The best way to keep your juices from browning too much and spoiling your gravy is to cook at a fairly low temperature: 300° F. The best way to tell when turkey is done the way you like it is to use a meat thermometer. Insert it in thickest part of thigh, next to body, without touching the bone. Most people like turkey that cooks until thermometer registers 185° F. If cooked at a low heat, it will be well done but not dry.

It is important to check turkey stuffing, particularly in large birds, to be sure it is thoroughly cooked. The reason for this is that the ingredients used in this stuffing are often the kind that encourage bacteria growth. So, to be on the safe side, insert a thermometer into the stuffing in the body cavity for 5 minutes. Temperature of the stuffing should reach 165° F.

Since turkey has become a year-round food, people are discovering that it is good, too, cooked without a stuffing. It is certainly a great deal easier to cook a large bird this way. Test for doneness in the same way as for a stuffed bird, but don't expect unstuffed turkey to take as long to cook as does that with stuffing in. If you want to bake stuffing separately while roasting a bird, see Stuffed Chicken in Easy Orange Sauce, which tells how to do it.

Freeze Some of Holiday Turkey and Fixin's

Try to use up leftover turkey before the taste begins to pall. Or follow this method of freezing and keeping for later use.

Make a gravy using the last of the drippings. Cut turkey meat into slices suitable for covering a slice of bread for a hot sandwich. Spread out on a large cookie sheet or some similar flat surface. Pour turkey gravy over the slices and set, uncovered, in freezer. When almost solid, mark squares with a knife. Finish freezing, then break apart in individual servings where knife markings were made. Store in a large plastic bag—so children can see what's in it—and remove as needed.

If you make your own cranberry relish, freeze in individual paper cups. When solid, store in a plastic bag and remove one at a time as needed. Serve with the hot turkey sandwiches.

If you cooked any especially good vegetables with your turkey dinner, freeze enough for one serving in lightweight plastic. Do it before, not after, dinner so there will be less nutrient loss. Keep a supply in a large heavy plastic bag so young people or a husband who may want to prepare a one-person lunch or dinner can take the makings of an individual hot turkey sandwich, cup of cranberry relish, and vegetables out of the freezer.

Making Your Own Bread Crumbs and Croutons

If you use a lot of crumbs, for fried dishes, meat loaves, and stuffings, it may be worth your while to buy day-old bread now and then (it's cheaper than fresh bread), make up a supply of crumbs, and store them in cans or jars. Crumbs you are going to use for poultry stuffing should be left coarser than should those you expect to use for breading. Those to be used for stuffings can also include both white and whole wheat remnants . . . in fact, they taste better if they do.

Spread slices of bread over oven shelves, turn oven to 400° F. and toast until crisp. When one side becomes a golden brown turn bread over. When both sides are golden, remove toast from oven. Spread out on a clean plastic table top—or on a large sheet of freezer paper—and crumble into the size crumbs you want with a rolling pin.

To Make Toasted Cubes or Croutons: Pile up 3 or 4 slices of stale bread and slice through the pile every ½ or ¾ inch in one direction; then reverse and cut in the other direction. Spread bread cubes over a cookie sheet and toast the same as above for making crumbs.

Turkey Stuffing

(Bread, Bacon, Onion, Celery, Nut, Raisin, and Apple)
Fills 14-to-18-lb. bird plus leftover to make 9 x 5 x 2½-inch loaf.

⅓ cup seedless raisins
2 Tbs. rum
1 tsp. papaya syrup (of substitute 1 Tb. apricot juice)
2 Tbs. orange juice
1 lb. lean bacon, diced (Check canned imported bacon prices. Sometimes their good quality makes them a better buy than domestic bacon.)
1 cup diced onion
2 cups diced celery
1 cup dry chestnuts, soaked 24 hours in water (or substitute other nuts)
¾ cup roasted, unsalted peanuts, coarsely crushed
1 32-oz. loaf stale bread, sliced, toasted, and crushed into crumbs
1 8-oz. pkg. herb-seasoned bread stuffing
½ lb. butter, melted, but not hot
½ lb. margarine, melted, but not hot
4 eggs
5 cups water
3½ cups peeled, cored, and sliced apples

Soak raisins overnight in mixture of rum, papaya syrup, and orange juice. Drain. Drink juice. Heat bacon in heavy saucepan. Add diced onion and celery and cook together until onion and celery are just tender but not browned. Combine all stuffing ingredients, mix well, stuff into turkey neck and body cavities. Sew or skewer shut.

Bake leftover stuffing in loaf, ring, or other shape. If there is room in the oven, you can bake at the same time that you cook the turkey—but only for 30 or 40 minutes—and baste several times with juices from the bird. Serve 2nd or 3rd day with sliced or creamed turkey.

Giblet Stuffing

Turkey or chicken heart, gizzard, and neck
1 tsp. salt
Pinch of pepper
2 cups of water

Combine all ingredients in a saucepan and simmer for one hour, or until gizzard is tender. Strain liquid and substitute it for all or part of liquid in any of the Pennysaver stuffing recipes. Chop heart and gizzard meat and add to stuffing if desired. If you do not use in the stuffing, add to bottom of turkey or chicken pan and let them brown in the drippings.

Quick and Easy Turkey Stuffing

½ lb. lean bacon, chopped
2 cups chopped celery
¾ cup chopped celery leaves
½ lb. butter or margarine (If bacon is very salty, use unsalted butter because prepared bread crumbs are also salted.)
2 cups chopped onions
2 8-oz. pkgs. herb-seasoned bread stuffing (mixed white and whole wheat if available)
2 eggs
2 cups lukewarm water

Cook bacon in heavy skillet until very lightly browned. Remove bacon with slotted spoon and set aside. Add chopped celery and celery leaves to skillet and lightly sauté in bacon fat. (If pan is too crowded, transfer half of celery to another skillet.) Add ½ pound of butter to skillet and melt. Gently simmer celery, celery leaves, and 2 cups of chopped onions in the butter for 10 minutes. Pour two pkgs. of stuffing into large mixing bowl. Lightly beat eggs together with lukewarm water, stir into bread stuffing and mix until each morsel of bread is dampened. Add cooked bacon and chopped celery and celery leaves and the butter in which they were simmered. Stir and stuff into turkey cavity.

Roast Half Turkey

½ of an 18-to-20-lb. turkey (see "Buying Poultry")
½ to ¾ amount of your favorite turkey stuffing required for a 20-pound bird, about 1½ to 2 qts.

Stuff the exposed cavity. Punch some holes in a sheet of heavy duty aluminum foil with a fork and lay the foil over the stuffing. Sheet should extend several inches beyond the edges of the turkey, all the way around. Cut two more sheets of foil, the same size, lay them on top of a flat rack—don't use a wire rack—in a large shallow roaster and invert the stuffed half turkey onto them, cavity side down. The sheet of foil you placed over the stuffing should hold it in place during the inverting process. Insert a meat thermometer into the thickest part of the thigh—don't let it touch the bone—and cook in a 300° F. oven until it registers 185° F. Check also to see if drumstick moves up and down easily and leg joint gives readily. If any part of the turkey becomes too brown during cooking, fold edge of foil up over it. If the skin is not as brown as you would like it to be when thermometer registers about 170° F., start basting with some butter. Serve in the same way as you would a whole bird. Serves 15 to 20.

Breaded Turkey Breast Cutlets

(*From ½ of 18-to-20-lb. turkey cut in parts for freezing*)

1 lb. turkey breast, very thinly sliced and pounded with wooden mallet
½ cup flour
½ tsp. salt
⅛ tsp. white pepper
2 eggs, lightly beaten
1 cup fine toasted bread crumbs
2 Tbs. butter or margarine
2 Tbs. cooking oil

Dredge slices of turkey meat with flour which has been seasoned with the salt and white pepper. Shake off excess flour, dip into egg, then coat on both sides with bread crumbs. Spread out in single layer and let dry for about 10 minutes. Heat butter or margarine and cooking oil in large, heavy skillet. When small bubbles appear, add turkey cutlets, a few pieces at a time, to pan and lightly brown on both sides. Don't let oils reach smoking heat . . . and don't crowd cutlets in pan. Serves 4.

Roast Turkey Leg, Thigh, and Wing

From 18-to-20-lb. turkey cut into parts and frozen uncooked, or purchased at a special sale of turkey parts

¼ tsp. salt
⅛ tsp. pepper
1 pinch dried rosemary
1 pinch dried thyme
1 Tb. butter or margarine
1 large drumstick and thigh and wing
½ cup red wine
1 cup Cranberry-Orange Relish (use double portion of recipe, page 222)

Rub salt, pepper, rosemary, thyme, and margarine into skin. Put in small roasting pan, pour wine into bottom, and cook in 400° F. oven for 30 minutes. Baste with wine in pan, turn heat down to 325° F. and continue cooking for 1 hour or until tender. Baste several times. If pan starts to get dry, add water, not more than ¼ cup at a time. There should be plenty of meat for 4 people, but whose bone gets some meat sliced off to make the fourth serving will have to be up to you. Serve with Cranberry-Orange Relish. Serves 4.

Turkey Turnovers

Turnovers can be prepared with some of holiday turkey while meat is still nice and fresh, then frozen, unbaked, for future use.

Turnover Filling:

3 cups diced cooked turkey
1 10½ oz. can cream of celery soup, undiluted
¼ cup minced onion
½ tsp. salt
¼ tsp. pepper
¼ cup sliced, cooked mushrooms

Combine all ingredients and use to fill turnovers.

Turnover Pastry:

3 cups all-purpose flour
1 tsp. salt
½ cup solid vegetable shortening
¾ cup soft margarine (entire amount of shortening can be vegetable)
⅓ cup ice water
1 bowl ice water for hands

Sift flour and salt into mixing bowl. Cut in shortening with pastry blender. Chill hands in bowl of ice water and keep them cold while you gradually work ⅓ cup ice water (more or less as necessary) into flour and butter mixture. Separate dough into two sections for easier handling. Lightly flour dough and roll out to ⅛-inch thickness on floured board or tabletop. Cut into circles about 5 inches in diameter. Place 2 to 3 Tbs. turkey filling on one side of each circle, fold the other side over, seal edges together with end of a small spoon handle—or some other dull instrument. Spread turnovers on cookie sheet and bake for 40 minutes, or until pastry is lightly browned, in 425° F. oven. Makes about 12 turnovers.

To Freeze: Freeze unbaked turnovers in single layers, wrapped in freezer paper. Bake frozen for approximately 10 minutes longer than if baked unfrozen.

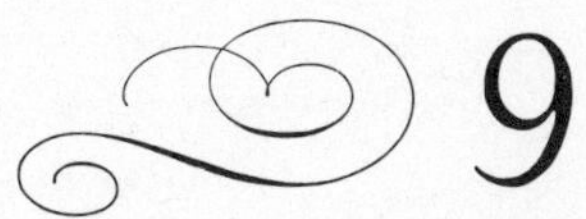

9

VARIETY MEATS AND VARIETY MEAT RECIPES

Affluent America is largely unaware of the threefold good in what the packing industry calls the "variety meats." But in the nations that we call backward, the have-not nations, the people for centuries have included these "variety meats" in their daily diets, and therefore long ago became aware of their goodness as to price, to health, and to taste.

What Are the Variety Meats?

The variety meats include such things as tripe, brains, sweetbreads, gizzards, tongue, feet and knuckles, heart and liver. They are readily available in any supermarket or butcher shop that counts the foreign born among its customers and, not so surprisingly, also in many restaurants that cater to gourmet tastes.

Dan and Arthur Lem, the latter a good family friend and an excellent Chinese cook, have included many such recipes in their *Hong Kong Cookbook*, and we all agreed that a few of those recipes ought to be included in The Pennysaver. You will find them among the recipes that follow, along with general instructions for preparing all of these meats. If your family is reluctant to try new and different meats, the Chinese method of cookery, with its interesting sauces and food combinations, should provide you with an easy means of introduction. You can also present these American combination dishes at your breakfast, lunch, or dinner table: fried brains and scrambled eggs, pickled tongue and Swiss cheese sandwich, and the intriguingly different taste of beef and kidney pie.

An important suggestion, already presented in the section on Veal, is to start by serving only variety meats that come from veal, since their flavor will be delicate and the texture tender and pleasing. Veal variety meats are more expensive than those from older animals, but it will be time enough to switch to the less expensive ones when your family has acquired a taste for them.

The Basics of Cooking Variety Meats

Variety meats are the most perishable of all meats available in retail markets and therefore should be cooked and eaten as soon after purchase as possible, preferably on the same day. We have included some individual recipes in this section that give cooking instructions in greater detail (as, for instance, the choice of liquids) but these are the basics:

Liver

Preparation: Remove heavy blood vessels and outside membrane if desired. Soak overnight in milk (discard the milk) for a sweeter flavor.

Braised: Coat with flour. Melt small amount of fat in heavy skillet and brown on both sides. Add just enough liquid to assure steam, cover tightly and steam 20–30 minutes per pound.

Broiled: Dip slices, ½ to ¾ inch thick, in melted butter, margarine, or bacon grease. Place on cold broiler rack and broil at moderate temperature (350° F.) for 3 minutes on each side or just long enough to brown lightly.

Pan-Fried: Coat slices in mixture of flour, salt, and pepper. Melt fat in heavy skillet and sauté liver over medium heat until lightly browned on both sides. (Coating with flour is optional.) Fat can be half butter for a nice flavor. Don't crowd in pan.

Deep-Fried: Have liver cut in long, thin strips. Coat in seasoned flour. Heat fat or oil in deep fryer to 350° F., place strips in frying basket, lower into oil and fry until light brown—a matter of a very few minutes. (Dip in egg and roll in bread crumbs after coating with flour, if desired.)

Chopped: Pan-fry in 2 or 3 Tbs. fat about 5 minutes. Let cool and then chop or run through grinder. Before chopping, combine with sautéed onion and hard-cooked eggs, if desired.

Heart

Preparation: Wash in warm water, trim away gristle and larger blood vessels.

Braised: Brown on all sides in hot fat over medium heat. Add salt and pepper and enough water to steam, cover tightly, reduce heat to low, and cook until tender. Beef heart needs 3 to 4 hours, veal heart 2½ to 3 hours. May be stuffed before browning, if desired.

Simmered: Place in deep pot, add salted water to cover. Cover pot tightly and cook same time as above.

Kidneys

Preparation: Wash in cold water, remove outer membrane, split through center lengthwise, remove inner fat and tubes. Cut up if desired.

Simmered: Place in deep pot, add water to cover. Place cover on pot and cook until tender, about 1 to 1½ hours for beef kidney, ¾ to 1 hour for veal.

Broiled: Dip in French dressing, melted bacon fat, butter or margarine. Place on cold broiler rack, broil 5 to 10 minutes on each side or until brown, at 350° F.

Brains and Sweetbreads

Preparation: Wash in cold water, remove blood clots, then soak in cold water for 30 minutes.

Simmered: Place in deep pot, cover with water and add 1 tsp. salt and 1 Tb. lemon juice or vinegar for each quart of water. Cover pot and cook 20 minutes. Then drain and rinse well. Remove membrane and blood vessels.

Pan-Fried: Roll in flour or dry bread crumbs. Heat small amount of fat in skillet and sauté until light brown and tender, about 20 minutes. Leftovers can be broken into small pieces and scrambled with eggs.

TONGUE

Preparation: Wash and then, if desired, soak corned, pickled, or smoked tongue in water for several hours to make flavor milder.

Simmered: Place in deep pot, cover with water, add salt if desired. Cover pot and cook until tender—3 to 4 hours for beef tongue, 2 to 3 hours for veal tongue. Then drain, dip in cold water, remove skin, and cut away bones and gristle at thick end. Serve either hot or cold. If cold, allow to cool in its own juices. Tongue is nice served with a spicy raisin sauce as a hot main course at dinner, or, cold, in sandwiches at lunch. Try it with Swiss cheese.

TRIPE

Preparation: None necessary because it is partially cooked before being sold.

Simmered: Place in deep pot, cover with water, adding 1 tsp. salt for each quart, cover pot and cook until tender, about 1 to 1½ hours.

Hong Kong Style Chicken Gizzards with Many Spices

U Sung Gai Kin

1 lb. chicken gizzards
4 qts. water
3 pieces star anise
2 cloves garlic
1 cinnamon stick
½ tsp. salt
½ tsp. sugar
2 scallions
2 Tbs. dark soy sauce

Simmer gizzards in 2 qts. water for 1½ hours; transfer to a colander and run cold water over them. Dry thoroughly with lint-free cloth towel and set aside. Discard water in which gizzards have cooked, rinse out the pot, and then bring the remaining 2 qts. of water to a boil. Add all remaining ingredients and slow simmer for 2 hours. Let cool to room temperature, then add the gizzards, cover and let stand 8 to 10 hours in refrigerator. Drain, making sure to save 1 cup of stock, and then prepare the following sauce:

SAUCE:

- 2 Tbs. oil
- 1 tsp. crushed garlic
- 1 tsp. white of scallion, chopped
- Cooked gizzards
- 1 cup stock
- ¼ tsp. salt
- ½ tsp. sugar
- ½ tsp. monosodium glutamate
- Dash pepper
- Dash sesame oil
- 1 Tb. cornstarch mixed in 1 Tb. cold water

Heat oil in large skillet until sizzling but not smoking, add garlic and scallion and stir until brown. Add gizzards, stir about 6 times, then add stock and bring to a boil. Add all other ingredients and stir until it has a bit-more-than-slightly thickened consistency, about 2 or 3 minutes. Serve on plate of decorative lettuce leaves and garnish with parsley.

Note: Gizzards are available from most butchers and in all stores that sell chicken parts. They cost about 25 to 35 cents a pound, depending upon where you live. Star anise, a much-used 8-pointed Chinese spice, is available in all Chinese groceries and in an ever-increasing number of American specialty food stores and quality supermarkets. If unavailable, aniseed may be substituted.

Kidney and Apple with Creamy Wine Sauce

1 large apple, peel left on, cored and cut into 4 round slices
2 Tbs. water
1 tsp. lemon juice
1 Tb. brown sugar
1 Tb. butter or margarine
1 kidney from very young veal, washed in cold water
1 cup flour
½ tsp. salt
⅛ tsp. pepper
1 Tb. butter or margarine
2 Tbs. cooking oil
1 cup red wine or sherry
4 slices white bread, toasted
1 cup heavy cream

Place sliced apples in bottom of shallow baking pan. Combine water, lemon juice, and brown sugar and pour over apples. Dot with 1 Tb. butter and bake at 350° F. for 20 to 30 minutes or until apple slices are tender. Leave in oven to keep warm until served.

Slice kidney down the middle and remove all fat and any tubes or membrane. (There won't be much that needs to be removed from a young veal kidney.) Cut into small cubes. Season flour with salt and pepper and dredge kidney cubes in the mixture. Heat 1 Tb. of butter or margarine and 2 Tbs. cooking oil in a large, heavy skillet. When the mixture is sizzling hot but not smoking, add floured kidney cubes and fry at medium heat until crisply browned on all sides. Add cup of wine or sherry and simmer for 5 minutes. Turn off heat and let kidneys and wine cool a little while you make toast. Stir cream into contents of skillet, then reheat over low heat. Place one baked apple slice on each piece of toast, spoon kidneys and sauce over them and serve at once. Serves 4.

Hong Kong Baked Sweetbread Foo Yung

Kok Foo Yung Ger No

4 pork brains
4 eggs
3 cups your own chicken broth
4 Tbs. cornstarch
1 tsp. monosodium glutamate
1 tsp. salt
1 tsp. cooking sherry
1 Tb. melted bacon grease
2 Tbs. chopped green onion (scallion) or parsley
Boiled rice

Wash brains twice in cold water, remove blood clots and tissue with point of small knife or with toothpick. Soak in cold water for 30 minutes.

Combine all other ingredients except onion or parsley and rice in mixing bowl and beat with egg beater until thoroughly mixed. (Dissolve cornstarch in ½ cup of broth before mixing if you prefer.)

Cut brains into small pieces and mix into the egg mixture, pour all into a well-greased casserole dish or baking pan and cook in preheated 350° F. oven for 20 minutes. Garnish with green onion or parsley and serve with boiled rice. Serves 4.

Hong Kong Curried Tripe

Gar Lee Ngow Bok Yip

3 Tbs. coconut or peanut oil
2 cups sliced onion
2 cloves garlic, crushed
1 Tb. crushed ginger root
1½ lbs. tripe, cut into ½ x 1 inch pieces
2 Tbs. curry powder
1 tsp. sugar
1 tsp. salt
½ tsp. pepper
4 cups beef stock, preferably your own
4 cups potatoes, cut French-fry style but only about 1½ inches long
1 cup green pepper slices, cut diagonally
1 cup red pepper slices, cut diagonally
Boiled rice
Parsley for garnish, chopped or in sprigs

Heat oil in large heavy skillet. When it starts to sizzle, add onions, garlic, and ginger and sauté until brown. Stir in tripe well, then add curry powder, sugar, salt, pepper and stock. Bring to a boil, cover, and simmer until tripe is tender but at least for 1 hour. Add potatoes, cook 15 minutes more, then add green and red pepper pieces and cook for a final 5 minutes. Serve over boiled rice with parsley as garnish. Serves 4.

Lee Aschettino's Honeycomb Tripe Neopolitan

A few pages back we told you how people in other lands transform the lowly and tremendously inexpensive variety meats into mouth-watering delicacies. Where they live makes no difference. Asia, Europe, South America, Africa . . . everywhere but in the United States it seems. What we consider gourmet variety-meat fare, they consider commonplace and everyday dishes. The preceding recipe tells one of the ways that tripe is cooked in Hong Kong. In this recipe we tell you one of the ways that tripe is cooked in Italy. We owe it to Lee Aschettino, the third-generation proprietor of a fine continental-cuisine restaurant with the unlikely name of Paddy's in the resort city of Long Beach on the South Shore of Long Island.

3 lbs. honeycomb tripe
2 Tbs. salt
1 large onion, minced
½ stalk celery, thinly sliced
Olive oil to cover
6 large raw potatoes, sliced
1 can (about 1 lb. 14 oz.) tomatoes
Pepper to taste
Oregano to taste

Place tripe in pot, cover with cold water and boil for 5 minutes. Change water, add salt, cover, and boil until tender, about 1 hour. Drain, cut into very small and thin bite-size pieces and set aside.

Place onion and celery in heavy 4 qt. pot, cover with olive oil and sauté just until onion is light golden in color. Add potato slices and canned tomatoes that first have been mashed in their own liquid, then tripe, pepper, and oregano. Cover and simmer until potatoes are tender, about 30 minutes. Serves 6 to 8.

Tongue with Sweet and Sour Raisin Sauce

1 2½-to-3-lb. smoked tongue
Water to cover
1 oz. mixed pickling spices

Place tongue in pot, cover with water, add spices, and bring to a boil. Then reduce heat, cover loosely, and simmer about 2 to 2½ hours or until tender. Test by piercing with fork at its thickest end. Remove from liquid. Allow to cool enough to peel and then do so. Slice and serve, topped with hot raisin sauce (recipe follows) and with vegetables on the side. Or place on 2 slices of bread, top with hot raisin sauce and serve as open sandwich, which is the way children usually like it best. Serves 6 to 8.

Note: It's delicious too, in cold sandwiches; either alone or in combination. Try it with Swiss cheese.

Sweet and Sour Raisin Sauce

½ cup seedless raisins
1 cup water
2 Tbs. butter or margarine
2 Tbs. flour
1 Tb. granulated sugar
1 Tb. brown sugar
1 Tb. lemon juice or to taste
Salt to taste

Simmer raisins in cup of water for 10 minutes. Remove with slotted spoon and set aside. Keep liquid hot. Melt butter or margarine in heavy skillet, add flour and cook together for 2 or 3 minutes, stirring constantly. Add hot water in which raisins were cooked all at once to butter and flour, stirring with a wire whisk as you add. Add granulated and brown sugar and lemon juice. Continue stirring until sauce is thickened and smooth. Add raisins and serve over tongue.

10

MEAT ALTERNATES . . . THE LEGUMES

Dry peas, dry beans, lentils, and peanuts (and other nuts) are high protein legumes that are excellent and inexpensive meat substitutes, especially if some protein from an animal source—meat, eggs, milk, or a milk product such as cheese—is eaten at the same meal. The meat-source food can be a small percentage and still raise the nutritional effectiveness of the legumes. The food we refer to as "the legume" is actually the seed from certain plants that have a seed pod opening on two sides.

Most of us think of beans and split peas in this context, but we sometimes overlook lentils entirely.

We think of the peanut as a nut and, although we eat two-and-a-half pounds of peanut butter per person a year in the United States, because it tastes so good, many of us don't really appreciate its possibilities as a protein substitute for meat, or that it's high in niacin content and makes an important Vitamin B contribution. Recipes throughout *The Pennysaver Cookbook* illustrate the peanut's versatility.

The USDA lists peanuts as one of our most plentiful foods.

Besides just plain peanut butter, peanut butter with jelly, chopped dates, or crushed pineapple, there are other good sandwich fillings including one of the animal source foods; peanut butter with bacon crumbles, peanut butter with mayonnaise, for example.

Peanuts, salted or plain, can be added to many foods. They can be baked in pies or cakes or cookies. (They taste delicious in oatmeal cookies or puddings instead of more expensive nuts.) Crushed, they can be used as toppings, too, instead of costlier nuts. Try making a peanut, instead of a pecan, pie. Crush them and sprinkle on vegetables, mash with sweet potatoes. The list could go on indefinitely. In short, the peanut is a good protein food, worthy of being substituted for meat, tasty and very, very versatile.

There's another legume which Americans know principally for its oil, or as stock feed and fertilizer: the soybean. But in the Orient, Tofu, made from soybean protein, has been one of the most important foods for centuries. It is growing in popularity throughout the world and can be found in some American supermarkets as well as all Oriental food stores.

Tofu, or soybean cake, is a rather bland, white, cheeselike substance that blends extremely well with many foods and seasonings. We have not included Tofu recipes in this book, since it is not available to everyone, but the proprietors of the Oriental food shops where it is sold are usually happy to give you suggestions for its use.

Legume (including nut) recipes are scattered throughout *The Pennysaver Cookbook*. Many will be found listed under a meat ingredient which the recipe contains. Using the suggestions for creative substitutions in these recipes, you can increase or decrease the proportion of legumes in many of these recipes to suit your needs.

Refer particularly to: Beef and Bean Shepherd's Pies, Chili Con Carne, Stuffed Peppers, Lamb, Lentil, and Eggplant Moussaka, Veal and Lentil Gourmet Combination, Split Pea Soup with Spinach and Vermicelli, Lentil Soup, Split Pea Soup with Ham, Hash Brown Parsnips with Bacon and Peanuts, Spinach with Nuts, Sweet Potato and Peanut Salad, Lentil Salad, Chicken or Turkey Meat Salad with Grapes and Almonds, Fish and Peanut Salad, Peanut Butter Cookies, Baked Apples with Honey, Nuts and Raisins.

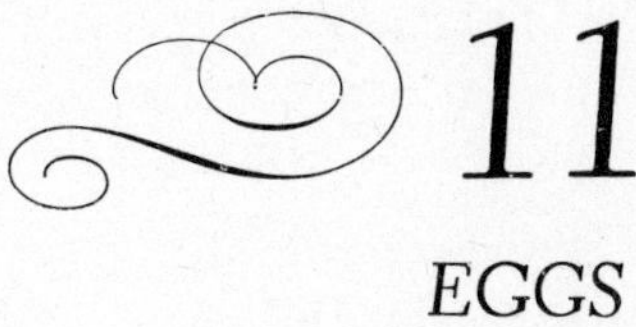

11

EGGS

From just about every standpoint, one of our greatest economy foods is the egg. To quote the United States Department of Agriculture:

"In addition to their versatility as a food, eggs are highly valued as a source of protein, iron, Vitamin A, and riboflavin, and are one of the few foods that contain Vitamin D. Because of the amount and quality of their proteins, eggs make a good alternate for meat."

Besides all that, the egg even provides its own covering.

USDA Shell Egg Grade Mark

The United States Department of Agriculture grade shield certifies that the eggs have been graded for quality and size under Federal-State supervision. The size may be shown within the shield or elsewhere on the carton. The grading service is provided on a voluntary basis.

How Grades AA ("Fresh Fancy"), A, and B Differ in Appearance

USDA quality standards are signified by U.S. grades AA (or Fresh Fancy), A or B. Which one is stamped on a carton of eggs is determined by checking such things as appearance and condition of the shell, and by observing the eggs under a candling light which shows the grader the interior condition of the egg. If the eggs are marked under the department's quality control program, a random sampling of eggs from every shipment is broken onto a flat surface so the height of the white can be measured and the yolk carefully examined.

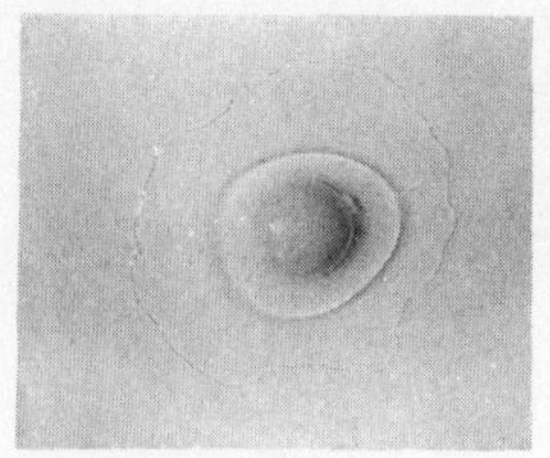

Grade AA
(*or Fresh Fancy*)
Egg covers small area; white is thick, stands high; yolk is firm and high

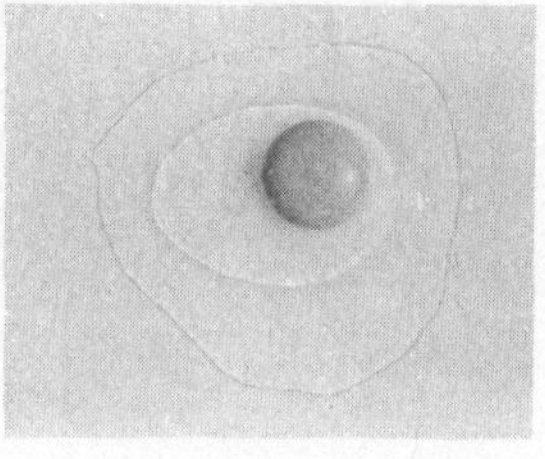

Grade A
Egg covers moderate area; white is reasonably thick, stands fairly high; yolk is firm and high

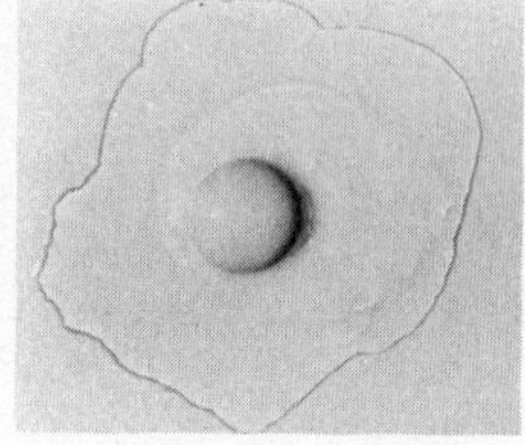

Grade B
Egg covers wide area; has small amount of thick white; yolk is somewhat flattened and enlarged

(Photos provided by the United States Department of Agriculture)

USDA Standard Weights for Different Egg Sizes

The most common egg sizes are Extra Large, Large, and Medium, but there are also Jumbo, Small, and Peewee. Following are the USDA standard weights per dozen used in grading eggs for size:

Jumbo weight	30 oz. per dozen (1 lb. 14 oz.)
Extra Large weight	27 oz. per dozen (1 lb. 9 oz.)
Large weight	24 oz. per dozen (1½ lbs.)
Medium weight	21 oz. per dozen (1 lb. 5 oz.)
Small weight	18 oz. per dozen (1 lb. 2 oz.)
Peewee weight	15 oz. per dozen (1 lb. less 1 oz.)

Eggs Are An Economical Food

When you consider that one dozen large eggs weighs one and one-half pounds, it becomes obvious that, ounce for ounce, eggs usually cost less money than meat (when large eggs sell for 60¢ per dozen, the price per pound would be 40¢.) When you consider that the egg is nearly 100 percent edible, no weight loss from bone and fat (only shell), the comparison is even more remarkable. To find out the price per pound of eggs divide the ounces per dozen into the price per dozen. Then, to get the most egg for your money, buy the size that costs the least per pound. To make it a little easier to figure—no one wants to do arithmetic in the middle of a crowded supermarket—if the larger eggs cost less than 7¢ more than a smaller size, the larger eggs are the better buy. Or turn it around the other way, if small eggs cost more than 7¢ a dozen less than the bigger eggs, buy the bigger eggs. For example, if large eggs sell for 60¢ a dozen and medium sell for 54¢ per dozen (both Grade A), the large eggs are the more economical.

There is another factor to consider, however. If your children leave part of a large egg, it's more economical to buy and serve them small ones.

Take advantage of this economy by combining eggs with other, more expensive, high quality protein foods to stretch those other foods, or combine them with the lesser protein foods to improve the quality. There are egg dishes that, by the addition of dibs and dabs of leftovers, are elevated to the "gourmet," or very special, class. These dishes not only are suitable for breakfast but lunch and dinner, too.

To Sum Up What to Remember When Buying Eggs

1. Only buy eggs that are kept under refrigeration. Heat lowers egg quality very quickly.

2. The size and color of an egg make no difference whatsoever to its eating quality.

3. A shield, showing the letters "USDA," certifies that the eggs have been graded for quality and size under Federal-State supervision.

4. Grades A or AA (Fresh Fancy) are ideal for any purpose; grade B eggs are suitable for general cooking and baking.

5. Eggs should not be cracked, they should be clean and packaged in an undamaged, clean container. (Eggshells are porous and eggs pick up flavors through them.)

About Commercially Frozen Egg Products and Dried Egg Solids

Dried egg products are becoming increasingly available in retail markets. They are sold as whole egg solids, egg yolk solids, and various blends.

Frozen egg products are used primarily in production of commercial products and for other large-quantity food preparation. Since they are occasionally found in retail markets, you should know something about them—as well as about the dried products.

1. The USDA inspection shield above will assure you that the frozen or dried egg product was produced in a plant under USDA supervision

and that it was required to be pasteurized, as well as being made from wholesome products under sanitary conditions.

2. To be on the safe side, use frozen or dried egg products only in dishes to be cooked for a long time on top of the stove or baked in the oven.

3. Thaw only the amount of frozen egg you need—in the refrigerator. Keep in the refrigerator and use within 24 hours.

4. Keep unopened dried eggs in a dry place where temperature is not over 50° F. (The best place is the refrigerator.) After opening, store in refrigerator in tightly closed container.

5. Reconstitute dried eggs according to package instructions, keep refrigerated, and use within 1 hour.

About Eggs and Breakfasts

One of America's nutritional problems seems to be breakfast. We—both adults and children—either eat none at all or we don't include enough nourishing food in what we do eat.

Habit and custom may be one of the reasons for our lack of interest in breakfast. Most of us have a very limited repertoire of breakfast menus. Rather than changing them, we just keep insisting that every member of the family eat what's given them. If they don't, we throw up our hands in despair and let it go at that.

Breakfasts that are nibbled at, then thrown out, are a waste of money. But, what is much more serious, they are also a waste of health. So try including some of the egg recipes in this section and other sections of the book; things you don't ordinarily think of as breakfast food.

Maybe a breakfast noneater in your family would find a custard interesting. Cereal cooked with milk, egg, and chopped dried fruit is more like pudding than breakfast food. For those in your family whose eggs just don't go down at breakfast, you may have to substitute something else that's nourishing: meat, cheese, fish. The egg can be added to dinner's dessert and some of dinner's protein served for breakfast: hot soup, for instance.

Another reason some of us hate to eat our breakfast egg may be the unpalatable way it is cooked. We tend to take out our resentment at having to get out of bed on the poor egg, subjecting it to heats that are much too high and generally overcooking it. The United States Department of Agriculture gives these very good general egg cooking instructions in its food management bulletin *Family Fare:*

Scrambled Eggs

"Break eggs into a bowl. Add milk as follows: For creamy scrambled eggs, add 1 Tb. milk for each egg; for dry scrambled eggs, add ½ Tb. milk for each egg. For a product with uniform yellow color, beat mixture enough to blend yolks and whites thoroughly. If you prefer scrambled eggs with flecks of yellow and white, beat only slightly. Season with salt and pepper.

"Pour the mixture into a heated frypan in which a little fat has been melted. Cook slowly, stirring occasionally to let the uncooked portion flow to the bottom. Cook until the mixture is set, but still moist.

"Or, if preferred, use a double boiler. Melt a little fat in the top part, pour in the egg mixture, place over simmering water in the bottom of the boiler, and cook as above.

"*Note: Use only clean, sound-shelled eggs in this recipe.*"

Variation

"Before cooking the mixture, add herbs, chopped onion, shredded cheese, or small pieces of cooked bacon or ham."

Eggs Cooked in Shell

"Put eggs in a pan; cover them completely with cold water.

"*For soft-cooked eggs,* heat water slowly to simmering. Cover pan and remove from heat. Let stand 3 to 5 minutes; allow the longer time for a larger number of eggs or for a firmer consistency.

"*Note: Use only clean, sound-shelled eggs in this recipe.*

"*For hard-cooked eggs,* bring water to simmering and simmer 20 to 25 minutes. Do not let the water boil. Serve the eggs hot or plunge them at once into cold running water and leave until cold.

"*Note:* The green discoloration that sometimes appears between the white and the yolk of a hard-cooked egg results from a chemical reaction, which is harmless. To help prevent this discoloration, cook eggs at low temperature, avoid overcooking, and cool promptly."

Fried Eggs

"Heat a small amount of fat in a frypan. Bacon or ham drippings may be used for flavor. Break eggs, one at a time into a saucer, and slip them into the fat. Sprinkle with salt and pepper. Cook over low heat, basting with the fat, until whites are firm.

"Or, if you prefer eggs with less fat, use this "Fry-poach" method. Melt a little fat in a frypan over low heat—just enough to grease the bottom. Add eggs one at a time, pour in 2 or 3 Tbs. of water, cover pan tightly, and steam until eggs are done. Season before serving.

"*Note: Use only clean, sound-shelled eggs in this recipe.*"

Poached Eggs

"Break eggs into a saucer or custard cup, one at a time, then slip them into gently boiling, salted water—enough water to cover the eggs in a shallow pan.

"Reheat water to simmering, take pan from heat, cover. Let stand 5 minutes, or until eggs are of desired firmness. Remove eggs from water and sprinkle with salt and pepper.

"*Note: Use only clean, sound-shelled eggs in this recipe.*"

Try our following Pennysaver recipes for a slightly different breakfast treat.

Fried Eggs with Chicken Broth

1 tsp. butter
1 Tb. minced green pepper
1 Tb. minced green onion (or any mild, sweet-flavored onion)
2 eggs
1 pinch salt
1 pinch pepper
1 pinch garlic powder
1 cube (1 to 2 Tbs.) reduced chicken broth. (See "Cooking Chickens for the Freezer and the Future.")

Melt butter in small teflon-lined or heavy sloping-sided skillet. Add vegetables, cook from 3 to 5 minutes at low to medium heat. Break 2 eggs over vegetables, sprinkle with seasonings. Place frozen cube of reduced chicken broth on white of egg and cover pan quickly with heavy lid. Turn heat to low and cook 2½ minutes without lifting the lid. Uncover (eggs should be soft cooked . . . if they are not done enough for your taste, quickly recover and continue cooking), lift any unmelted frozen cube off and set aside. Serve eggs at once with buttered toast.

Omelet with Sliced Meat or Fish Loaf

1 tsp. butter
3 tsps. cooking oil
4 slices leftover meat or fish loaf
3 eggs, lightly beaten with 1 Tb. water, wine, or beer
Salt and pepper according to seasoning in loaf

Heat butter and oil in large, heavy iron skillet. Add slices of loaf and very lightly brown on both sides. Pour egg around slices and add salt and pepper. Lift edges of egg and meat loaf so uncooked egg can run underneath. When egg is cooked on the bottom, set pan under broiler flame (be sure it does not have a handle that will burn) and very lightly brown top. Serve at once on warm plates. Serves 4.

12

SAUCES

You don't have to paint pictures or write books or music to be creative. There is excellent opportunity for it in your kitchen. Chances are, without realizing it, you already have re-created some of the most famous of the basic French sauces, demonstrating the twofold economy of creative cookery in making sauces using broths saved from other dishes. Using the broths or drippings from foods you cook to create delicious sauces—instead of throwing them out—is a very good way to save both nutrients and money.

Recipes in the book explain how to make your own beef broth from bones and scraps, page 76, chicken broth, page 130, or fish broth, page 108. But there will often be times when you have broths in which you cooked meats and vegetables; broths into which nutrients leaked out into the liquid . . . use them! Of course, some of these nutrients will get away from you during storage and recooking but care on your part can cut down on such losses. Don't leave perishable broths standing around. Chill them quickly, cover them, and get them into the refrigerator or the freezer.

Making Sauces

Proportions of Fat, Flour, and Liquid: The most frequently used thickening agent is flour, whether it's for a gravy, a sauce, or a soup. The more you use, the thicker the sauce. The less you use, the thinner. Remember the word "O-N-E" and you won't go wrong.

ONE CUP OF THIN SAUCE

1 Tb. fat
1 Tb. flour
1 cup liquid (water, milk, wine, broth, or any other liquid)

ONE CUP OF MEDIUM SAUCE

2 Tbs. fat
2 Tbs. flour
1 cup liquid

ONE CUP OF THICK SAUCE

3 Tbs. fat
3 Tbs. flour
1 cup liquid

As you see, the formula is simple. Just remember three ones for a thin sauce. Then, for a thicker sauce, add one more each of fat and flour; thicker yet . . . one more again. But the liquid remains the same.

To Cook: Cook the flour and fat together in a skillet or saucepan for at least two minutes, heat the liquid to the boiling point—or just under boiling in the case of milk or cream. Using a wire whisk, stir fat and flour constantly with one hand while you add the hot liquid, all at once, with the other. Continue stirring and beating with the wire whisk until sauce is thickened and smooth.

There is disagreement among cooks over whether or not liquid must be hot. The answer is that "some like it hot, some like it cold." Use whichever works best for you, but be sure to beat it with a wire whisk. It's possible it's the instrument, not the temperature, that makes the biggest difference.

Instead of mixing the flour with the fat, some people find it easier to drizzle the flour into a cold liquid, beating constantly until smooth. This mixture is then combined with melted fat and stirred constantly, with a whisk, until thickened and the flour cooks. (We find this method takes longer cooking to get rid of the raw flour taste than does the first.)

The Easiest Ways to Thicken Sauces: The easiest way of all to thicken a sauce is to use a thick canned or frozen soup—which you actually thin with broth or whatever it is that you want thickened. Some delicious sauces, gravies, and soups can be made this way. Nutritionally, the good thing about them is that your vitamin-laden liquid broths aren't wasted; you simply add them to the canned or frozen soup, stir until smooth and heat.

There also are very good prepared mixes to which you sometimes merely add liquid (use your meat or vegetable broths whenever possible) and sometimes are required to do a little more. These mixes are often too strong if you use the entire packet for one small sauce. There are many interesting uses you can make of the packet remnants; use some of them in salad dressings, some in steak or barbecue sauces, some in meat loaves. Use your imagination and experiment but remember this very important rule: *taste as you go along.* Just add a bit at a time until you know what the results will be.

How to Create Your Own Easy Sauces: Using the proportions 2 Tbs. flour and 2 Tbs. butter and the cooking instructions on page 172, make the following different sauces simply by sometimes making the cup of liquid something different and by adding different seasonings. (While being creative with sauces, remember this: they give you a great opportunity for supplementing calcium intake by using milk and cheese.)

1. MEDIUM THICK WHITE SAUCE (the French call it Béchamel Sauce)
   The liquid: 1 cup milk
   Seasonings: Salt and pepper to taste

2. MEDIUM THICK CREAM SAUCE
   The liquid: 1 cup half and half
   Seasonings: Salt and pepper to taste
   ¼ tsp. onion salt

3. MEDIUM THICK CHEESE SAUCE (the French call it Mornay Sauce)
The liquid: 1 cup milk
Seasonings: ½ to ¾ cup grated cheese
1 tsp. prepared mustard (optional)

4. MEDIUM THICK MUSTARD SAUCE
The liquid: 1 cup milk
Seasoning: 1 Tb. prepared mustard

5. MEDIUM THICK TOMATO CREAM SAUCE (the French call it Sauce Aurore)
The liquid: 1 cup milk
Seasoning: 2 Tbs. tomato paste

Try adding your own touches to these sauces, such as the "French" touch of stirring extra butter, 1 tsp. at a time, into any of the above the minute they are removed from heat. Each tsp. of butter must melt and be stirred in before another is added.

6. MEDIUM THICK FISH SAUCE (the French call this Sauce Velouté)
The liquid: ¾ cup strained fish broth
Seasoning: ¼ cup wine (optional)

7. MEDIUM THICK CHICKEN SAUCE (the French call this Sauce Velouté also; the liquid in Sauce Velouté may be fish, chicken or veal broth, and some also include beef and vegetable broth in the list.)
The liquid: ¾ cup strained chicken broth
Seasonings: ¼ cup wine (optional)
¼ cup finely chopped mushroom stems

8. MEDIUM THICK BEEF SAUCE
The liquid: 1 cup strained broth made when boiling beef, then reduced to desired richness

Other Simple Sauce Suggestions

1. Easy Wine Sauce

The liquid: ¼ cup wine

Seasoning: ½ tsp. oregano

Mix wine and oregano and use to marinate, then to baste a broiled steak. Pour juices out of pan, add to 1 Tb. butter in skillet, and boil until blended. Spread over cooked steak or reserve to rub into a roast or season a gravy.

2. Easy Soy Sauce

The liquid: 2 Tbs. soy sauce

Rub just as it is into meat—steak or roast. Reserve drippings and use for the base of another sauce. Add wine or pineapple juice or both.

3. Vinegar and Oil Dressing

The liquid: ¼ cup vinegar and ¼ cup olive oil
(above proportions can be changed to suit your taste)

Seasonings: 1 clove garlic
1 pinch sugar
¼ tsp. salt
⅛ tsp. pepper

Hollandaise Sauce

4 egg yolks
1 tsp. lemon juice
1 Tb. cold water
½ lb. butter, cut up into little pieces and permitted to get warm
¼ tsp. salt
1 pinch white pepper

Place egg yolks, lemon juice, and cold water in top of double boiler. Whip together, using hand eggbeater or wire whisk. Place top of double boiler over bottom in which water is simmering. It should not touch the top section. (This sauce must be cooked very slowly and never allowed to get very hot or the ingredients won't blend properly.) When egg yolks are beginning to thicken just a bit and are hot, add butter, one little bit at a time, waiting for each piece to melt completely before adding the next, beating each one in with whisk. When all butter has been added, remove from heat, add seasonings and serve.

Note: There are many sauces having the same base as hollandaise, but, with the addition of each new ingredient, a new name is added. Get the feel of the egg yolk and how to make it combine and thicken with the butter, then try making these two additions:

MOUSSELINE SAUCE: Add ½ cup whipped cream to hollandaise.

SIMPLE BÉARNAISE SAUCE: Substitute 1 Tb. tarragon vinegar for lemon juice, season with pinch of cayenne pepper.

Mayonnaise

2 large egg yolks (use only very fresh eggs that have been kept under refrigeration)
½ tsp. salt
1 tsp. lemon juice or wine vinegar
1 cup oil

All ingredients and utensils (including beaters of electric mixer) should be room temperature.

Put egg yolks in a bowl, stir for one or two minutes, add salt and lemon juice or vinegar and beat together on medium speed until well blended. Using a spoon, start adding oil, a drop at a time, to the egg. Don't stop beating and keep pushing the yolk from the sides into the center of the bowl. When sauce starts to thicken, you can increase oil you are adding to a thin stream. When all the oil has been added, you can stop beating.

Variations: Many different sauces are made simply by adding one or more ingredients to mayonnaise. This mayonnaise base can either be one you make yourself, using the above recipe, or a commercial product you buy at the supermarket. Following are a few suggestions of things to add to ½ cup of mayonnaise:

RUSSIAN DRESSING:

2 to 4 Tbs. catsup

EASY TARTAR SAUCE:

1 tsp. mustard sauce
1 Tb. sour cream (optional)
2 Tbs. sweet pickle relish, drained

COLE SLAW SAUCE:

¼ cup whipped cream
1 Tb. vinegar
1 tsp. sugar

Easy Butter Sauces

Butter, all by itself, is an excellent sauce to spread on a steak, on poultry, on roasts, on fish. Add a variety of other things and blend into a tablespoon or two of butter for interesting taste variations. Try these:

1. Leftovers of other sauces
2. Drippings from broiling fish or steaks
3. Chopped garlic
4. Chopped onion
5. Mustard powder or sauce
6. Anchovies or sardines
7. Crab, shrimp, or lobster meat, finely chopped
8. Herb seasonings
9. Coral and roe from lobster
10. Horseradish
11. Paprika

13
SOUP RECIPES

Fish Broth and Vegetable Soup

½ cup of chopped vegetables for each person to be served (vegetables previously used in making broth)

½ cup of strained broth (before reducing) for each person to be served. (See recipe for basic broths in fish section of recipes.)

Combine, heat and serve.

Variations

VEGETABLE-MUSHROOM SOUP

Add 1 10½-oz. can cream of mushroom soup

VEGETABLE SHRIMP SOUP

Add 1 1-oz. can frozen cream of shrimp soup

VEGETABLE-CHEESE SOUP

Add 1 10½-oz. can cheddar cheese soup

Beef Shanks with Tomato Soup

1 Tb. cooking oil
8 slices of beef shanks (8 oxtail joints can be substituted)
2 1-lb. 12-oz. cans tomatoes
1 large onion, chopped
2 large carrots, scrubbed but not peeled
Salt, pepper, and marjoram, rosemary, or sweet basil to taste

Heat cooking oil in heavy skillet and brown shanks on all sides. Transfer shanks to a large soup pot, add scrapings from skillet, cans of tomatoes, 2 tomato cans of water, chopped onion, and unpeeled carrots. Bring to a boil, turn down to a slow simmer, and cook for 2½ hours. Stir every now and then to keep from sticking to bottom of pot. Remove carrots before they become mushy. Slip skins off, slice, reheat in butter, and serve as a vegetable with the pieces of shank.

Add water or cook soup down to make a nice consistency. Taste, and add seasonings a little at a time. Serve soup in bowls, then serve chunks of shank with sliced carrots.

A loaf of French bread, thickly sliced, is all you need to make this dish a complete meal. Serves 4 with leftover soup.

Note: *Leftover soup can be further reduced and used as is or as a base for a very good tomato sauce.*

Split Pea Soup with Spinach & Vermicelli

Frozen Split Pea Soup (See Split Pea Soup with Ham)
¼ cup vermicelli broken into small pieces
1 slice bacon cut into small pieces
6 small, tender spinach leaves

Put ½ cup of water into large, heavy pot. Add block of frozen soup, turn to very low heat, cover, and heat until block starts to defrost. Stir frequently to help speed process.

Boil vermicelli according to instructions on package and drain. Start bacon cooking in heavy skillet. Add spinach leaves and sauté lightly with the bacon. Remove spinach from pan and cut into very small pieces. Drain grease from bacon on absorbent paper and crumble for soup garnish.

When split pea soup is completely defrosted and very hot, add vermicelli and spinach and serve. Garnish with crumbled bacon. Serves 4 to 6.

Note: If your family balks at eating the dark, leafy greens that are so packed with nutrition, add them in bits to other soups . . . and to vegetable salads.

Lentil Soup

1 cup cooked lentils (See Lamb, Lentil, and Eggplant Moussaka)
2 cups chicken broth
1 cup leftover cooked vegetables (broccoli, string beans, or cooked greens are especially good)
Grated Parmesan cheese

Combine and heat, stirring frequently. Serve with French bread. Sprinkle grated Parmesan cheese into soup. Serves 4 to 6.

Note: Fresh vegetables can be cooked and added with the water in which they were cooked if you do not have leftovers to use up.

Split Pea Soup with Ham

Make with ham bone and broth from Boiled New England Dinner with Ham

1 ham bone
Broth from boiled dinner . . . add water to make 4 quarts
1 1-lb. box quick-cooking split peas (or lentils)

Put bone and liquid in large soup pot. Wash split peas and add. Bring to a boil, turn down to simmer, and cook for 1½ hours or until peas are soft. Stir frequently, particularly at end of cooking time to be sure peas do not stick to bottom of pot. Set ½ aside.

This hearty soup, served with a salad and a filling dessert makes a satisfying meal. Serves 4 to 6.

Freeze half of soup that was set aside (see "Freezing Measured Amounts of Broths") and use it to make Split Pea Soup with Spinach and Vermicelli.

14

VEGETABLES, FRUITS, AND SALADS

Buying Fresh Fruits and Vegetables

The perishable nature and distance from grower to consumer of fruits and vegetables make handling and transportation costs expensive. As a matter of fact, fruits and vegetables have the largest marketing bill of all the five main food products.

From the standpoint of nutrition and flavor, as well as economy, the ideal way to purchase fresh fruits and vegetables is directly from the grower. There are still a few farms tucked away in the most unexpected places. Look in your telephone book yellow pages under "Farm Products" and you might discover there's one right around the corner from you. But most of us aren't so lucky and we're faced with a choice between a neighborhood fruit and vegetable store and the supermarket.

Before ruling out the neighborhood vegetable store in favor of lower supermarket prices, try it. If the independent store is owned by someone who knows good produce and who is so passionately devoted to it that he gets up at three o'clock in the morning and drives his truck to a large produce market to select personally each bunch of radishes and head of cabbage, you will probably do well to shop there.

In the long run, it pays to buy good quality fruits and vegetables. Even though the initial cost is greater, there will be less waste to be cut away and thrown out when you prepare them for cooking. There will be less left on the plates to be thrown out, because there's just no comparison between the taste of top quality fruit and vegetables and inferior quality that probably started out by being picked too green, then may have been stored too long and displayed too long exposed to heat and air. And, of course, there's always the biggest—though hidden—saving; your family's better health that comes as a result of being given food containing sufficient nutrients.

Controlled Atmosphere Storage and Improved Transportation Are Lengthening the Seasons: A form of cold storage known as "controlled atmosphere," is partly responsible now for stretching out the perishable foods' seasons and moving them closer together. As science further perfects this storage method—used in transport as well as storage—seasonal buying gradually may disappear and fresh foods will be released as needed.

Some of the produce kept in controlled-atmosphere storage may come out almost field fresh, but, unless it is kept constantly under refrigeration—in the store as well as in your home—it may spoil very quickly. If you buy exceptionally nice produce out of its normal season, play it safe. Hurry it into the refrigerator and keep it there. If it's in a package, check the label for storage instructions. Of course, it may not be out of season at all. Instead, it may come from a far-off land, where our winter is their summer. This is another advantage we are beginning to enjoy from improved storage and transportation.

If you don't have enough refrigerator space and you find your fruits and vegetables are spoiling, arrange to shop two or three times a week for these things. That way, the produce market, not you, will absorb the loss from spoilage . . . and you'll enjoy the benefits of eating fresh food.

Buying Fruits and Vegetables in Quantity: Many fruits and vegetables (citrus fruit, onions, potatoes, apples, etc.) are cheaper if you buy them in already-packaged quantities. This, however, is not necessarily an economy. You may need refrigerator space for some of it. Unless you can see pretty well what's inside the container, the bottom and center as well as the top—you may be buying food that's anywhere from 10 to 50 percent on the verge of going bad.

Should You Buy Fresh or Frozen or Canned Fruits and Vegetables? From the standpoint of taste, nutrition, and price, at the height of each fruit and vegetable's growing season, it's unquestionably best to buy it fresh . . . especially if it's grown nearby. However, when it's not in season it's a good idea to check the price on canned and frozen varieties.

We don't recommend that you use a very large percentage of your freezer space for fruits and vegetables because you may save more by using it for meat. The obvious exceptions to this recommendation are those who have access to large quantities of top quality fruits and vegetables at very cheap prices; such people probably will own large farm-style freezers and know all about the various ways of preserving foods when they are in season.

Freeze Individual Pieces of Fruit for Garnishes: There are a few fruits that add so much to the appearance and taste of many dishes when used as a garnish or decoration that you should always try to keep a supply of at least one variety in your freezer. Freeze them individually, either plain or sugared, spread them out on cookie sheets, then, when solid, put them in small plastic bags or other containers from which you can remove a few at a time as needed.

Thompson seedless grapes (remove from stems), blueberries, strawberries, and Italian prune-plums (cut in half, seed removed) are excellent for this purpose and don't take up too much room.

What to Look for When Buying Fresh Fruit and Vegetables: Generally, good-quality ripe fruits and vegetables are nicely developed, plump and unwrinkled, heavy for their size, and have a rich, healthy-looking color. The fragrance of many of them also is a good indication of quality.

The United States Department of Agriculture booklet, *How to Use USDA Grades in Buying Food*, has this to say about fresh fruits and vegetables:

"This grade mark may be used on *fresh fruits* and *vegetables*. When you see it, it means good quality produce. And it means that the product was packed under the supervision of an official Government grader. [Authors' note: The continuous inspection shield, see page 27, is also used on some fresh fruits and vegetables and some tree nuts.]

"Although most fresh fruits and vegetables are sold at wholesale on the basis of U.S. grades, not many are marked with the grade when they are sold in the grocery store. [You may see them, however, in the food circular and newspaper advertisements: Authors.]

"The typical range of grades for fresh fruits and vegetables is U.S. Fancy, U.S. No. 1, and U.S. No. 2. For some products, there are grades above and below that range. For instance, grades for apples are U.S. Extra Fancy, U.S. Fancy, U.S. No. 1, and U.S. Utility.

"The grades are based on the product's color, size, shape, maturity, and number of defects. The lower grades are just as nutritious as the higher grades. The difference is mainly in appearance, waste, and preference."

Peak Seasons and Other Helpful Things to Know About Fruits and Vegetables

(The following information on peak seasons can serve as a helpful guide if you keep in mind the constant changes being wrought by science, improved transportation—which still doesn't completely alter the fact that foods available in one part of the country may not always be available hundreds of miles away—and other factors.)

Apples: The wide variety of apples with their equally wide variety of seasons makes them available the year around. Avoid immature, shriveled-looking apples or any with soft, mushy spots. Their fragrance should be fresh, not heavy. Don't buy bruised apples unless you get them for next to nothing directly from the orchard where a windstorm has just knocked them down . . . and you plan to use them within a few hours.

For eating: Delicious, Jonathan, McIntosh, Stayman, and Winesap

For pies: Gravenstein, Grimes Golden, Jonathan, and Newton

For baking: Rome Beauty, Northern Spy, Rhode Island Greening, Winesap, and York Imperial

Apricots: A few imported during December and January but domestic crop peaks in June and July. Apricots must be tree-ripened. Avoid green-colored or runty-looking ones.

Artichoke: Peak crop comes in April and May although some are available the year around. Artichokes should be heavy in relation to size. Avoid those with brownish, dried-looking leaves or spots of mold.

Asparagus: Available from mid-February with peak from April to June. Avoid loose tip, dirty-looking green color or a heavily ridged stalk.

Avocados: Available all year. Avoid cracked surfaces, sunken spots or very small fruit (in which the seed is disproportionately large). Colors differ but should be healthy-looking. Fruit when ripe will give slightly if pressed gently between cupped hands.

Bananas: Available year round. Buy when yellow and green for use in a few days; yellow with brown flecks for immediate use. Avoid fruit that is bruised or a grayish color.

Beans (Green Snap): *Available all year.* Avoid faded, flabby, or mildewed beans.

Beets: Available year round. Avoid droopy, dull beets.

Blueberries: Available from May through September. Blueberries should be dark blue with a silvery bloom. Avoid tiny berries, damp baskets, an excess of stems and leaves.

Broccoli: Available year round but less abundant in July and August. Avoid overmature broccoli on which yellow flowers are beginning to open and on which stems look old and tough.

Brussels Sprouts: Peak of season is from October through December, although they are available most of the year. Avoid sprouts that are a yellowish color, loose-leafed, wilted, or wormy-looking.

Cabbage: Most summer cabbage is "new" crop (which is available the year round) but some of what we buy in the winter is from cold storage. Avoid wilted, discolored cabbage or cabbage with too much loose "wrapper" leaf. There is smooth-leaved green cabbage, crinkly-leaved green Savoy, and red cabbage. The outer, greener leaves contain more Vitamin A than do the paler, inner ones. The heart of cabbage is also nutritious. Serve pieces raw as an appetizer or chopped in salads.

Carrots: Available year round. Avoid those that are flabby or poor-colored.

Cauliflower: Available year round but peak crops are from September through January. Avoid heads that are not crisp and firm or show signs of mold or are black speckled.

Celery: Available year round. Avoid wilted or discolored celery.

Cherries: Available from May through August. Lamberts should be dark red to be ripe and sweet; other varieties from deep red to black. Avoid those with leaking flesh, decay, and shriveled flesh or stems.

Chicory, Endive, Escarole: Available most of year but peak crops are in winter and spring. Avoid wilted or discolored heads.

CITRUS FRUIT:

Grapefruit: Available all year; peak crop January through May

Lemons: Available year round

Oranges: Available year round with following peak seasons:

Parson Brown and *Hamlins* available in October;

Navels are available from November until May;

Pineapple oranges from late November through March;

Temple oranges from early December to early March;

Valencias from March through October.

Tangerines: Available November to March; peak in December and January.

Color is not the best indication of sweetness in oranges and grapefruit. State laws require that both fruits be mature before being picked. The skin should be relatively smooth-textured and small-grained. The fruit should be firm and heavy for its size.

Tangerines should be lustrous deep yellow or orange.

Small skin blemishes on citrus fruit don't effect quality, but fruit with soft spots, bruises, or mold should be avoided.

Corn: Available most of the year but peak crops are from May into September. Avoid dried out or wormy husks or tiny, immature kernels.

Cranberries: Available from September through January, but November is the peak month. When berries are top quality and price, you may want to freeze 2 or 3 boxes.

Eggplant: Available in limited quantities most of the year, eggplant reaches its peak in late summer. Avoid those that are soft, shriveled, decaying, or not a rich, dark purple color.

Grapes: There is almost always one variety or another of grapes available. The following listing tells when and briefly describes each variety.

GREEN-COLORED GRAPES *should have a yellowish tinge to be at their sweetest:*

Almeria (medium large; greenish white) September to November;

Niagara (large, round to egg-shaped; white to amber) September to October;

Olivette Blanche (elongated; green) June to August;

Thompson Seedless (medium-size, elongated; greenish-white) June to November. This is the only completely seedless grape;

White Malaga (large; greenish-white to yellow) September to November.

RED, BLUE- AND BLACK-COLORED GRAPES *to be at their sweetest, should have no green coloring:*

Cardinal (large; dark red) June to August;

Catawba (medium-size, oval; purple-red) September to November;

Concord (medium-size; blue-black) September to October;

Delaware (small; light red) August to September;

Emperor (large, elongated; light red and reddish-purple) November to May;

Red Malaga (large, spherical; pink to reddish-purple) July to October;

Ribier (large, round; black) July to February;

Tokay (large, oval; bright red) August to January;

White Malaga (large; greenish-white to yellow) September to November.

Examine stem end of grapes. If unhealthy or watery with a great many grapes falling off, don't buy.

Greens: A large number of greens, both domestic and wild are available throughout the year. Some of the best known are: beet tops, chard, collards, cress, kale, dandelion, mustard, spinach, turnip tops. Use only those that are fresh, young, tender, and free from blemishes (and insects) if you want a sweet, mild, palatable flavor. Greens are important for Vitamin A.

LETTUCE

Available in one variety or another year round; peak months are generally May through August. The four most common varieties are:

Iceberg: Large, round and solid; medium green outer and pale-green inner leaves. Avoid heads that are very hard, have irregular shapes or are unusually pale in color;

Butterhead: (includes Big Boston and Bibb varieties) is smaller than iceberg, looser, darker green with yellowish, buttery soft center leaves that form a rosette;

Romaine: tall, cylindrical plant with crisp, dark-green leaves in loosely folded, but fairly compact head;

Leaf Lettuce: This includes many varieties, none with a compact head. Leaves are broad, tender, succulent, and vary in green color. It may be raised in greenhouses and sold locally.

Avoid lettuce with discolored leaf tips or soft decay or rust spots. Look for healthy appearance and a good color for the variety. There is more vitamin content in deep green outer leaves or loose-leafed varieties.

MELONS

Cantaloupe (Muskmelon): Some imports early in spring; domestic crop available from May through September;

Casaba: Available from July to November;

Cranshaw: Available from July through October; peak months are August and September;

Honey Dew: Imported during winter and spring; peak domestic crops from July through October;

Persian: Available in August and September;

Watermelon: Some available from early May through September; peak crops are in June, July, and August.

Melons are very hard to judge for sweetness. If one side of a watermelon is turning yellow, it's probably ripe. Cantaloupe should be yellow to gold with well-defined netting. There should be no stem fragment left on a cantaloupe, but on some other melons it stays on. Unless you're experienced in choosing ripe melons, better play it safe, buy from a good market and ask the advice of one of the experienced clerks.

Mushrooms: Available year round in varying amounts. Peak in fall and winter. Mushrooms should be firm, fresh-looking, and free from blemishes. Caps are rounded when fresh, tend to open and flatten out as they get old. Only buy those produced and sold commercially.

Nectarines: Available from June through September. Avoid fruit that is hard, dull or shriveled-looking. Healthy, mature fruit with a little green ground color will ripen at room temperature.

Onions: Some variety of both green and dry onions will be available year round. Some varieties of onions cost much more than others do so you should know the intended use before buying, then ask your vegetable man which are the "sweet" onions suitable for eating raw and which are the stronger-flavored cooking varieties. The most common variety is the "globe" used generally for cooking. It usually has a yellow skin, but it can be white or purple, which makes it easy to confuse with other varictics. Very large onions, regardless of color, are usually sweet.

Avoid dry onions that have wet or soft necks or fresh sprouts. Green onions (and leeks) should have fresh, crisp, green tops. The white portion should extend two or three inches up from root.

Parsley: Generally available year round. Don't buy if wilted. Parsley should be eaten, not just used to make a dish look pretty, because it is an excellent source for Vitamin A.

Parsnips: Available most of the year; parsnips are best eaten in late winter as the flavor becomes sweeter after long exposure to cold. Avoid parsnips that have large, coarse, and badly wilted roots. Well-formed small to medium parsnips that are firm and smooth are the best.

Peaches: Available May to October. Green-colored peaches do not ripen.

Peaches should be firm, with creamy to yellow undercoloring. Deep red colors do not necessarily mean the peach is sweet-ripe. If hard, hold at room temperature until they begin to soften and turn sweet. Then eat or refrigerate.

There are many varieties of peaches that fall into two general types;

clings, used primarily for canning, and freestone, which is the one most often eaten raw.

Pears: Available, with the help of cold storage, from August through May. Buy pears when they are firm but just beginning to soften. When necessary, finish ripening at room temperature, then refrigerate.

Colors vary according to variety.

Avoid wilted or shriveled pears, those with weakening of the flesh near the stem or spots on the sides and blossom end.

Peppers (sweet green): Available most of year but peak crop is late summer. Avoid peppers that are wilted, light for their size or have soft spots on the sides. When inexpensive and nice, clean and freeze a few for garnishes.

Pineapple: Available the year round; at peak supply in April and May. Picked when mature but green in color, pineapples must be ripened at room temperature until they are: golden yellow, orange yellow, or reddish brown (depending on variety). They should be heavy for their size. Avoid fruit with dull yellowish-green color and dried appearance; bruises or soft or moldy spots or an unpleasant odor.

Plums and Prunes: Plums are available from June to September; prunes from August through October. There are a number of varieties of plums and they differ in appearance. Prunes are rather small and purplish or bluish-black. Buy both prunes and plums while still firm but beginning to soften. Avoid fruit that's excessively soft, or very hard, has broken skin or brownish discoloration.

Potatoes: Available year round. "New" potatoes most often refers to those harvested and marketed during the late winter or early spring. They are excellent for boiling. Most potatoes come under the general purpose category and, with the aid of air-cooled storage, are available all times of year. Avoid potatoes with deep eyes, damaged or wrinkled skins, green areas, mold, or sprouts.

Squash: (*Summer,* including varieties harvested when immature. Summer squash include: yellow crookneck, large yellow straightneck, greenish-white patty pan, and slender green zucchini and Italian marrow.) Some are available at all times of the year. Avoid squash that is droopy-looking or has a dull skin.

Squash: (*Fall and Winter,* those varieties that are marketed when fully mature. Acorn, butternut, buttercup, hubbard, delicious, and banana.) Winter squash reaches its peak from early fall until late winter; acorn squash is available year round. Avoid tender or sunken spots or a soft rind. Winter squash should be heavy for its size.

Strawberries: Available in varying amounts from January into the fall; peak supply in May and June. Avoid mold, soft spots, excessive seedy areas. Berries should be bright, lustrous red, and have their cap stem still attached.

Sweet Potatoes: The two types of sweet potatoes are available in varying amounts year round. The most common type of sweet potato is the "moist" type which has soft, moist, orange-colored flesh and bronze or rosy skin. "Dry" sweet potatoes have pale-colored flesh, are low in moisture, rather mealy, and have a yellow or light-brown skin. Avoid damp or soft spots, discolored or shriveled appearance. Sweet potatoes should be well shaped and firm.

Tomatoes: Available in varying amounts throughout the year; imports add to supply from late winter to early spring. Buy tomatoes that are uniformly pink, red, or yellow in color. When necessary to ripen, hold at room temperature before—never after—refrigerating. Fruit should be firm and plump without breaks or bruises. Cherry tomatoes, though usually more expensive than other varieties, contain a higher content of Vitamin C for their size. Sometimes, too, children who won't eat regular tomatoes will eat the small, cherry variety.

Turnips and Rutabagas: Turnips are available most of the year. Rutabagas are available in fall and winter and (from cold storage) sometimes in the spring, too. (These cold storage rutabagas are sometimes covered with a thin layer of paraffin to prevent loss of moisture.) Turnips are white fleshed with a purple top. Rutabagas are their big yellow-fleshed relatives.

Turnips should be small or medium, smooth, round and firm.

Rutabagas should be larger, heavy for their size, fairly smooth, firm, generally round or elongated and without decay.

Cook Vegetables the Healthy, Tasty Way

From the standpoint of taste, texture and nutrition, vegetables probably are the most abused of all our foods. They are all too often overcooked, reduced to an ugly, soggy, watery mess, then placed on dinner plates to detract from the meat or fish and thin the gravy.

This is all done with the apparent notion that simply by providing the required number of vegetables, no matter whether or not any one is willing to eat them, the nutritional obligations have been met.

Here are some things to remember if you want vegetables to be nutritional and taste good, too:

1. Wash vegetables thoroughly. Soak broccoli and Brussels sprouts for 1 hour in cold, salted water to remove any insects.

2. Cook vegetables for the briefest time possible, then eat them at once.

3. Try to add no more liquid than will be absorbed by the time vegetables are cooked. Substitute other liquids, such as well-seasoned broth, for the cooking water sometimes for a taste treat. Young, tender greens will sometimes cook in just the water left on the leaves after washing. Put them in a tightly closed pan so no steam escapes and cook just until tender, but not mushy, season with butter, salt, and pepper and eat at once. Tomatoes can be cooked in their own liquid in much the same manner.

4. Try the Chinese way of frying or braising sliced vegetables in just a little oil, butter, or margarine until crunchy tender.

5. Root vegetables such as carrots require more water than do the vegetables with a greater liquid content. But the younger root vegetables are, the less time—and therefore the less water—will be needed. Bring them to a boil, turn down to a simmer, and cover tightly. With a little care, you can even cook carrots and small potatoes (in their skins) until they are just done and the liquid disappears. But not the flavor. The flavor and a great many nutrients remain in the vegetables. Nothing's thrown down the drain.

6. Whenever possible, cook and eat the skins of vegetables.

7. Add calcium, flavor, and taste appeal in the form of a cheese sauce. Add a little protein and flavor with a sprinkle of nuts or crumbled fried bacon.

8. Don't cut and bruise vegetables with dull knives.

9. Prepare canned and frozen vegetables according to package or can instructions.

10. Try the Pennysaver vegetable recipes which illustrate the above suggestions. They also provide many different ways to include sources of Vitamin A, Vitamin C, and the other vitamins, too, that help round out the nutrient variety of your daily meals.

Vegetable Recipes

Sautéed Asparagus and Mushrooms

2 lbs. asparagus, white end cut off, washed, and sliced on the diagonal
¼ lb. fresh mushrooms, cleaned and sliced
1 Tb. cooking oil
1 Tb. butter or margarine
Salt and pepper to taste

Be sure asparagus and mushrooms are clean and dry. Heat cooking oil and butter or margarine in heavy skillet. When very hot and bubbles are beginning to form, add asparagus and mushrooms. If necessary, use two skillets to avoid crowding the vegetables in the pan. Sauté, stirring frequently, just until crisp-tender. Season with salt and pepper. Serve at once. Serves 4.

Broccoli Almandine

1 small bunch of broccoli
½ tsp. salt
1 cup hollandaise sauce, see page 175
¼ cup slivered blanched almonds

Wash broccoli, cut off coarse end of stalk, and slice lengthwise. Put in heavy saucepan, add water to a depth of about ¼ inch, and add salt. Bring to a boil, cover, turn down to a simmer, and cook just until crisp-tender. Check occasionally to be sure water is not boiling dry. Keep just enough water in saucepan so it will be absorbed when broccoli is done. While broccoli is cooking, make hollandaise sauce according to instructions. Crisp almonds in a hot, lightly greased skillet. Turn off heat when they start to turn golden. When broccoli is done, serve on heated plates, top with hollandaise and sprinkle with crisp almonds. Serves 4 to 6.

Variation: Add a little grated cheese to hollandaise.

Hong Kong Sweet and Pungent Cabbage

Tim Seun Shee Toy

4 Tbs. oil
1 clove garlic, crushed
1 cup shredded green pepper
1 cup shredded carrot
4 cups shredded cabbage, preferably celery cabbage
½ cup water
3 Tbs. vinegar
3 Tbs. sugar
1 tsp. monosodium glutamate
½ tsp. salt
Dash pepper, or to taste
1 tsp. cornstarch dissolved in 2 tsps. cold water
Dash sesame oil
Boiled rice
1 cucumber, sliced but unpeeled

Heat oil in frying pan. When sizzling, add garlic, green pepper, and carrot and stir-fry for 3 minutes over medium heat. Add cabbage and stir-fry 3 minutes. Then add water and vinegar, cover, and boil 3 minutes more. Add sugar, monosodium glutamate, salt and pepper, raise heat to high and stir another 3 minutes. Add cornstarch mixture and stir about 1 minute or until thickened. Finally stir in the sesame oil and stir once or twice to glaze, about 3 seconds. Heap over hot boiled rice on serving platter, surround with garnish border of cucumber slices. Serves 4.

Green Beans and Bacon

2 slices of bacon, chopped
1 lb. young green beans, washed and sliced diagonally
¼ cup water

Start bacon cooking in heavy skillet or saucepan. Add beans and stir until each piece is coated with bacon grease. Add ¼ cup of water, cover and cook just until water is all absorbed and beans are crisp-tender. Serve at once. Serves 4.

Creamed Greens

1½ lb. very young and tender greens
¼ cup boiling water
½ tsp. salt
1 cup of warm hollandaise sauce (use variation of your choice, page 176)

Thoroughly wash greens, cut away any tough leaf ribs. Put greens in heavy saucepan and add boiling water and salt. Return water to a boil, turn down to simmer, cover pan and cook for 5 minutes. Gently mash greens down into the hot water and finish cooking uncovered for 2 or 3 minutes or until greens are tender but not mushy. If any water is left, drain it off. Chop greens into bite-size pieces and stir in the warm hollandaise sauce. Serves 4.

Mixed Vegetables Cooked in Broth

1 green pepper, cleaned and sliced
2 carrots, scraped and sliced
2 small sweet onions, sliced
2 stalks celery, sliced
½ cup your own chicken or beef broth (or substitute canned broth)
1 cup sour cream or plain yogurt
Salt to taste

Combine all ingredients except sour cream or yogurt and salt in a heavy saucepan and bring to a boil. Turn down to a low simmer, cover, and continue cooking for 15 minutes without removing lid. Check to see if vegetables are crisp-tender. If not done, recover and continue cooking for about 5 minutes more. If necessary, add more broth—use water if you don't have more broth—but just enough to keep vegetables from burning. When done, add sour cream or yogurt. Taste. Add salt if necessary. Stir and continue cooking on low heat until cream is warm. Don't overheat. Serve at once on warm plates. Serves 4.

Pickled Leftover Vegetables

1 cup leftover cauliflower, broccoli, or sliced beets
½ cup sliced onion
2 Tbs. wine vinegar
1 tsp. olive oil (optional)
1 clove garlic
¼ tsp. salt
⅛ tsp. pepper
½ tsp. sugar
2 Tbs. water

Put leftover vegetables and sliced onion in a small bowl. Cauliflower and broccoli can be combined if you happen to have them both at the same time, but beets should be prepared in a separate dish because the red color runs out of them. Mix vinegar, olive oil, garlic, salt, pepper, and sugar with water and pour over vegetables, mixing as you pour so oil will not separate. Any of the seasonings can be increased or decreased according to taste. Cover bowl and refrigerate. Serve pickled leftover vegetables as a garnish or on an antipasto tray or as a canapé . . . serve with toothpicks, not crackers. Sliced pickled beets can be cut with a cookie cutter to give them a more decorative shape when using as a garnish.

Rainbow Mixed Vegetables

An End of Week Casserole

1 cup cauliflower cut in pieces
½ sweet red onion, sliced
1 carrot, sliced
1 stalk celery, sliced
1 floweret of broccoli
Any other small amounts of vegetables left in refrigerator at week's end
2 cups chicken or beef broth (your own or canned)
1 tsp. butter
Salt and pepper to taste
Pinch of garlic salt

Combine all ingredients except butter and seasonings in heavy saucepan. Bring broth to a boil, cover saucepan, turn down to a simmer, and cook until vegetables are crisp-tender and most of liquid has been absorbed. If liquid has not been absorbed when vegetables are done, leave lid off and simmer it away. Add salt and pepper and pinch of garlic salt, spread butter over the hot vegetables and serve on warm plates. Serves 4 to 6.

Hashed Brown Parsnips with Bacon and Peanuts

1 lb. parsnips, peeled
2 slices bacon, diced
1 medium onion, sliced
1 Tb. butter or margarine
¼ tsp. salt
⅛ tsp. pepper
2 Tbs. crushed peanuts

Boil parsnips in water to cover until tender, 20 to 40 minutes. Heat diced bacon in heavy skillet and add sliced onion. While onions start cooking, slice parsnips. Add parsnips, butter, salt and pepper to skillet. Fry on medium heat until crisply browned on one side, then turn over, using spatula. When other side is brown, serve. Sprinkle with crushed peanuts. Serves 4.

Baked Sweet or White Potatoes

A large potato, either sweet or white, that is heavy for its size and short and plump, rather than long and thin, will take about one hour to bake in a 450° to 500° F. oven. The water content, the shape, and, in the case of sweet potatoes (or yams), the sugar content, all affect the length of time needed to bake potatoes well done. Test for doneness after about 45 minutes (unless potatoes are small) by sticking a fork into the thickest part of the potato to see if it is tender.

Baking potatoes of either variety is about the easiest and the best way to prepare them, especially if you eat the skins. Scrub thoroughly, and put in a preheated oven—you don't even need a dish—take out when done and eat plain or with a little butter and salt.

Nutritionists consider sweet potatoes one of the outstanding Vitamin A vegetables. The white potato seems to be sort of betwixt and between. It doesn't have *quite* enough Vitamin C to be grouped with the top group, but it comes close, and besides that, with the exception of Vitamin A, it rates pretty well in most of the other nutrients. So the nutritionists sometimes group the white potato with Vitamin C vegetables, sometimes with the "other" vegetables, but they say, "other vegetables, including potatoes." So, since *they* try so hard to point out that the potato is nutritionally worthwhile, don't *you* overlook it.

Yams and Pineapple Casserole

1 1-lb. 6-oz. can yams, or sweet potatoes, drained and sliced
1 14-oz. can pineapple chunks, drained
Syrup from pineapple can
½ to ¾ cup liquid from canned yams
⅛ tsp. salt
½ cup light syrup
3 Tbs. brown sugar
¼ cup butter or margarine
1 Tb. lemon juice

Arrange yams and drained pineapple chunks in alternating layers in well-greased, shallow 1½ qt. casserole. Combine all remaining ingredients in a saucepan and simmer for 5 minutes, stirring frequently. Pour over yams and pineapple and bake in 375° F. oven about 30 minutes or until sauce is thick and dish is very lightly browned. Serves 6 to 8.

Mashed Rutabagas

1 to 1½ lbs. rutabagas, peeled and diced
1 tsp. sugar
1 tsp. butter or margarine
Salt and pepper to taste
⅛ tsp. nutmeg
1 Tb. finely minced parsley
½ tsp. lemon juice

Boil diced rutabaga in water to cover for 20 to 30 minutes or until fork tender. Add tsp. sugar to cooking water. Drain, mash, add butter or margarine, salt and pepper to taste, nutmeg, minced parsley, and lemon juice and thoroughly mix together. Serves 4 to 6.

Variation

MASHED RUTABAGAS AND WHITE POTATOES Prepare rutabagas as above and combine with an equal amount of mashed white potato. Serve instead of potato.

Spinach with Nuts

1 10-oz. pkg. frozen spinach
¼ cup water, boiling
½ tsp. salt
1 Tb. butter or margarine
¼ cup pine nuts or slivered, blanched almonds

Add spinach to boiling water in heavy saucepan, add salt and cook until water returns to boil. Cover saucepan and continue boiling for 3 minutes, or until frozen spinach can be pulled apart. Cut up in small pieces, cook without lid until most of water is absorbed. If this doesn't happen in 5 minutes, drain spinach. Add butter and stir until melted. Serve and top each serving with nuts. Serves 4.

Tomatoes Stuffed with Leftover Vegetables

4 medium tomatoes, centers scooped out, inverted and drained
2 Tbs. tomato centers, chopped and drained
1 cup mashed potatoes (if you use leftover potato, add a little warm milk and beat with electric mixer)
1 egg, slightly beaten
1 cup leftover peas, corn, lima beans, or a combination of any or all
1 Tb. grated onion
Salt to taste
⅛ lb. sharp Cheddar or a milder cheese, depending on preference

Sprinkle a little salt in tomato cavities and over the chopped tomato. Beat mashed potato and egg together, add all other ingredients except cheese, and fill tomato cavities with the mixture. Slice cheese and spread over stuffed tomatoes. Fit tomatoes into a small, lightly buttered casserole (they should fit closely enough to hold each other up), pour ¼ cup water around them and bake in oven preheated to 325° F. for about 30 minutes, or until tomatoes are cooked and cheese is nicely browned. Serves 4.

Variation: Tomatoes can be stuffed with cooked corn, or succotash, or peas with just a little butter and seasoning added.

Creamed Turnips

1 lb. turnips, peeled and sliced
Salt and pepper to taste
4 Tbs. butter or margarine
4 Tbs. flour
1½ cups milk
½ cup chicken broth (your own or substitute canned broth)
2 Tbs. sour cream (optional)
Paprika

Boil sliced turnips in water to cover. Drain. Salt and pepper to taste. Melt butter or margarine in large, heavy skillet. Add flour and cook for 2 minutes, stirring constantly. Heat milk and chicken broth almost to boiling and add all at once to flour and butter mixture, stirring constantly with wire whisk. Stir until sauce is smooth and thickened. Continue cooking at low heat for about 5 minutes. Add turnips, turn off heat and stir in sour cream. Serve and sprinkle each serving with a small amount of paprika. Serves 4.

Stuffed Zucchini

using leftover stew as base for stuffing

3 zucchini, 6 to 8 inches long, and solid
1 tsp. salt
1 Tb. olive oil (cooking oil of your preference may be substituted)
1 medium onion, finely chopped
½ medium green pepper, finely chopped
1 cup leftover stew cut in small cubes
1 6-oz. can tomato paste
¼ lb. Cheddar cheese, sliced (substitute any cheese that makes a good topping)

Put zucchini in large, heavy pot, add water to half cover, and add salt. Cover, bring to a boil, and simmer for about 15 minutes or until beginning to get tender. Don't overcook.

While zucchini cooks, heat olive oil in a heavy skillet and lightly sauté onion and green pepper. Stir in stew and tomato paste and mix thoroughly. Remove zucchini from pot. When cool enough to handle, slice lengthwise and scoop out seeds. Chop and stir them into mixture in skillet. Pile mixture into cavities and over tops of zucchini halves, top with sliced cheese, arrange in a shallow roasting pan and bake in oven preheated to 350° F. for 30 minutes, or until cheese is melted and lightly browned.

Salads

Don't be restricted in your saladmaking to the standard lettuce, cucumbers, green peppers, onions, and tomatoes. Add zest and savor by including snips of very young, very tender spinach or other vitamin-packed dark green leafy vegetables that we usually only serve cooked, or:

Use some of the tiny leaves from the well-nourished dandelions that pop up on your lawn. Bits of nasturtium leaves add a very different biting zest.

Add also very thin slices of zucchini and not quite so thin pieces of red cabbage. Try mixing your lettuces, and remember that the darker green, outside leaves are the ones that pack a vitamin wallop.

For a seemingly different salad, leave the skin on cucumber and slice it paper thin. Use a vegetable slicer and only do this with cucumbers that are very firm and not watery.

Slivers of cabbage, cauliflower or broccoli heart add crunchy goodness as do tiny raw flowerets from very fresh cauliflower and broccoli. Left-over pieces of cooked broccoli, cauliflower, string beans, asparagus, and beets make nice salads, particularly if marinated in a vinegar and oil dressing.

Slices of cucumber, carrot, celery heart, broccoli heart, and cabbage heart can be substituted for crackers as dip-dunkers or things upon which to put spreads. If you keep the dips and spreads low calorie, this is excellent for dieters as well as providing vitamin-rich taste interest.

Very Fresh Salad with Anchovy Dressing

½ head of lettuce
2 small flowerets of broccoli
Cabbage heart
2 very small, tender leaves of spinach
2 or three very small, young string beans
1 tomato
Other vegetables you may want to include, such as carrots and asparagus

Wash lettuce, dry, and tear into bite size. Wash and dry other vegetables and, with the exception of the tomato, cut them into small bits or slices and put in a salad bowl. Reserve tomatoes to put on after dressing has been added.

Note: Make this salad on the day you buy vegetables so you can add some slivers of those that are good raw only when very, very fresh. This way, you don't have the additional expense of buying a bunch of each type in order to make the salad. Just take a little bit of each of your week's supply of vegetables.

Anchovy Salad Dressing

2 Tbs. wine vinegar
½ tsp. sugar
Pinch of pepper
1 clove garlic
1 2-oz. can anchovy fillets in pure olive oil

Put vinegar, sugar, pepper, clove of garlic, and oil from anchovies in a jar. Shake, pour on salad and toss until vegetables are well coated. Decorate with anchovies and tomato wedges. Serves 4 to 6.

Note: Instead of opening a can of anchovies and draining the oil off into the garbage, then perhaps buying some olive oil to marinate the anchovies in for a dressing, make use of every bit of the contents of every can of anchovies you open, including the delicious oil.

Mixed Salad

1 small tomato chopped
½ small cucumber, thinly sliced
1 green onion, including darker green upper half (not the leaves), thinly sliced
6 medium and small tender leaves of romaine lettuce, torn into pieces
½ cup shredded red cabbage
½ medium green pepper, minced

Salad Dressing

2 Tbs. wine vinegar
1½ Tb. salad oil
1 tsp. soy sauce
½ tsp. honey
1 pinch paprika
¼ tsp. onion powder

Put all salad ingredients together in a salad bowl. Combine salad dressing ingredients in a small saucepan. Set saucepan on warm part of stove (don't turn on heat), so ingredients will blend. Stir until thoroughly mixed, pour over salad, toss so that all of vegetables are coated with dressing and serve. Serves 6 to 8.

Tomato and Cucumber Salad

2 small tomatoes, firm ripe, sliced
1 medium cucumber, ripe but not watery, sliced
¼ cup mayonnaise
2 Tbs. sour cream
1 Tb. watercress, finely chopped

Combine tomatoes and cucumbers in a salad bowl. Mix mayonnaise and sour cream, stir into vegetables, sprinkle watercress over top of salad and serve at once. Serves 4.

Macaroni and Cottage Cheese Salad

3 cups cooked elbow macaroni
½ lb. cottage cheese
½ pt. sour cream
1 onion, finely chopped
½ cup finely chopped green pepper
1 carrot, grated
Chili powder to taste
Salt and pepper to taste
Lettuce
1 cup radishes

Combine all ingredients except lettuce and radishes in a salad bowl, mix well, and chill. Serve on beds of lettuce with radishes as a garnish. Serves 4 to 6.

Coleslaw with Raisins and Carrots

2 cups finely shredded cabbage
¼ cup seedless raisins, soaked overnight in
¼ cup orange juice, then drained
½ cup grated carrot
½ cup mayonnaise
2 Tbs. wine vinegar
2 tsps. sugar
⅛ tsp. pepper
½ tsp. salt
1 Tb. grated Parmesan cheese (optional)

Combine shredded cabbage, raisins, and grated carrot in salad bowl. Mix mayonnaise and vinegar together until blended, add sugar, pepper, salt, and Parmesan cheese. Stir well and mix into slaw. Serves 4 to 6.

Raw Vegetable and Apple Salad

There can be many versions of Waldorf salad and this is just one of them, to serve as a guide for others of your own creation. Make them when bright red eating apples and celery are at a peak of crisp, crunchy goodness.

4 raw apples, cored and diced
1 cup shredded cabbage
3 stalks celery, minced
1½ tsps. lemon juice
1½ tsps. sugar
1½ cups mayonnaise
1½ tsps. shredded parsley

Combine apples, cabbage, and celery in a mixing bowl. Blend lemon juice and sugar into the mayonnaise and add to the fruit and vegetable mixture. Mix gently but well. Garnish with parsley. Serves 6.

Sweet Potato and Peanut Salad

1½ cups cooked sweet potato, diced
1 medium tomato, ripe but very firm, chopped
¼ cup crushed roasted peanuts
½ small onion finely minced
2 Tbs. Planters peanut oil
1 tsp. lemon juice
2 pinches pepper
¼ tsp. salt
1 pinch garlic powder
Crisp lettuce leaves

Mix all ingredients except last one together. Serve on individual salad plates, piled on lettuce leaves. Serves 4 to 6.

Lentil Salad

1 cup cooked lentils (see Lamb, Lentil, and Eggplant Moussaka)
½ cup mayonnaise
2 Tbs. catsup
Lettuce leaves

Squeeze most of liquid out of lentils by putting them in a colander or other perforated utensil and mashing with a spoon. Mix lentils with mayonnaise and catsup. Chill and serve in a mound on crisp lettuce leaves. Serves 4 to 6.

Chicken or Turkey Meat Salad with Grapes and Almonds

1 to 1½ cups leftover chicken or turkey meat, diced
1 cup sweet green seedless grapes
½ to 1 cup diced celery, with most of strings removed
¼ cup slivered almonds
⅓ cup sour cream
⅓ cup mayonnaise
Crisp lettuce leaves

Combine poultry meat, grapes, diced celery, and almonds. Thoroughly mix sour cream and mayonnaise and stir into salad. Pile the salad mixture onto individual lettuce leaves on small plates or on a cupped bed of leaves in a serving bowl. Serve at once. Serves 4 to 6.

Chicken or Turkey Meat Salad Mold

1 envelope unflavored gelatin
½ cup boiling water
10 Tbs. cold chicken broth (your own, if you have it)

Make gelatin according to package instructions, but adding chicken broth instead of cold water. Stir in Chicken or Turkey Meat Salad (above), pour into a mold and chill until firm. To unmold, prepare serving platter you want to use, dip mold for 15 seconds (time yourself) into hot water. Place serving platter face down over mold, flip platter and mold over together. Salad should slide out onto platter. If it does not, press very hot towel over outside of mold and shake it, sharply. Serves 4 to 6.

Variation: 1 pkg. lemon gelatin mix can be substituted for unflavored gelatin.

Fish and Peanut Salad

2 cups flaked fish (or canned tuna, drained)
1 cup diced celery
1 cup seeded green grapes
½ cup toasted whole peanuts
⅔ cup mayonnaise
1 Tb. lemon juice
1 tsp. grated onion
½ tsp. salt (omit if using canned tuna)

Combine first four ingredients in a mixing bowl.

Blend mayonnaise, lemon juice, grated onion, and salt. Add to mixture and toss lightly. Serve in bowl or on lettuce leaves on individual salad plates. Goes well with cottage cheese and potato chips. Serves 4 to 6.

Pineapple and Cottage Cheese Mold

2½ cups crushed pineapple
¾ cup water, or enough to make 1¾ cups liquid when combined with pineapple juice
1 3-oz. pkg. lemon gelatin
Juice of 1 lemon
1 lb. cottage cheese
½ cup sour cream

Separate pineapple from its syrup, add the latter to water and heat.

Add gelatin and dissolve. Add lemon juice and cool until gelatin mounds on a spoon. Fold in pineapple, cottage cheese, and sour cream. Pour into mold, chill, and serve. Serves 6 to 8.

Pomegranate Mold

1 3-oz. pkg. lemon or lime gelatin dessert
¾ cup boiling water
1 cup cold lemonade
½ medium pomegranate, very ripe
1 cup creamed cottage cheese
½ cup peanuts, coarsely crushed
½ cup whipping cream
1 tsp. granulated sugar
6 large lettuce leaves

Make gelatin according to instructions on package, but use ¾ cup instead of 1 cup boiling water and substitute cold lemonade for the cold water listed in instructions. Pour ½ of gelatin mixture into a mixing bowl and divide balance among six 5-oz. individual molds. Remove fruit from pomegranate. Put it on absorbent paper towel to dry and be very careful not to mix any bits of the bitter yellow skin with it.* Sprinkle the fruit into the molds and refrigerate. Stir cottage cheese and peanuts into remaining gelatin in mixing bowl and refrigerate until mixture starts to get firm and gelatin in it is no longer runny. Whip cream, stir in sugar, then gently mix into cottage cheese and gelatin mixture in mixing bowl. Divide into individual molds on top of pomegranate-filled lemon gelatin. Let set for several hours or overnight, unmold by dipping molds for 10 to 15 seconds into hot water and inverting onto lettuce leaves arranged on salad plates. Serves 6.

* *Note about pomegranates:* This interestingly flavored and very beautiful fruit is not expensive when in season and is beginning to appear in more and more markets. Just one small pomegranate will go a long way to add taste and color excitement to a plain dish. Every bit of the yellowish-white skin that separates the red seeds, which are the edible fruit, must be removed before eating as it is very bitter. The inner part of the red seed is very crunchy and may startle those eating it for the first time.

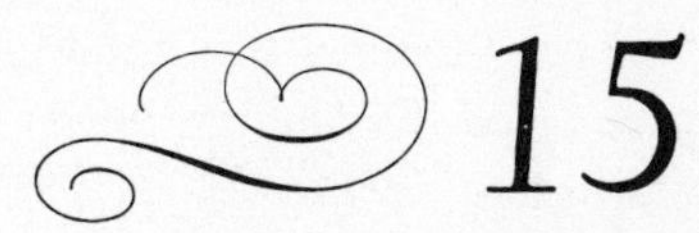

15

BAKED GOODS AND OTHER DESSERTS

Desserts should fill in nutritional gaps in day's eating. The recipes in this section contain milk, eggs, fruit, and cheese. They will not be just an additional expense to satisfy a craving for sweets. As between-meal snacks for children or as a dinner dessert, they will round out the menus and fill in nutritional gaps in the day's foods.

Apple-Oatmeal-Raisin-Cookies

¼ lb. stick (½ cup) of butter or margarine
¼ cup brownulated sugar
⅓ cup granulated white sugar
2 eggs
1 cup applesauce
1 cup quick-cooking rolled oats
1¼ cups all-purpose flour
½ tsp. salt
1 tsp. baking powder
½ cup raisins

Mash butter in bottom of large mixing bowl. Add brown and white sugars and thoroughly blend in, creaming until mixture is light and fluffy. Use electric mixer to beat in eggs thoroughly, adding them one at a time. Stir in applesauce, then rolled oats, mixing well. Sift flour, salt, and baking powder together. Stir into moist mixture just until flour disappears. Add raisins. Drop onto lightly greased cookie sheets by the teaspoonful, allowing plenty of space for cookies to spread out. Preheat oven to 350° F. and bake cookies for 15 minutes or until done. Makes 3 dozen.

Variation: Instead of raisins, use bits of chopped dried fruit—prunes, peaches, or apricots—that have been soaked overnight in applesauce.

Breakfast Food Cookies

½ cup shortening
½ cup brown sugar (packed)
½ cup white sugar
1 egg, beaten well
1½ cups flour
½ tsp. salt
1 tsp. baking soda
1 cup dry cereal (Wheaties type and size. Larger size cereals can be crumbled slightly.)
1 tsp. vanilla

Thoroughly mix shortening and sugars. Add egg and beat again. Mix dry ingredients (including Wheaties) together and add to first mixture. Add vanilla. Drop on lightly greased cookie sheet. Bake in 350° F. oven for 10 to 12 minutes. Makes 30 cookies.

Note: Children who won't eat their breakfast cereal in the usual way may take to it, with a glass of milk, in cookie form. See also: Peanut Butter Cookies and Apple-Oatmeal-Raisin-Cookies.

Peanut Butter Cookies

¾ cup shortening
¾ cup granulated sugar
¾ cup brown sugar
2 eggs
1 tsp. vanilla
¾ cup peanut butter
2½ cups flour
1½ tsp. soda
½ tsp. salt
1 to 3 Tbs. hot water

Thoroughly cream shortening and sugars. Add eggs and vanilla. Stir in peanut butter. Sift dry ingredients together and mix into creamed mixture. Add hot water as seems necessary to make a smooth dough. Roll dough into balls (small) and place on ungreased cookie sheet. Flatten balls with tines of fork, making crisscrossed design if desired. Bake in 350° F. oven about 10 minutes. Makes about 4 doz. cookies.

Plain Egg Muffins

Serving with jelly and a glass of milk will turn these muffins into a dessert.

2 cups sifted all-purpose flour
2 Tbs. sugar
2½ tsps. baking powder
¾ tsp. salt
1 well beaten egg
¾ cup milk
⅓ cup oil or melted shortening

Sift dry ingredients into bowl. Combine egg, milk, and oil or shortening and add all at once to flour mixture. Stir just until flour is moistened. Fill 12 greased muffin pans ⅔ full. Bake at 400° F. about 25 minutes.

RAISIN, NUT, OR DATE MUFFINS Add ½ to ¾ cup raisins, chopped walnuts, or chopped dates to mixture. Before adding, coat raisins, nuts, or dates with 2 Tbs. flour. This helps keep the fruit from settling to the bottom.

BLUEBERRY MUFFINS Prepare muffin batter, using 3 Tbs. less milk than recipe calls for. Add 1 cup fresh or *well-drained* canned or frozen berries mixed with 2 tsps. sugar. Mix lightly into batter. You can, if you prefer, coat berries with 2 Tbs. flour instead of sugar.

Whole Milk Biscuits

Spread with jelly or honey and serve with milk for snack or dessert.

2 cups sifted all-purpose flour
3 tsps. baking powder
½ tsp. salt
⅓ cup shortening
⅔ to ¾ cup milk

Sift flour, baking powder, and salt together. Cut shortening into flour mixture, using back of a fork, until well mixed. Add milk all at once and stir just until mixed. Shape mixture into ball with hands, pat onto lightly floured board, and pat out to ½ inch thick. Cut with biscuit cutter dipped into flour, and bake on ungreased baking sheet in hot oven, 450° F., for 10 to 12 minutes. Makes 15 biscuits.

Variation:

BUTTERMILK BISCUIT Sift ¼ tsp. baking soda into other dry ingredients, and substitute buttermilk or sour milk for the whole milk.

Note: Use cool utensils for mixing pastry and run cold water over your hands to cool them before handling dough.

Baked Apples with Honey, Nuts, and Raisins

4 large apples, cored with one end left in
4 Tbs. raisins
2 walnuts, meats removed and broken into chunks
4 Tbs. honey
Cinnamon
Milk or light cream

Peel skin from top of each cored apple to give more exposed area for honey to penetrate and place them in an oven pan. Pack 1 Tb. raisins into bottom of each cavity and top with ¼ of walnut meats. Spoon 1 Tb. honey into each cavity and over peeled top of apple. Sprinkle each apple with a pinch of cinnamon. Bake in 350° F. oven for 40 to 60 minutes—until apple is fork tender. If bottom of pan starts to burn, add ½ cup water. Serve with milk or light cream, either hot or cold. Serves 4.

Baked Apple with Spiced Honey

6 large baking apples
6 Tbs. honey, or more to taste
6 sticks cinnamon

Core apples, place in shallow baking pan, and fill cavities with honey. Put a cinnamon stick in center of each apple, place pan in oven, cover bottom of pan with ⅛ inch of water and bake at 350° F. for 50 minutes or until tender. Baste frequently with sauce from pan. Add more water if necessary. Serves 6.

Dough for One- or Two-Crust Pie

ONE-CRUST PIE

1 cup flour
½ tsp. salt
⅓ cup solid vegetable shortening
2 Tbs. (more or less) ice water

Sift flour and salt together. Cut shortening into flour with pastry blender until well mixed but grainy looking. Chill hands in bowl of ice water, add 2 Tbs. (more or less) ice water gradually to flour mixture, working it in with hands kept chilled and dry. Add only enough ice water to make firm but workable dough . . . it should not be sticky. Shape dough into a ball, dust lightly with flour, cover rolling pin with cloth cover—or place dough between 2 sheets of waxed paper—and roll out. Fit carefully into piepan. Lift edges and smooth out air bubbles. Trim pastry, leaving enough extra to fold edge under and shape into a fluted, upright rim. Prick bottom and sides with a fork. Bake at 450° F. oven for 12 to 15 minutes, or until golden brown.

Two-Crust Pie

Double ingredients called for in one-crust pie shell. Divide and form into 2 balls, one slightly larger than the other, and roll out. Slash smaller circle to let steam escape when pie is baking. Fit larger circle into piepan and fill. Cover with small circle, fold edges of crusts under and press together to seal. Bake according to pie recipe instructions.

Extra Piecrust

Combine scraps into a ball, lightly flour, and roll out on piece of freezer paper. Cut it into decorative designs with cookie cutters or use a small real leaf for a pattern.

To Use a Leaf Pattern

Choose a pretty leaf—be sure it is a nonpoisonous variety—and freeze it. When very stiff, press it, vein side down into rather soft dough. Remove the leaf and with a very sharp, thin-bladed knife, cut around the outer outline of leaf, using a slashing, not a pulling, cut. Lift the knife between each slash, otherwise it will pull the dough out of shape. After cutting outline—you can emphasize veining on leaf with the dull side of a dinner knife—put sheet of dough in freezer. When stiff, leaves will easily lift out. You can float a large leaf or several small ones in the center of a pumpkin pie or on tops of baked custard cups, not putting them on until the last 10 or 15 minutes of baking, when filling or custard is firm enough to hold them up and pastry won't burn. Freeze any that are left over between sheets of wax paper.

Fruit Compote Pie

A good substitute for mince at traditional feasts

¾ cup dehydrated apples
½ cup seedless raisins
6 Tbs. rum
8 Tbs. orange juice concentrate
6 Tbs. lemonade
⅓ cup prunes
⅓ cup dried apricots
⅓ cup dried pears
¼ tsp. ground cinnamon
¼ tsp. ground nutmeg
¼ tsp. ground cloves
2 Tbs. candied citron
½ tsp. salt
3 Tbs. honey
2 Tbs. tomato catsup
½ cup lightly packed light brown sugar
1½ tsps. cornstarch

Wash dehydrated apples and soak overnight in 2 cups of water. Wash raisins and soak them overnight in a marinade made by combining the rum, orange juice concentrate, and lemonade.

Remove any pieces of core left in apple. Combine apples with other fruits, including the liquids in which apple and raisins soaked. Stir in all other ingredients except cornstarch. Simmer, uncovered for 20 minutes. Dissolve cornstarch in 1 Tb. water, add to fruit mixture, stirring constantly until the sauce thickens. Turn heat to low and continue cooking for 10 minutes, stirring frequently. Pour into unbaked 9-inch piecrust shell, cover with pastry top. Seal edges of top and bottom crust together and flute with a stand-up fluting. Use scraps of pastry dough to make a flower design on top of pie. Cut some small gashes in top crust with a sharp, thin knife, making gashes a part of the floral design.

Cover fluting with strips of aluminum foil carefully folded over it. Lay strips of foil over floral design. Put pie in oven preheated to 450° F. In 2 minutes turn down to 425° F. and continue cooking for 10 minutes, turn down to 350° for 35 minutes or until done. Remove foil strips last 10 minutes. Serve pie hot or cold. Serves 8 to 12.

Rich Pumpkin Pie

Put a little cream into the filling instead of piling a lot of whipped cream on top of the pie

1 1-lb. 13-oz. can pumpkin. *Use the whole can. You can freeze what you don't eat for future use. It will make* 1 9-inch and 1 8-inch *pie and* 6 5-oz. *cups of custard.*

¾ cup sugar
1 tsp. salt
1½ tsps. cinnamon
¾ tsp. ginger
¼ tsp. nutmeg
5 eggs, beaten lightly
½ cup whipping cream
2½ cups milk
1 9-inch unbaked pie shell, and
1 8-inch unbaked pie shell *
8 leaves cut from extra piecrust *

Lightly beat first 9 ingredients together in a large mixing bowl. Fill two pies and fill custard cups about ⅞ full. Put pies in oven preheated to 450° F. After first 10 minutes, turn down to 350° F. and continue cooking 25 to 40 minutes longer. When pie fillings look as if they are no longer runny, test by sticking a thin knife blade into the very center—which cooks last. If the blade comes out dry, the pie is done.

* See Dough for One- or Two-Crust Pie.

Set custard cups in water. If there is room in oven, put them in when you turn heat down to 350° F. Test pudding centers for doneness when you test the pies; since they will be deeper, they may take longer to bake.

Float one shapely pastry leaf on each pie and custard cup as soon as the pumpkin mix is cooked enough to hold it up. Don't put it right in the center of the pie, or you won't be able to test for doneness. Pies serve 8 to 12; custards serve 6.

Note: Don't bake everything at one time if there will not be free circulation of hot air in your oven.

Before starting to bake, set pies on circle of aluminum foil about 1½ inch wider all the way around than each pie. If crust starts to get too brown on the edge, fold foil up over it.

Instead of Whipped Cream Topping: The small amount of cream included in this pie filling gives it a very nice, rich taste. Whipped cream or ice cream in addition makes it a little too rich, especially after a traditional holiday feast, for people are beginning to ask for lighter desserts. Try topping with ice milk for those who feel the pie is incomplete without something up there.

Best Apple Pie

8 to 10 medium-sized tart apples
¾ to 1 cup sugar
1 tsp. cinnamon
¼ tsp. nutmeg
Dash salt
Pastry for 2-crust 9-inch pie
2 Tbs. butter

Pare and core apples and slice thin. Combine sugar, cinnamon, nutmeg, and salt. Place apples in crust-lined piepan, just to cover bottom, for a first layer. Sprinkle layer with 4 Tbs. or so of sugar mixture. Dot with ⅓ of the butter. Add more apples for another layer, sprinkle more sugar, dot with more butter. Add more apples, and continue until pie shell is heaped with apples. (Apples cook down when baking—so be generous, and have a good-sized pie with lots of layers. Adjust top crust over apples, use tines of fork to seal the two edges together. Poke holes with the tines in the middle of crust. Trim off excess crust. (Use up extra pie crust by making small tart shells, which, when baked, can be filled with jelly.) Bake pie in 400° F. oven for 50 minutes or until done. (Tarts take 15 minutes in 400° F. oven.)

Note: Before sealing the two crusts together, wet fingers with cold water and dampen the bottom crust. To make the crust shiny, brush before baking with 3 Tbs. warm milk. Serves 8.

Lemon Meringue Pie

1½ cups granulated sugar
4 Tbs. cornstarch
4 Tbs. flour
½ tsp. salt
2 cups boiling water
3 beaten egg yolks
⅓ cup lemon juice
Baked pie shell (9-inch)

Mix sugar, cornstarch, flour, and salt together in medium to large saucepan. Gradually add 2 cups boiling water, stirring constantly. Cook, stirring constantly, over high heat until mixture begins to thicken, then turn heat lower and continue cooking until very thick. Add 3 beaten egg yolks and cook 2 minutes longer on low heat. Take off heat, cool 5 minutes, and add the lemon juice. Mix well and put aside to cool, stirring it once or twice before putting it into a baked pie shell.

Note: Have lemon juice squeezed and egg yolks separated and beaten before you start. Save the egg white for the meringue. When adding the beaten yolks to the hot thick mixture, take 2 or 3 spoonfuls of the hot mixture and add *it* to the yolks. Mix and then return yolks with mixture to the large saucepan. This way the egg will consolidate right into the mixture, instead of separating as sometimes happens when there is too sudden a change in temperature.

MERINGUE:

3 egg whites
1/8 tsp. salt
1/3 cup granulated sugar

Have medium-sized bowl, eggbeater or mixer beater cool—but not refrigerator cold. Put egg white and salt into bowl and start beating. Gradually add the granulated sugar and beat until fluffy, but not too dry.

Spoon meringue onto cooled lemon pie, place in preheated 350° F. oven for 10 to 12 minutes, or until nicely browned. Serves 8.

Crumbled Cracker Fruit Cake

1 Tb. butter
1 1-lb. 4½-oz. can crushed pineapple, drained
½ cup applesauce
½ cup cranberry-orange relish, see recipe page 222
2 cups unsalted soda crackers, crumbled
¼ lb. margarine, melted
¼ cup whipping cream
½ tsp. sugar
1/8 tsp. vanilla or to taste

Grease inside of 5 x 9 x 2½-inch loaf pan with 1 Tb. butter. Mix crushed pineapple and applesauce and spread 1/3 of mixture over bottom of pan. Dot with 1/3 of cranberry-orange relish. Top with 1/3 of crumbled crackers. Repeat layers two times and pour melted margarine over top layer of crumbled crackers. Bake 1 hour in preheated 375° F. oven. Serve warm or cold.

Whip cream, add sugar and vanilla, and spoon over individual slices of cake. Serves 8.

Note: Substitutions to use up leftover canned fruits or jams can be made in this cake so long as you drain the fruit and keep the proportions the same.

Cranberry-Orange Relish

½ cup raw cranberries
2 sections of ripe, thin-skinned orange, including skin
¼ cup sugar
½ tsp. lemon juice

Grind cranberries, orange sections and peel in food chopper, using medium blade. Mix in other ingredients and refrigerate in covered dish for at least three hours before serving. Use with poultry recipes or Crumbled Cracker Fruit Cake. Makes about one-half cup of relish.

Marge Cecil's Fruit Cake

1 cup margarine or butter
2 cups brown sugar (packed)
5 eggs, beaten
2 cups sifted flour
1 tsp. nutmeg
1 tsp. cinnamon
½ tsp. allspice
½ tsp. soda
¼ tsp. salt
½ cup cold coffee
3 Tbs. molasses
1 cup dried figs, chopped
1 cup citron, chopped
1 cup currants
1 cup dates, pitted and chopped
1 cup raisins, seeded

Cream margarine or butter and sugar together. Add beaten eggs, and blend well. Combine flour, nutmeg, cinnamon, allspice, soda, and salt. Mix cold coffee and molasses together and stir until blended. To the egg mixture, add all but ½ cup of flour mixture alternating with the coffee and molasses mixture. Combine fruit, pour the remaining ½ cup flour over it. Mix until fruit is well coated with flour and add to the cake batter. Bake in well-greased and wax-paper-lined 3 x 5 x 9½-inch loaf pans. Other pans may be used, or use a ring mold if you prefer. Preheat oven to 300° F. Place pan of hot water on oven bottom to maintain moisture while baking cakes. Check water pan at the end of an hour to make sure pan has not gone dry. Add more hot water if necessary. Bake cakes for 1½ hours. If edges of cake start to turn brown before the middle looks done, lower heat to 275° F.

When cakes are done, invert pans on paper towels or cake rack until thoroughly cool. Wrap cakes in waxed paper and replace in clean baking pans for storage. Fruit cake tastes better if allowed to ripen for 2 to 4 weeks before eating. If brandy-flavored cakes are desired, dribble brandy over cakes several times at no more than 3-day intervals. Don't get the cakes too wet at any time. Use about 2 Tbs. brandy per cake each time. Rewrap cakes and keep in a cool place, but not necessarily the refrigerator. After cakes are cut, however, it will be necessary to keep them in refrigerator. Use a damp knife for cutting them to insure getting firm slices and not crumbs.

Note: 1 package fruit-cake fruit mix may be substituted for any 2 cups fruit.

White Loaf Cake

2 cups all-purpose flour (sifted before measuring)
½ tsp. salt
1 tsp. baking powder
¼ tsp. nutmeg
1 cup margarine
1½ cups sugar
4 eggs (well beaten)
½ cup milk
1 tsp. vanilla
½ tsp. almond or lemon flavoring

Measure sifted flour, sift again with salt, baking powder, and nutmeg. Set aside. Thoroughly cream margarine, adding sugar gradually and continue creaming until mixture is very smooth. Add eggs, well beaten, and beat mixture again. Add sifted flour mixture alternately with milk and flavorings. Mix well after each addition. Bake in well-greased, wax-paper-lined loaf pans of any moderate size for 50 minutes in a preheated 350° F. oven. When cake begins to pull away from the edges, and a toothpick inserted in the cake comes out clean, remove cake from oven and invert cakes on rack or paper towels to cool. Remove pans from cake after 15 minutes. Continue cooling, rewrap in foil or plastic wrap and store in freezer or refrigerator until needed. Makes 3 medium-sized loaves.

Note: This cake is good without frosting and can be used in any number of ways:

Substitute for shortcake when making strawberry shortcake.

Make a plain pudding into a fancy dessert by lining a loaf pan with sliced cake, pouring prepared puddings into center, and topping with whipped cream.

Serve this cake topped with fruit or ice cream or chocolate sauce spooned evenly over slices.

Strawberry Shortcake

2 cups sifted all-purpose flour
2 Tbs. sugar
3 tsps. baking powder
½ tsp. salt
½ cup margarine
⅔ cup whole milk
1 beaten egg
2 Tbs. butter
4 cups sugared sliced strawberries
1 cup whipping cream, whipped

Sift together dry ingredients, cut in margarine with back of a fork, until mixture is mixed very well. Combine milk and beaten egg. Add all at once to dry ingredients, stirring just enough to mix. Shape into large ball, place on floured board and pat out to ½ inch thick. Cut large "biscuits"—at least 3 inches in diameter. (Use a bowl to cut around if cutter is not available.) Bake on ungreased baking sheet in 450° F. oven for 10–12 minutes. Split cakes with serrated knife, lightly butter bottom half. Spoon sugared strawberries on, add 1½ Tbs. whipped cream, top with other half, cover with whipped cream. Top with half a strawberry and serve. Serves 6.

Note: Use cool utensils for mixing pastry and run cold water over your hands to cool them before handling dough.

Caramel Custard

4 eggs, lightly beaten
2 Tbs. white granulated sugar
1 Tb. brown sugar
1¾ cups milk
¼ cup cream (or milk)
¼ tsp. vanilla
¼ tsp. nutmeg
¾ cup brown sugar

Combine beaten eggs, white and brown sugar. Combine milk and cream and heat in a saucepan almost to boiling. Add very slowly to beaten egg, stirring constantly. Stir in vanilla and nutmeg. Spread ¾ cup of brown sugar over bottom of a 1½ quart casserole or mold, and pour custard mix over it. Set in a large pan of hot water, put in oven preheated to 325° F. and bake for 40 minutes. Test for doneness by carefully inserting a thin-bladed knife into center of custard. If it comes out clean, the custard is done. The depth of the custard determines the length of time it will take to cook. Chill quickly, cover and refrigerate. When custard is very cold, it can be inverted onto serving platter, or served directly from mold into small dishes. Serves 8.

Rice Pudding

2 cups cooked rice
1½ cups milk
¼ tsp. salt
⅓ cup sugar
1 tsp. vanilla
3 eggs (beaten)
½ tsp. grated lemon rind
1 tsp. lemon juice
½ cup raisins

Combine all ingredients except lemon rind, lemon juice, and raisins in medium-size bowl. Grease a baking dish and pour pudding mixture into it. Bake in preheated oven (325° F.). After pudding has been baking for 20 minutes, add the lemon rind, lemon juice, and raisins, and stir gently for ½ minute. Adding the raisins at this time insures that they will be mixed into the pudding and won't sink to the bottom as sometimes happens. Bake 30 minutes longer. Serves 8.

Baked Bananas and Cream

3 very ripe bananas,* peeled and sliced
3 Tbs. honey
3 tsps. lemon juice
1 tsp. butter, melted
2 Tbs. coconut
¼ cup whipping cream
4 drops pure vanilla

Arrange sliced bananas in shallow baking dish. Sprinkle with a mixture of the honey, lemon juice, and melted butter and bake in 400° F. oven for 10 minutes. Spread coconut out on a cookie sheet or in a piepan and toast in oven for 5 to 10 minutes—at 400° F.—or until very lightly browned. Whip cream, using very cold dish and beaters and stir in

* Watch for very ripe bananas on sale—brown spots on skin don't affect quality of fruit if eaten immediately—and buy for one meal only.

vanilla. Do not sweeten. Divide bananas into dessert dishes, top with whipped cream, sprinkle with toasted coconut and serve. Serves 4 to 6.

Hot Honeyed Grapefruit for Dessert or a Hurried Breakfast

1 Tb. honey, or to taste
1 grapefruit, sections removed, skinned, and each one cut in half
1 pinch of salt

Combine honey, grapefruit, and salt in a saucepan and heat. Turn off heat and let stand for a few minutes to blend flavors. Serves 2.

Tipsy Doodle

This is a good dessert to make when you want to throw away bottles that have just a little nice wine left in them. You can substitute any congenial assortment.

1 tsp. vermouth
1 tsp. sherry
1 tsp. Riesling
2 Tbs. honey
2 Tbs. undiluted frozen lemonade
¼ tsp. nutmeg
1 ripe red apple
½ of 3-oz. box lemon gelatin dessert
1 3-oz. box raspberry gelatin dessert
1½ cups boiling water
¾ cup apple cider
Ice cubes
¼ cup whipping cream

Mix 3 wines, honey, lemonade, and nutmeg and stir until nutmeg is well blended. Core apple, cut in small, thin slices and soak in wine mixture while making gelatin. Put lemon and raspberry gelatin into a bowl, add boiling water and stir until dissolved. Add ice cubes to the ¾ cup apple cider to make one cup of liquid and stir liquid and cubes into warm gelatin. Refrigerate until gelatin starts to thicken, then remove apple slices from marinade with slotted spoon and stir into it. Spoon gelatin into parfait glasses, leaving plenty of room for cream topping. Refrigerate and cover.

Whip cream just before serving. Stir wine marinade into it, immediately divide over desserts and serve. Serves 8.

Apple and Blue Cheese Gelatin

1 3-oz. pkg. orange gelatin dessert
1 1-Tb. envelope unflavored gelatin
2 Tbs. cold water
1½ cups boiling water
2 cups cold apple juice
2 cups, finely chopped, peeled apple
¼ cup grated blue cheese
2 Tbs. cream cheese
¼ cup mayonnaise

Put orange gelatin in a 1-qt. or larger mold. Soften unflavored gelatin in 2 Tbs. cold water and add to the orange gelatin. Pour the boiling water over the two gelatins and stir until they are completely dissolved. Add 2 cups cold apple juice and refrigerate.

Combine chopped apple, blue cheese, cream cheese, and mayonnaise. Mash and blend together with a large spoon.

When gelatin is set but not stiff, spoon in alternate layers with apple-cheese mixture into parfait or other stemware glasses. Refrigerate until time to serve. Serves 6.

Grape Zip

1 package lemon-flavored gelatin
1 cup boiling water
1 cup grape juice

Dissolve gelatin in boiling water. Cool 5 minutes. Add grape juice. Blend well. Chill until cold and syrupy. Place bowl in another bowl filled with cracked ice or ice water and whip like cream. Gelatin, when whipped, practically doubles in bulk. Pile lightly in sherbet glasses. Chill until firm. Serves 4 to 6.

End Your Day with One of These Easiest, Tastiest, Most Nutritious Desserts

Did the children rush out in the morning without drinking their orange juice?

Did Father skip a customary lunch-time glass of milk because he was entertaining a client?

Did you, Mother, get so caught up in the rush you didn't drink any orange juice OR milk and besides that did you neglect the family's Vitamin A for a day or two?

All is not lost! There's still the TV and bedtime snack.

Use it as a nutritional backstop. When you're pondering what to serve, don't forget the concentration of calcium you get from the ten pounds or so of milk it takes to make one pound of cheddar-type cheese.

Serve Fruit in Season With Cheese of Your Choice: Eat some seasonal fruit with a few slices of cheese, chill the fruit if you like it that way *but remove the cheese from the refrigerator and let it warm for at least a half-hour at room temperature, thus releasing the aroma and heightening the flavor,* and you have one of the world's great dessert combinations.

If this is not already one of your standard desserts, start with the cheeses your family is accustomed to, then branch out and discover the adventure of shopping for and eating cheeses that are strange to you. (Someone got the variety count up to 200, then quit.)

Apples, bananas, and grapes are traditionally eaten with cheeses that you slice . . . but if you just need a little more calcium than you've already consumed during the day, cottage cheese goes just great with almost any fruit. Besides your good Vitamin C sources such as citrus fruit and strawberries, don't forget the double dividend of both Vitamins C and A that you get from cantaloupe, mangoes, and papayas.

Ice Cream Sundae Combinations Without End: There is no end to the sundae combinations that can be concocted in most kitchens. You couldn't do better than to make fruit sundaes one of your mainstay desserts or snacks. Keep vanilla ice cream in your freezer, buy fresh fruit when in season, and top the ice cream with the fruit, with or without sugar as taste dictates. When you can't find the fresh fruit you want at a reasonable price, buy it canned or frozen. Here are some suggestions:

Apricot Sundaes:

Buy very ripe apricots, chop, pour over vanilla ice cream, top with a sprinkle of coconut.

Mix chopped apricots with canned mandarin oranges, pour over orange ice and top with sprinkle of coconut.

Cantaloupe Sundaes:

Make a circle of cantaloupe slices, put a scoop of vanilla ice cream or orange ice in the center and sprinkle ripe blueberries over the top.

Blackberry, Blueberry, Stawberry Sundaes:

Any ripe, sweet berry, either plain or mashed with a little sugar, makes an excellent topping for ice cream. Vanilla ice cream is most frequently used in these combinations, but there aren't any rules so use your imagination.

Peach Sundaes:

Canned or fresh or frozen peaches, or just the thick syrup from the canned variety are excellent with ice cream. The juice from canned peaches can be combined with that from maraschino cherries—add a little brandy and lemon juice if you like—and simmered together for a few minutes. The result is a wonderful sundae sauce.

When buying and serving fruit for your end-of-day catch-up of neglected nutrients, don't overlook those that aren't included on the Vitamin A or C lists. They are nutritious, too. To demonstrate in how many ways these other fruits are good for you, we listed a few examples from the United States Department of Agriculture's *Home and Garden Bulletin No. 72, Nutritive Value of Foods* to show how their nutritional cross-indexing compares with that of an orange. We hope this listing, which is shown below, will spur you to add the goodness and spice of variety to your eating pleasure.

HOW A FEW COMMON FRUITS COMPARE, NUTRIENT-WISE, WITH AN ORANGE

Fruit: (raw)	*Food energy*	*Carbohydrate*	*Calcium*	*Iron*	*Vitamin A value*	*Thiamine*	*Riboflavin*	*Niacin*	*(Vitamin C) Ascorbic Acid*
	Calories	*Grams*	*Milligrams*	*Milligrams*	*International Units*	*Milligrams*	*Milligrams*	*Milligrams*	*Milligrams*
Orange 2⅘-in. diameter	60	16	49	.5	240	.12	.05	.5	75
Peach 2-in. diameter	35	10	9	.5	1,320	.02	.05	1.0	7
Pear 2½-in. diameter	100	25	13	.5	30	.04	.07	.2	7
Pineapple 1 cup, diced	75	19	24	.7	100	.12	.04	.3	24
Apple 2½-in. diameter	70	18	8	.4	50	.04	.02	.1	3
Banana 6 x 1½-in.	85	23	8	.7	190	.05	.06	.7	10
Grapes 1 cup (Malaga, Muscat, Thompson Seedless, Emperor and Flame Tokay)	95	25	17	.6	140	.07	.04	.4	6

Even though the number of nutrients recognized by scientists appears to have jumped from "over 40" to "over 50" during the course of our writing the *Pennysaver Cookbook*, we, Dan and Inez Morris, would like to recommend the addition of one more, perhaps the most important of all the values to be derived from eating:

ENJOYMENT

Index